A PROFESSIONAL FOREIGNER

ADST-DACOR DIPLOMATS AND DIPLOMACY SERIES

Series Editor: MARGERY BOICHEL THOMPSON

Since 1776 extraordinary men and women have represented
the United States abroad under widely varying circum-
stances. What they did, and how and why they did it, remain
little known to their compatriots. In 1995 the Association
for Diplomatic Studies and Training (ADST) and DACOR,
an organization of foreign affairs professionals, created the
Diplomats and Diplomacy book series to increase public knowledge and appreciation of the professionalism of
American diplomats and their involvement in world history. In *A Professional Foreigner*, the seventy-fourth volume
in the series, career Foreign Service Officer Edward Marks
recounts many tales of how an ordinary diplomat spends his
life in other people's countries, wherein lie the charm and
distinction of the professional diplomat's life.

A Professional Foreigner

LIFE IN DIPLOMACY | *Edward Marks*

An ADST-DACOR Diplomats and Diplomacy Book

Potomac Books
An imprint of the University of Nebraska Press

The opinions and characterizations in this book are those
of the author and do not necessarily reflect the opinions
of the United States government, the Association for
Diplomatic Studies and Training, or DACOR.

Library of Congress Cataloging-in-Publication Data
Names: Marks, Edward, 1934– author.
Title: A professional foreigner: life in diplomacy /
Edward Marks.
Description: Lincoln: Potomac Books, an imprint of the
University of Nebraska Press, 2023. | Series: ADST-DACOR
diplomats and diplomacy series | Includes index.
Identifiers: LCCN 2022034589
ISBN 9781640125513 (hardback)
ISBN 9781640125827 (epub)
ISBN 9781640125834 (pdf)
Subjects: LCSH: Marks, Edward, 1934– | Diplomatic and
consular service—United States—History—20th century. |
United States. Foreign Service—Officials and employees—
Biography. | Ambassadors—United States—Biography. |
Diplomats—United States—Biography. | BISAC: BIOGRAPHY
& AUTOBIOGRAPHY / Political | POLITICAL SCIENCE /
International Relations / Diplomacy
Classification: LCC E840.8.M256 A3 2023 |
DDC 327.73009/04092 [B]—dc23/eng/20220831
LC record available at https://lccn.loc.gov/2022034589

Set in Arno Pro by A. Shahan.

In memory of my partner on the trip, Aida.

Over the years at various posts people would eventually casually ask how we met — with an unstated query about my distinctly provincial Detroit origins and her much more glamorous Iranian-Armenian looks and nickname as the Persian Princess. This has always given me the opportunity to respond with very deliberate Foreign Service casualness, "Why, at a cocktail party in Nairobi."

When you set out for Ithaka

ask that your way be long,

full of adventure, full of instruction.

—C. P. Cavafy,
"On the Road to Ithaka"

CONTENTS

ILLUSTRATIONS

ACKNOWLEDGMENTS

Aida Nercess, known to her family as Shakey and to our friends as the Persian Princess, was born in Tehran, Iran. In Nairobi, Kenya, she joined me in my life and career and passed away in Washington DC, some years after our career, but not our life together, ended. Most of the grace we exhibited in our long joint career was due to her.

Although much of this story is recounted in the first person, the real protagonists were my colleagues in the Foreign Service, if not the Foreign Service itself. My experiences were not unique and were usually shared with others. The book mentions only a few names, but there were many, many more who played a role in this story: bosses who made work a thrill and a challenge, colleagues who were friends and partners, and juniors who humored me.

Writing this book took me into unknown territory where I desperately needed knowledgeable and sympathetic guides. The two most important were Charles Stuart Kennedy and Margery Thompson, both key figures in the Association for Diplomatic Studies and Training (ADST). Stu brought me into his awesome oral history project soon after I retired, thereby capturing memories before they got lost. Margery took on the tedious task of guiding this innocent author through the wilds of manuscript preparation.

INTRODUCTION

One day in 1965 I was called into the office of Harvey Cash, my boss in the U.S. consulate in Nuevo Laredo, Mexico, and given an assignment to assist an American citizen in some sort of difficulty. He was being held prisoner in a local brothel for failure to pay his bill. The consul, trying not to giggle, assigned me—his very junior vice consul—to sort it out.

Most Americans do not think of the Texas-Mexico border as "foreign" in the same way they do Paris or Tokyo. But it has peculiarities that one doesn't find often in, say, Ohio. For instance, prostitution is legal in Mexico, and border towns all have brothels. Arriving somewhat nervously at the establishment in question, I was met by the madam, a rather respectable-looking middle-aged lady. She showed me my American citizen, a man in his late thirties or early forties, sleeping quietly in bed. He had shown up about two days earlier, already reasonably drunk, and had spent a couple of days buying drinks and other services and paying everyone's bill. After about two days of this, the manager thought she better get some more cash in hand, but it now appeared that he had run out. By then he was practically comatose, so they cleaned him up and put him in a bedroom, allowing him one drink a day so he would come down gradually. She presented me with a bill for roughly $700, which was a lot of money in 1964.

I called his family and discovered that he was the scion of a wealthy Southern family who had indulged in this sort of adventure several times before. (The first reaction on the telephone was, "Oh no, not again!")

With the family's authority I negotiated the price down a bit, received money from the family, paid the bill, and transported the man in the consulate car to the railway station across the border in Laredo, Texas, where I put him on a train heading home. By then he was sober, if not in very good shape, and quite unrepentant.

So how did I get involved in this multicultural human relations problem? Serendipity or chance or whatever, I suppose, which determined the pathway of my adult life. I was in the communal bathroom of my fraternity house in Ann Arbor in the autumn of 1955 when chance struck. A fraternity brother came into the bathroom to perform his ablutions—it was a Friday night and a football weekend, and we were preparing for the usual weekend jollities available on such occasions. Taking the washbowl next to mine, he commented that he had just mailed his application for the Foreign Service exam. My ears perked up, as they say in the old novels, and I immediately asked what that was and how to do it. He explained the simple procedure: merely obtain the requisite postcard application form from the post office or some such place, fill in your name and address, and send it in. By doing so you would be registered for the next written Foreign Service examination.

This was all quite wondrous to me, as I had no idea of the existence of the exam, much less how to sign up for it. In fact, my knowledge of the Foreign Service itself was quite limited. First generation Americans from Detroit did not, in those days, run to much knowledge of such subjects, despite pursuing a major in political science.

But the information was most welcome. I was in the penultimate semester of my undergraduate career at the University of Michigan with no real thoughts as to my postgraduate future. I rejected the thought of medical or dental school, was not interested in law, couldn't see myself as an engineer or talented enough to be an architect (although I had suspicions it could be a very classy profession), and turned my nose up at business administration or pharmacy (these forming the boundaries of conceivable careers for first-generation Jewish American youths from Detroit in the early 1950s). I had some vague thoughts about an academic career (pipes and tweeds and books), but I was so generally lax in my academic work that I realized it was not to be.

What I really wanted to do was to ensure that I did not have to return home. Instead, I wanted to go out into that wider world that I knew was there. Vague thoughts about joining a large international company and traveling the world as an international business executive crossed my mind. I was enjoying life as a senior, expecting to be drafted into the army after graduation. Serious worrying about the future could come later. Without realizing it, I was considering two years' prospective army service as a sort of *Wanderjahr*.

The tip about the Foreign Service exam proved to be decisive. I signed up for it, and from then until the day I retired some forty years later, my life flowed along the organized path of a professional civil servant, subspecies career diplomat. I showed up for the written exam, then for the oral examination when instructed, filled out the requisite medical and background forms, and in due course presented myself in Washington DC to join an intake class of newly commissioned Foreign Service officers. In September 1956, as I flew from Los Angeles, where my parents were living and where I had gone after graduation to await the call to Washington to take up that role, I remember a feeling of pure glee. Life was beginning, and Detroit was now forever in the past.

1

Taking the Oath

I had no clue as to what I was getting into, but I was lucky. It turned out that the Foreign Service was a happy experience for me. There have been disappointments and frustrations along the way, of course, but nothing tragic and nothing overwhelming. I never did get to be the co-drafter of the treaty that ended the Cold War (although I was around when it happened), or, to tell the truth, to co-draft any treaty. Still, all in all, there were some days and some results of which I am not ashamed. I console myself today, in retirement, by noting that while it was the tribunes who got the credit, it was the centurions who carried the day. And I often remind myself of a friend's observation that life was good when one was actually being paid to live a life and do work so eminently enjoyable.

What did I think I was doing when I joined the Foreign Service? I knew absolutely nothing about the career and life I was about to enter. My family and cultural background were quite distant from the world of diplomacy. I had no personal role models. The only government official I knew, and that not well, was an IRS inspector who married an older cousin. She was at least ten years older than I, and he another five years or so. This is a significant age difference when one is young, and we were not a close family.

It is difficult now to recall how provincial much of America was then, especially ethnic communities. The perspective on the world was narrow, reflecting the particular history and situation of the ethnic group in question. Television was just beginning to become widespread, and the move to the suburbs was just beginning. Travel outside the community was extremely limited by today's standards, even within the larger city. Travel outside the city even within the state of Michigan had been limited to an uncle's farm about forty miles away, or a lake somewhat closer (both now suburbs of Detroit). Trips to places as exotic as Chicago, New York, and Miami Beach by more prosperous relatives, friends, and acquaintances were rare enough to be subjects of discussion. We lived across the river from Windsor, Ontario, a city located in a foreign country and in which I actually had living relatives, and yet we hardly ever crossed that river. By the time I left Detroit definitively to go to Ann Arbor, I still had no real experience outside of the northwest quadrant of the city, an informal Jewish ghetto of a type common in midcentury America. The United States of the late 1940s and the 1950s was undergoing a dramatic, revolutionary transformation (see David Halberstam's *The Fifties*), but the effects were only beginning to filter into the relatively closed ethnic communities of America.

Movies and books were our only windows on the world. My immediate friends and I were enamored with the literature of the "Lost Generation"—of Hemingway and Fitzgerald—but neither literature, popular culture, or the movies really spent much time on diplomacy and diplomats. Diplomats occasionally appeared in books and movies but almost always as marginal characters and usually not particularly attractive ones at that. Stuffiness was the primary characteristic of most of them, regardless of age, and often the diplomatic character tried to tell "our hero" why he couldn't do what he was proposing. Usually this was something dangerous or scandalous or both, and of course the hero disregards the "safe bureaucratic" advice and proceeds to achieve his objective with great élan. This fictional treatment of diplomats lives on.

At university I had majored in political science, mostly international affairs. However, almost all courses were oriented toward policy or contemporary affairs and made little attempt to describe or explain the role and what we now call the "lifestyle" of diplomats and other international fauna. I doubt if political science departments do any better nowadays, and there is probably no reason why they should. I have

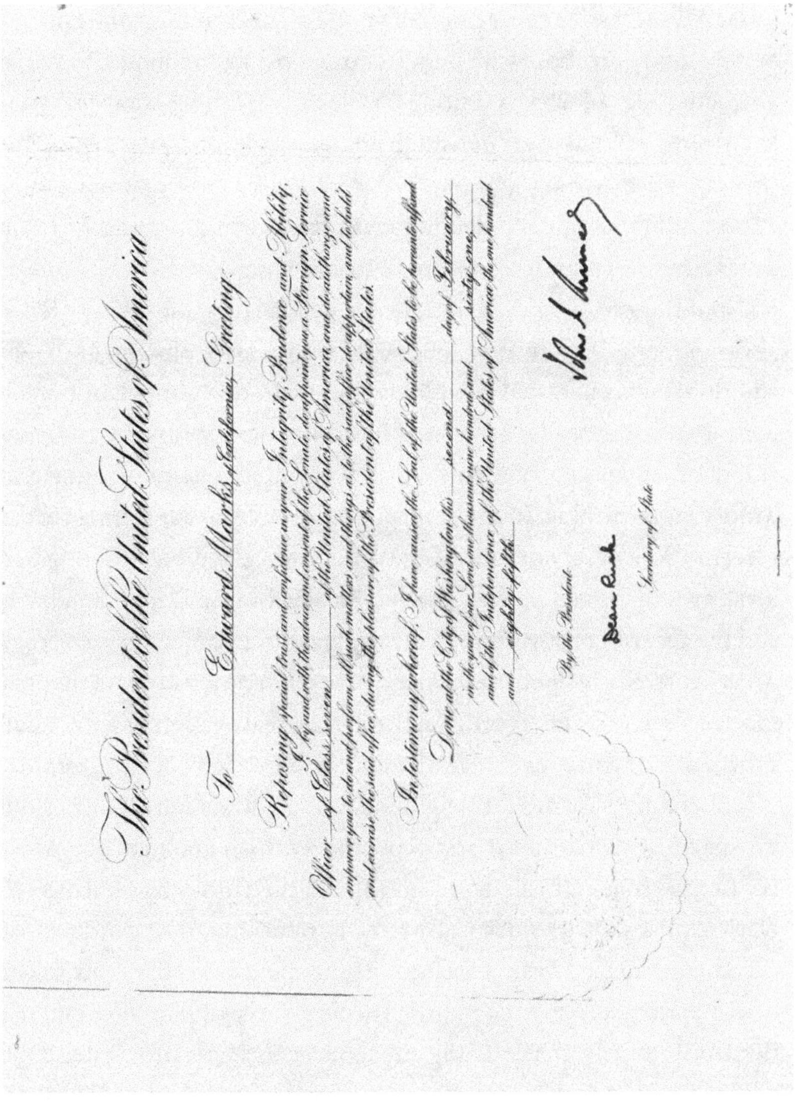

The President of the United States of America

To Edward Marks, of California, Greeting:

Reposing special trust and confidence in your Integrity, Prudence and Ability, I, by and with the advice and consent of the Senate, do appoint you a Foreign Service Officer of Class seven of the United States of America, and do authorize and empower you to do and perform all such matters and things as to the said office do appertain, and to hold and exercise the said office, during the pleasure of the President of the United States.

In testimony whereof, I have caused the Seal of the United States to be hereunto affixed.

Done at the City of Washington this second day of February in the year of our Lord one thousand nine hundred and sixty-one and of the Independence of the United States of America the one hundred and eighty-fifth.

By the President:

Dean Rusk

Secretary of State

Fig. 1. Author's commission as an officer in the Foreign Service of the United States. Author's collection.

observed successive generations of young officers entering the Foreign Service, and only those with family or other personal connections have any better idea of what is waiting for them than I did. (Many today do have more definite ideas derived from television and the movies, but they are mostly wrong.)

So I didn't have many definite ideas about where I was going. My motivation was founded on a desire to leave home and Detroit and go out into the wide world. This is, by the way, a common (although not always admitted) motivation among Foreign Service officers (FSOs). In addition, I was interested in international affairs and wanted, in a vague but very real way, to play a role in history. I was not excessively egotistical and did not expect a large role, but I did want at least to be present at history in the making. In addition, public service was a much-respected ideal in those days, not long after World War II, and a strong sense of idealism still existed in many circles. Finally, I was a Depression baby, and the security of government service was attractive.

As I entered my senior year at Ann Arbor, I occasionally gave thought to what I would do afterward, but the imminence of military service had provided an excuse for procrastination. The Foreign Service examination therefore fell onto fertile ground, although friends scoffed at the prospects of success for a first-generation Jewish graduate of a non–Ivy League school. In all innocence, I took the written examination in Detroit on a snowy Friday in December, returning to Ann Arbor that evening in the back seat of a Chevrolet coupe driven by a law student who, I discovered years later, had also been successful in the examination. As it turned out, my timing was superlative. It was late 1955, and the old Ivy League WASP Foreign Service was being reformed, reorganized, and greatly expanded. There was now definitely room in the American Foreign Service for people like me.

And it was an exciting time to join the Foreign Service. The Cold War was in full progress and the era of decolonization and the "winds of change" was about to take off.

Several experiences during my entry process into the Foreign Service forever marked my attitude toward it. The first involved the oral examination, which took place after I had successfully passed the written test. I took it in Cincinnati, traveling by train from Ann Arbor. My interviewing panel consisted of three FSOs—the first I had ever met and whose names I cannot remember. It was the classic examination of that period, consisting of a series of rapid-fire questions. I had been primed that there might be some questions intended to be potentially embarrassing, but the only one that could be so considered in my case was about my brief stint in the U.S. Postal Service (part-time during my freshman year at Wayne State University in Detroit; I was fired for tardiness). What I do remember was that the questions alternated between subjects I had studied in school and some I had not. I specifically remember that they asked me about the Compromise of 1850, a subject I was able to discuss in some detail (but probably could not now). I wasn't launched very far into my answer when they stopped me, because it was clear I knew about the subject, and they were not really interested in the substance of my reply.

In a sense they were probing my educational strengths and weaknesses and how I handled them. As it happened, I had been given another bit of useful advice before I left Ann Arbor for the examination. Do not be afraid to say you do not know and avoid any attempt to bluff—the examiners are older, have had more training and experience, and outnumber you. Your chances of getting away with anything are not good. This was timely advice, and I have often passed it on to candidates since.

(Later I had a chance to confirm this. When I returned to the State Department after my military service in early 1959, I was put to work sorting personnel documents, as I had a few weeks before I was to join a class of newly appointed FSOs. I ran across the memorandum on my interview [which you are not supposed to see], and a key remark: "Mr. Marks did not attempt to bluff when he did not know the answer." I had been given a key bit of good advice and had had enough sense to follow it.)

The second incident occurred when I joined an entering officers' class (called A-100) at the Department of State's Foreign Service Institute in Washington in September 1956. There were thirty-five of us, from all over the country, seven of whom were women. I was twenty-two years old and only a few months out of college. I was the second youngest (by a couple of months) and awed by my colleagues, most of whom had vastly greater experience and education. Apart from the one other recent graduate, the class was filled with real adults with military and wartime service, graduate degrees, and lots of real-life experience.

I now realize how very young I was, with a narrow background in the Detroit Jewish community—almost a dictionary definition of provincial. At the University of Michigan I had barely scratched the surface of what was on offer. And then, all of a sudden, I had come to Washington to join the diplomatic service. I had left home for good, by choice, and it was obviously the best of all possible worlds. I had been elected into a "very good club" and couldn't have been happier. I felt privileged and lucky to be among that group, and that feeling has never left me.

And then my self-satisfaction came to a screeching halt about two weeks into the course, when I received my draft notice. In my excitement about entry into the Foreign Service, I had forgotten about my Selective Service status, and the mills of the draft board had ground their way to me. I had spent the summer as a management intern at Prudential Life Insurance in Los Angeles waiting for the call from Washington and had neglected to inform my draft board of my impending entry into federal government service. In the mid-1950s, with no war underway or in sight, that fact might have been enough to obtain a draft deferral. However, I had been too feckless or too thoughtless or maybe just too inexperienced to do so, and so, shortly after I arrived in Washington the draft notice followed. After the sixth week of the A-100 course I was off to the army. My leaving became an event, as my class decided to give me a going away party in the *Bierskellar* of the Old Europe Restaurant in upper Georgetown.

Washington in 1956 had some curious local customs and laws. For instance, it was illegal to carry a drink from one table to another. We were a numerous crowd occupying a number of tables and by about one in the morning we were getting fairly raucous and moving back and forth among the tables, despite the owners and the waiters telling us to stop. We did not. Instead, we started singing German songs: "Lili Marlene," of course, "Deutschland Uber Alles," and even tried to sing "Hoerst Wessel Lied"—though few of us knew any of the words. Most of us in fact hadn't a clue as to what we were singing. Those I looked up to as adults were letting loose as if at a fraternity party.

Then the police showed up and we were expelled from the Old Europe. Some of us wandered through the streets of Georgetown and ended up at somebody's apartment, where we drank a little bit more. It ended at about three in the morning. It was a Thursday night, and we had Friday morning class at the old Foreign Service Institute (located where the diplomatic entrance of the State Department is now). I didn't make it to class at all in the morning, and neither did the class president.

We were in class soon after lunch when the door opened, and one of the school secretaries looked around the room and pointed at me and the class president. We were taken to the office of an august person—a Foreign Service inspector.

"All right, what happened?" We blinked. He then explained that the State Department had received a call from the gentleman who owns the Old Europe saying that a group of young diplomats had behaved badly last night, singing Nazi songs. The police had been called and the group expelled from the restaurant. The restaurant owner wanted the department to know that he was a German Jewish refugee from the thirties and was preparing to go to the newspapers with the story. The inspector then showed us the morning *New York Times*. On the front page in the bottom was a little article headed, "State Department Aide Criticizes Orthodox Jews." (A State Department Arabist had given a speech in New York, and some in his audience were upset by his remarks.) Suitably chastened, my classmate and I described our evening to the inspector, as best we could remember, and I have always remembered his reaction.

In the first place, he accepted our story without comment, in other words took our story as given, merely making the obvious comment that we had been quite stupid. He then instructed us, "All right, you go down and talk to the man about it. Explain it, do what you can, apologize but don't crawl."

We, of course, crawled all over the place. We went to the restaurant, where the owner declined to shake our hands but did invite us to sit down. We then apologized and tried to explain. I made sure he knew I was Jewish, and we abased ourselves more than a little bit, making a deservedly profuse apology. The owner accepted our apology, shook our hands, and said we could come back again.

We had not only behaved badly and stupidly but also improperly, because we were no longer private citizens. It was a sobering lesson in which I first learned the obligations involved in the old expression "taking the king's shilling."

Several days later I left Washington as a newly inducted private in the Army of the United States. What a change in status—from a diplomatic officer in the Foreign Service of the United States of America to E-1 in the Army of the United States! My military service—my *Wanderjahr*— would actually consist of two years of clerical duty at the U.S. Army Infantry Training Center at Fort Jackson, South Carolina. Draftee service in the U.S. Army in the mid-1950s was not a completely unpleasant experience, and it did contribute to my education and development, as I knew as little about the army as I did about the Foreign Service. My entire military service was spent at Fort Jackson, where I was kept on as a company clerk in a training company.

While hardly adventurous or dramatic, the experience included extensive contact with a broad range of other Americans of differing classes and backgrounds, especially from the South. Of particular interest and fondly remembered were the career soldiers of the Old Army—that is the regular army of the pre–World War II era. The old sergeants let me sit with them at their morning coffee breaks in the mess hall. These were the sort of people featured in the novel *From Here to Eternity*, and their gossip over coffee about Fort Benning in '38 and Hawaii in '39 perfectly matched the atmosphere of that book and the resulting movie.

First Sergeant Jeffcoat also gave me a lesson in the responsibility that goes with taking an oath. It was during the civil rights crisis in 1957, when President Eisenhower sent federal troops to Little Rock, Arkansas, to enforce the Supreme Court ruling on school integration. One of our company officers, a ninety-day-wonder second lieutenant from rural Texas, fumed about the court's decision and muttered childish remarks about resigning his commission and resuming the struggle. I responded, equally petulantly I suppose, by saying that in that case I would go back to Michigan, put on a black hat, and come down to administer another whipping to Southern pretensions. (I think I actually said it much more bluntly.) Sergeant Jeffcott, however, a tall, lean thirty-year regular from Tennessee, looked at the young lieutenant and merely said, "I'm a regular, I go where the president sends me." The ensuing silence was deafening.

I later ran across the novel *Soldier in the Rain*, which was turned into an entertaining movie with Jackie Gleason, a young Steve McQueen, and an even younger Tuesday Weld. While the novel's story did not replicate my personal adventures, it did quite accurately catch the mood and atmosphere of my "war" and my "army" at Fort Jackson.

Entering the Foreign Service, I had expected to spend those two years in some exotic, far-off corner of the world. But, to tell the truth, South Carolina in the mid-1960s had its exotic aspects for a northern city boy like me. It is now fashionable in some circles to bemoan the loss of the democratic social experience of life in the barracks. While that attitude can be overdone, I personally remember with gratitude, mixed with nostalgia, the experience of living in the socially and racially integrated society of an army post, especially given its sharp contrast with the wider world of a still segregated America just outside the gates.

It also left me with an abiding interest in the military and in professional soldiers and, as a former Specialist 4th Class, a permanent sense of disorientation and amusement when I later mingled with senior military officers.

But the military interlude was only that, an interlude. Soon I was back in Washington and beginning my life as a professional diplomat—an officer in the Foreign Service of the United States.

2

About Diplomats

He ordered another bottle . . . in honor of a career so
comfortable that it is called The Career and a ministerial
department so superior that it is called The Department.

—ROGER PEYREFITTE, *Les Ambassades*

Professional diplomats are professional foreigners. They spend much of
their life living in other people's countries, not as tourists or immigrants
or even as business expatriates. They do so as government officials of a
foreign country and government. They are formally "foreign" to their place
of residence at any given time. They are foreigners not only by choice
but also by definition, and their status states so expressly. The legendary
and usually misunderstood status of diplomatic immunity makes that
clear. No one but a diplomat on assignment is officially, formally, and
legally exempt from the local legal regime. The diplomat is an officially
recognized professional foreigner.

Professional diplomats are, by and large, articulate and verbal folk. Not
surprising, as what they do professionally is interact with other people to
seek, explain, or learn something. Diplomats occupy that last three feet
between governments, as governments talk to each other. At the same
time, diplomats traditionally fulfill the dual functions of canaries in the
coal mine and public opinion polltakers.

One of their functions, therefore, is to be constantly passing on the
product of these interactions to colleagues and superiors and to the rest

of their government. (Diplomats belong to government bureaucracies, even though many don't want to admit it.) There is also the requirement to record for the official record—for government is about records. This obligation applies to all bureaucrats, but to diplomats even more so, because they are so dispersed geographically. The U.S. diplomatic system consists of the headquarters in Washington and some three hundred offices scattered around the world: embassies, missions, consulates general, and consulates, plus the occasional temporary office or special mission. All that information gathered, all those "demarches" made, all those conversations and observations have to be recorded and reported.

Accordingly, diplomats write a lot: dispatches (in the old days), cables, memoranda, letters, notes, "nonpapers," and nowadays emails and perhaps even tweets. We scribble, scribble, scribble to earn the accusation King George threw at Edward Gibbon. Because of this requirement, and because of the academic and intellectual origins of most diplomatic practitioners, high-quality literacy has always been a point of pride as well as a career requirement.

Contemporary technology, from television to the internet and the web, has provided additional ways of doing the same thing; it doesn't change the function of the diplomat, but merely adds to it. After all, even tweets and email messages have to be "written" by somebody and read by someone else. The importance of writing skills remains, although somewhat less apparent. The files and the history of American diplomacy are filled with these efforts, and some are legendary, from the nineteenth-century telegram "Emperor Dead" to George F. Kennan's history-making "Long Telegram." Battalions of U.S. diplomats have spent years straining to achieve that kind of immortality.

The Foreign Service as a professional community and a culture is self-consciously proud of its literary skills. This attitude is attested to by the number of diplomats who are published writers, including the huge number of diplomatic memoirs by diplomats of all nations—a minor genre by itself. And then there are the legions of wannabees. While not all diplomats really believe they produce work of high literary quality, almost all believe they at least produce work above the standard production of regular public servants. Writing skills have long been a major item in the annual officer efficiency reports, and woe betide the officer whose written work (now combined with speaking and labeled communication skills) is not praised in glowing terms by his superiors. One traditional manner in which to administer the stiletto has been to quietly imply that the rated officer's writing skills were somehow not up to the Foreign Service standard.

The above is background to explaining one of the unexpected joys of my assignment as principal officer to the American consulate in Lubumbashi, Republic of Zaire, in 1974. As the principal officer (boss), I was the person who decided upon and controlled the messages sent out to the Department of State. The reporting function, as noted, is a high-priority and prestigious activity in the Foreign Service, and now my name would be in the signature line of telegrams and airgrams. (We used to send a document called a dispatch—as in diplomatic dispatch—but somehow in the 1970s this was felt to be *démodé* and old-fashioned, so the written document was renamed an airgram, which implied that it traveled faster and was more modern. Actually, it traveled by the classic diplomatic pouch or mailbag and was processed in the State Department and other embassies in pretty much the same way as dispatches.)

By tradition, all diplomatic correspondence is "signed" by the head of mission (ambassador or chargé d'affaires) or principal officer (consul general or consul) and, in the case of outgoing messages from the Department of State, by the secretary of state. This practice is extended to monthly reports, ranging from the mileage of official vehicles to the number of passports issued and the arrival and departure of staff, as well as to weighty submissions on the prospects for war. Messages are written by legions of officers and staff and approved by an only slightly smaller group of supervisory officers authorized to approve draft documents for transmission. (The secretary of state actually reads only a handful of the thousands of messages, if that many, that go out every day over his or her signature, despite what some innocent or ignorant commentators like to pretend.)

From the beginning of modern diplomacy in the seventeenth century, the term "foreign service" has been used to characterize this special aspect of diplomacy; it was something done over there, in foreign countries. Practitioners—diplomats—were in government service over there, in "foreign" service. Increasingly in the modern world the term became a noun, and the United States formally adopted it early in the twentieth century when Congress created the Foreign Service of the United States—the official title of the American diplomatic service.

Most countries provide professional education for their diplomats. Some countries even provide education about diplomacy and foreign affairs to ordinary citizens. Not the United States. Therefore, it should not surprise anyone that the American public in general remains essentially ignorant about these subjects, though this ignorance does not in any way inhibit commentary from anybody and everybody.

As this book is about the observations of someone who practiced diplomacy as a government professional, it might be useful to lay out some terms and definitions. (Experienced practitioners may wish to skip this section.) Much confusion abounds in the popular mind about the subject of diplomacy. It has been famously noted that English is a tricky language, requiring a good deal of care to ensure that what is said is what is meant. Even at the level of single words, confusion can occur as words often have multiple meanings. One good example is "diplomacy," which, in addition to its formal reference to a specialized activity of governments, has entered into common parlance to denote personal qualities involving pleasing, tactful manners.

However, even in the context of its original meaning, there is much confusion among several terms that many people think are synonyms: foreign affairs, foreign policy, and diplomacy. Using some fairly standard dictionary definitions, we find that

- "foreign affairs" means "matters having to do with international relations and with the interests of the home country in foreign countries";

- "foreign policy" introduces a further distinction, "the diplomatic policy of a nation in its interactions with other countries";
- "diplomacy" is defined as "the art and practice of conducting negotiations and regular communications between nations" in order to implement those policies and pursue those interests.

We thus have a neat progression, from the general subject (foreign affairs) to a specific manifestation (foreign policy) to implementation (diplomacy).

The meaning of diplomacy is further complicated by two meanings in general usage, in that "a government's diplomacy" sometimes means a government's foreign policy and sometimes, in the operational sense, refers to the conduct of business between and among governments conducted through bureaucratic institutions, individuals, and processes.

Obviously, these terms and what they represent are overlapping. The continuing and inevitably intimate relationship between foreign policy and diplomacy, between the objective and the means, ensures that they can never be completely separated. For instance, U.S. foreign policy since World War II has included support for democracy; therefore, American diplomats pursue activities supporting democratic governments or encouraging democracy. But back when President John Quincy Adams stated that the United States does not go abroad in search of monsters to destroy, American diplomats and American diplomacy did not pursue that objective.

Diplomacy is the instrument of communication, not the message communicated. George Kennan, who thought about his profession as seriously as he did about foreign affairs and foreign policy, noted that "the classic function of diplomacy [is] to effect the communications between one's own government and other governments or individuals abroad, and to do this with maximum accuracy, imagination, tact, and good sense." In other words, the medium is only part of the message.

But the medium must have a corporeal form; in fact, it has two. The first is the activity itself, when officials—from presidents to embassy third secretaries and the occasional special representative—practice diplomacy, that is, conduct official communications between governments.

The second form is an established institution and the actual people who inhabit it. Even the internet, seemingly intangible as it is, requires some form of physical instrument to access it. For diplomacy that physical instrument is a diplomatic service ("the diplomatic and consular personnel of a country's foreign office"), which in the case of the United States is the Foreign Service of the United States (a governmental institution comprising government employees, established by law as part of the Executive Branch) and a ministry of foreign affairs, which in the case of the United States is the Department of State.

These departments and their personnel constitute one of the major tools in the foreign policy toolbox; others include the intelligence and military communities and the Treasury Department. Most countries try to organize these instruments in the form of a professional cadre—recruited, trained, and educated for their task as representatives and interpreters of their country's foreign policy. But diplomacy has never been a popular, or even well-understood, activity in most modern democratic countries. After the remarkable performance of Benjamin Franklin, who spent over eighteen years in "foreign service" in London and Paris, the United States proceeded to conduct its diplomacy with an ad hoc mixture of personalities chosen largely through the political tradition of the spoils system. By the end of the nineteenth century, however, the reform movement in the United States accepted the necessity of a professional foreign service for preserving the country's independent existence

That awareness produced the Rogers Act of 1924, which created the professional Foreign Service of the United States. Changes and reforms were introduced over the years of the twentieth century as the country moved from its traditional policy of hemispheric isolationism to world leadership. The current organization and mission of the Foreign Service were mandated by Congress in the Foreign Service Act of 1980, which stated:

1. A career Foreign Service, characterized by excellence and professionalism, is essential in the national interest to assist the President and the Secretary of State in conducting the foreign affairs of the United States; [and]
2. The scope and complexity of the foreign affairs of the Nation have heightened the need for a professional foreign service that will serve the foreign affairs interests of the United States in an integrated fashion and that can provide a resource of qualified personnel for the President, the Secretary of State, and the agencies concerned with foreign affairs.

So perhaps the problem of definition is not really that difficult. We only need to turn to the relevant legislation and listen to our elected leaders. They say the business of the Foreign Service is to "conduct diplomacy on behalf of the United States" and to "serve the foreign affairs interests of the United States." If Congress can understand this clear distinction, why can't everyone else?

Diplomats as a class have suffered from bad press for a long time. Back in the seventeenth century, Sir Henry Wotton famously quipped that a diplomat is "an honest gentleman sent to lie abroad for the good of his country." And Napoleon declared, "Ambassadors are, in the full meaning of the terms, titled spies." Against that backdrop, practitioners of diplomacy have worked hard to make their profession more respectable. In 1716 French diplomat François de Callières published *De la manière de négocier avec les souverains* (*On the Manner of Negotiating with Sovereigns*, often translated as *The Practice of Diplomacy*), a seminal text in the development of modern diplomacy and accompanying professional ethics.

Facilitating that process over the course of the nineteenth century, European governments took on the form of the modern nation-state. Governmental functions became increasingly regulated and standardized, and ethical standards began to emerge to govern bureaucrats in the performance of their duties. The belief that civil servants needed ethical guidelines arose naturally from their role as professionals exercising specialist knowledge and skill. As such they are capable of making judgments, applying their skills, and reaching informed decisions in situations that the general public is not qualified to review. How the use of this knowledge should be governed when providing a service to the public can be considered an ethical issue, to be managed or regulated by a set of standards or code of ethics.

Such a code gives officials and practitioners boundaries to stay within during their professional careers. But no set of guidelines can cover all ethical or moral considerations. As Francis Fukuyama observes in *The Origins of Political Order: From Prehuman Times to the French Revolution* (Farrar, Straus & Giroux, 2011): "In most political hierarchies, principals hold authority and delegate the implementation of their policies to agents, whom they appoint. Many governance dysfunctions arise because the agents have different agendas from the principals."

The obligation of the career public servant becomes even more complicated in the case of the diplomat, for whom the agent-principal relationship takes two forms: internally, within the bureaucracy representing his or her agency; and externally, where the diplomat is the agent for the government as a whole.

Writing in the May 1961 *Foreign Service Journal* on "Diplomacy as a Profession," George Kennan declared: "This is the classic function of diplomacy: to effect the communication between one's own government and other governments or individuals abroad, and to do this with maximum accuracy, imagination, tact and good sense." Or to put it another way, the job of a diplomat is to maintain communications between two separate political entities, as the representative of one to the other.

One element of this mission is obvious: the responsibility for delivering the "message" to the other government. But the mission also requires the bringing back of messages from the "other," as well as corollary information—intelligence, in other words. The diplomat is thus charged with a double task: studying and comprehending the nature of the outside world and communicating with other governments concerning his or her own government's interests and aspirations. As Kennan put it, the diplomat's job is to be "the bearer of a view of the outside world." And for that reason, any general code of ethics for diplomats must include a subset addressing their role as intermediary agents.

Although morality is often a matter of judgment, most commentators would classify most governments as essentially amoral in their external behavior. As Lord Strange observed, "Diplomacy as an institution can never have morals markedly superior to those of the governments whose tool it is; though, owing to the force of its corporate traditions, they are likely nowadays to be never worse, and usually rather better."

Despite the distinction between foreign policy and diplomacy, the inevitably intimate relationship between power politics and the functions of diplomacy means that the two can never be completely separated, at least in the mind of the general public.

Quotations along those lines are numerous. Here are just a few from Ambassador Charles W. Freeman's *Diplomat's Dictionary* (U.S. Institute of Peace Press, 2010):

- Diplomacy is to do and say the nastiest things in the nicest way. (Proverb)
- Diplomacy: the patriotic art of lying for one's country. (Ambrose Bierce)
- Diplomacy is to speak French, to speak nothing, and to speak falsehood. (Ludwig Boerne)
- Diplomats approach every problem with an open mouth. (Arthur Goldberg)
- In their own mind's eye, diplomats are imperturbable, courteous, painstaking, capable of seeing all sides of a problem, and firm and conciliatory, depending on the situation. In the view of many members of the general public, they are callous, cynical, standoffish, superficial, and vacillating. (Charles Roetter)

This jaundiced view of diplomacy, largely by nonpractitioners, has been reinforced by a modern popular attitude that focuses on one aspect: its secrecy. Americans in particular remain influenced by Woodrow Wilson's famous call for "open diplomacy," which contributed to a popular image of diplomats as untrustworthy double-dealers.

In some respects, the depreciation of diplomacy in the modern world reflects a lack of faith that it can really make a difference. As Hans Morgenthau notes: "There is nothing spectacular, fascinating, or inspiring, at least for the people at large, in the business of diplomacy." Seeing nothing spectacular occurring—in the modern world of TV and films and the internet, where people are bombarded every minute by the spectacular—many conclude that nothing is happening. The rare occasion when a Henry Kissinger flies in secret to a China is, in other words, rare.

While diplomats perform many of the same functions as other bureaucrats, they are unique in also serving as official communicators and interpreters between the external and internal worlds of a given nation-state. This responsibility gives them a Janus-like character that tends to highlight the role of personality in carrying out their mission. As Secretary of State Elihu Root once wrote: "More fights between natural persons come from insult than from injury. . . . Nations are even more sensitive to insult than individuals. One of the most useful and imperative lessons learned by all civilized governments in the practice of international intercourse has been the necessity of politeness and restraint in expression."

The role of the official observer and reporter—the interpreter of Secretary of State Dean Acheson's "vast external realm"—has always been fundamental to the definition of a diplomat throughout the historic development of communications technology. From the oral briefing, the handwritten dispatch, and the telegram to today's email and encrypted phone conversation, diplomatic reporting is a form of dialogue or conversation between the diplomat in the field and his or her master back in headquarters.

Though the conversation is official, it does not necessarily constitute policy. Rather, it is often about "informing and shaping policy through prophetic reporting and analytical writing," as Hannah Gurman observes in *The Dissent Papers: The Voices of Diplomats in the Cold War and Beyond*

(Columbia University Press, 2012). More bluntly, it is about the sausage making.

It is in the performance of this function that the distinction between the master and the agent arises. While the state may act amorally, the agent is required to conduct this dialogue in accordance with some standard of professional ethics—or else abandon any pretense of being an objective public servant. Such a dereliction of duty will eventually destroy his or her effectiveness, both with foreign interlocutors and among peers and colleagues. Only the trustworthy diplomat is useful to his or her government.

During the McCarthy era, dedicated officers like Jack Service and John Paton Davies—the old "China Hands"—were hounded out of the Foreign Service simply for reporting honestly on developments and trends in postwar China. And Wikileaks' release of thousands of confidential documents may have done comparable damage to the ability of U.S. diplomats to gather information, since local contacts are much less likely to speak candidly when they fear being quoted publicly.

Though different in motivation, both these types of threats strike at the very essence of a diplomat's professional ethic: the obligation to report, comment, and advise objectively. It is always tempting to prepare a report to satisfy the views of the recipient, or to justify the decisions made or about to be made by headquarters. Indeed, many senior officials, especially political figures, expect this. Instead, after firmly presenting his or her own country's views and policies externally, the truly professional diplomat must turn around and "report" objectively on the local response—without slanting his or her observations and comments to satisfy the report's recipients.

In their seminal 1953 study, *The Diplomats, 1919–1939*, Gordon A. Craig and Felix Gilbert decry "the growing tendency of home governments to give attention, and preferment, to those diplomats who reported what their superiors wanted to hear rather than to those whose analysis of the developing situation has been justified by history." This is a persistent temptation for all governments, but especially in democracies with lively domestic political environments. After all, the careers of the political leadership depend upon policy success, or at least avoidance of blame for failure. Moreover, because political leaders tend to value personal loyalty, career officials who introduce opinions and information at variance with the official policy line risk adverse consequences.

Another temptation for any diplomat in the field is to gild his or her own lily. (Has any drafter of a memorandum of conversation ever reported losing an argument?) And then there is the ever-present threat of "localitis": giving too much weight to the pressures and temptations of the local environment and at times becoming overly enamored of the host country.

The intellectual center of gravity of this professional perspective has two dimensions: the need to balance the present against the future, viewing the world objectively from both perspectives, and the need to protect one's credibility as an agent by not uttering falsehoods deliberately. The first half of the equation may seem obvious, though commentators have often ignored it. But as for the second, the distinction between misleading one's interlocutors and not lying to them is subtle and lost on many.

Self-delusion is dangerous for countries as well as individuals, and the diplomat's job is to introduce into political and policy deliberations the realities of that "vast external realm" which lies outside our borders. As Edmund Burke observed two centuries ago, "Nothing is so fatal to a nation as an extreme of self-partiality, and the total want of consideration of what others will naturally hope or fear." The ability to resist that tendency requires a robust adherence to ethical principles by Foreign Service officers.

This challenge is particularly daunting for diplomats operating in a totalitarian or authoritarian society. They must find ways to publicize and address human rights violations and other abuses of power, while still maintaining access to the local tyrant and his aides.

Today's world is full of places requiring this sort of compromise by the United States and other Western governments: from Syria to Saudi Arabia to North Korea, to numerous Big Man governments throughout

Africa, to several Latin American countries, and to Russia and China. On the one hand, a diplomat's failure to "make nice" can lead to being declared persona non grata and expelled from the country. If such an outcome is the result of specific instructions to press for democratic values and human rights, then so be it. That is what happened to my boss in Zaire, Ambassador Deane Hinton, in 1976. But in the absence of such directives, each diplomat must figure out how to conform (more or less) to the local ground rules for behavior.

For an example of the other end of the spectrum, consider what happened to U.S. ambassador to Iraq April Glaspie in 1990. Carefully following her instructions during a meeting with Iraqi president Saddam Hussein, she laid out the U.S. position regarding the Iraq-Kuwaiti border dispute. When Hussein invaded Kuwait soon thereafter, leading to the Persian Gulf War, some accused her of having given a green light for the invasion by the way she phrased her message.

No one who was not there can really say what transpired, but in light of Ambassador Glaspie's professional reputation and her own reporting on the event, most knowledgeable commentators dismiss such charges as unfair, if not irresponsible. That has never stopped the Monday-morning quarterbacks and those seeking scapegoats, however. As ever, diplomats are the favorite targets for politicians, journalists, academics, and other bureaucrats.

Such situations illustrate the conflict between the amorality of the state—especially in the practice of realpolitik—and the professional morality of the diplomatic agent. In a fundamental sense, a diplomat cannot thread this needle effectively without at least some adherence to professional ethics. Admittedly, this is far easier said than done. But even an immoral government is badly served by an immoral agent.

From two quarters comes welcome evidence that appreciation for the importance of dissenting views is not yet a lost cause, despite the lingering wounds of the McCarthy era and the persistent demands of party politics. In 1968, as the Vietnam War raged, the American Foreign Service Association began conferring two annual awards to recognize and encourage constructive dissent and risk-taking within the Foreign Service: the W. Averell Harriman Award for constructive dissent by junior officers (FS-6 through FS-4) and the William R. Rivkin Award for mid-level officers (FS-3 through FS-1). These awards were joined the following year by the Christian A. Herter Award, honoring constructive dissent by senior Foreign Service officers. All three of these awards have proven to be helpful to most recipients' careers, not harmful, much to the surprise of many cynics.

Separately, in 1971 the Department of State instituted what it calls the Dissent Channel, through which any employee may submit a message to the secretary on any subject. This mechanism remains unique, by the way; no other federal department or agency has anything similar. Despite continuing skepticism about the real-world impact of the Dissent Channel on U.S. diplomacy, many State employees have used it to criticize specific U.S. policies and propose alternatives.

These two initiatives constitute at least a formal recognition of the need for diplomats to pursue professional ethical obligations that may transcend work requirements.

All of this came home to me later when I arrived in Lubumbashi in August of 1974. As principal officer I was now the approving authority for all messages going out of the U.S. consulate in Lubumbashi. To paraphrase, it was a modest authority, but my very own.

I decided to take advantage of this situation. Modeling myself on an old tradition of the diplomatic *tour d'horizon* and of Janet Flanner's "Letter from Paris" series in the *New Yorker*, I wrote the first dispatch/airgram of the year in January 1975 with the title "Letter from Lubumbashi." It was a potpourri of comments and observations intended to provide readers with a feeling for the atmosphere and daily life of this remote corner of the world. As no one in the department nor the ambassador in Kinshasa complained or criticized my effort (in fact the ambassador said some nice things), I decided to make this a regular habit whenever I was in situations that permitted me to produce these letters without editing or the need to obtain approval from anyone else. After Lubumbashi

I produced a number in Guinea-Bissau and Cape Verde. As a student at the National War College at Fort McNair in Washington, I was not producing any official communications, but I wrote a "Letter" anyway, which was printed in the *Foreign Service Journal*. I dropped the habit for the next five years or so while working in Washington but renewed it when assigned as deputy chief of mission in Colombo, Sri Lanka. As my ambassador was a kindred spirit, he permitted me to write these "Letters from Colombo" as official exercises. I wrote similar papers, often for my own satisfaction, covering different situations, such as my time at the U.S. Mission to the United Nations in New York and after retiring at the U.S. Pacific Command in Hawaii. Even though they have been rewritten to varying degrees, I hope this material retains some of the immediacy of the originals, as I tried to avoid Monday-morning correction of my original impressions and comments.

I don't consider this book a classic memoir; there is little personal material in it and not much about my own professional career. There are no diplomatic secrets in these chapters, although I hope they possess some insight into a few of the minor byways of modern history. The goal is that they present some insight of a workaday American professional diplomat—a Foreign Service officer—what we think and what we do all day. They are the observations of a professional foreigner.

Unlike many of my colleagues, I did not participate in the traumatic national experience of Vietnam, did not become involved in major global issues like arms control and European integration, and did not serve in major capitals such as Moscow, London, or Tokyo.

Not that I wouldn't have wanted to, but things didn't work out that way for me—serendipity ruled. I was present in the decolonization era in Africa (but always seemed to be at the opposite end of the continent from the hottest developments), was intimately involved in the early days of the U.S. government's antiterrorism programs, observed close-up the unfolding of a nasty and tragic ethnic conflict in one of the most charming countries in the world, and saw the end of the Cold War at UN headquarters in New York. Not as much history nor as central a role as

I might have wished for, but not bad when viewed from the perspective of my youth in Detroit.

The book's personal recollections attempt to explain diplomacy as a daily activity. This is important, as the subject is grossly misunderstood by the public and in fact by much of the political class. As explained earlier, the word "diplomacy" has two general meanings. The most common refers to personal manners; "diplomatic" means well-mannered and sophisticated. It can be used as a compliment or a criticism (implying a preference for form over substance, if not outright two-faced behavior). The second and more fundamental meaning refers to the conduct of business between national governments. Most people really only know the first meaning, although some think it also covers the second. Which is why experienced and sophisticated people from the business, political, and academic worlds believe they are equipped to be diplomats, and so seek presidential nominations to be ambassadors. They think that diplomacy is a form of public relations requiring the personal skills covered by the word "diplomatic" when referring to personal qualities. They are wrong, but as everyone but professional diplomats is interested in maintaining this fiction, it survives and flourishes.

The following chapters tell of my years of apprenticeship and later years of other postings. Some other "places" I served were not foreign in any geographic sense but rather in cultural terms: the National War College, the United Nations in New York, and the United States Pacific Command in Honolulu. I assure readers that the military world can, indeed, be a very "foreign" place to civilians. The UN certainly does strike most Americans as foreign, even though located in Manhattan; but it is a world of concentrated diplomacy. There is no local government at the UN headquarters, no local population needing to be addressed with the tactics of "public diplomacy," no local or expatriate business community to service—just a self-contained world of diplomats. (And journalists, of course, but they are like pilot fish—always around.) But the very foreign atmosphere existent in UN headquarters does mean that an assignment there for an American diplomat is an assignment on "foreign service."

3

Apprenticeship

Upon discharge from the army in December 1958, I returned to Washington and to the Foreign Service Institute in Roslyn, Virginia, just across the river from Georgetown. The legendary FSI registrar, Mrs. Edrie Wray, welcomed me with a smile and the words, "Well, how are you? Welcome back." For a few minutes I was a notable figure.

As the next A-100 Class was not due to start for several weeks, I was set to doing busywork in the files of personnel, where I ran across the memorandum of my oral interview. A little look into the mirror, that. Nothing dramatic except, as mentioned earlier, I had been well advised not to try to bluff—an honest admission of ignorance to a question had gone down well with the interviewers. After a few weeks of this not very glamorous activity I joined my second A-100 Class (a dubious distinction shared with only one other FSO of my acquaintance) in order to finish the required junior officer program. As there was little substantive professional content to the course at that time (I don't know if it has much more today), this was a mere formality, although it had the downside of having to repeat the weeklong segment at the Department of Commerce. This was a program of such stupefying dullness that on the morning of the fourth day the entire back two rows of "students" collapsed into uncontrollable laughter akin to a state of hysteria.

The A-100 class ended, and off I went to my first assignment, as a program officer in the Foreign Special Program of the Bureau of Cultural and Educational Affairs (CU). It was not exactly what I had been

27

looking forward to, but then I still really did not know what work in the Foreign Service actually consisted of, or what my options were. In a moment of timidity, when first invited to join the Service back in the summer of 1956, I had indicated a preference for my initial assignment to be in Washington, and I got what I requested. There I was, organizing three-month U.S. visits for artists, academics, journalists, politicians, and others from Asia. CU was not exactly the sexiest part of the Department of State, although over the years I learned to appreciate how the U.S. government's cultural exchange programs like Fulbright and others played a truly influential role in contemporary history. Over the years, the hundreds of thousands of people who traveled and studied under the sponsorship of the U.S. government's exchange programs played a significant role in how the world has turned out. Lots of reasons have been given for the West's victory in the Cold War, but surely the steady, long-term exposure of the world's rising leadership class to a no-warts-hidden United States was one of them. At the end of the century, the concept of public diplomacy was all the rage, and there we were doing it in the 1960s without the trendy title. Was it Molière who had one of his characters surprised to find he had been speaking prose all his life without knowing it?

In any case, I went to work in my first Foreign Service assignment and almost immediately felt at home. My boss, Reid Bird, was the first FSO I got to know, and he remained my model for many years. I realized that I had stumbled into a good place. That first impression never left me, and thirty-six years later I retired still holding that view. It was later in Brussels in the early 1970s that John Heimann, a colleague and close friend, articulated our common conclusion—fostered by good Belgian beer—that it was truly a blessing to be paid to do such interesting work and lead such an enjoyable life.

My first overseas assignment set the pattern for the rest of my career—a small post in the Third World on the periphery of mainstream diplomacy. I was a vice consul and junior officer with a lady boss, Margaret McClellan, in a two-officer commercial section in the Consulate General in Nairobi, Kenya. I was not unhappy to go to Kenya, still a British colony, although I had asked for Asia. When called by the personnel placement officer informing me of my Nairobi assignment, I blurted out, "Don't you people read the preference report?" As I said earlier, I was very inexperienced.

In those days they did not pay a great deal of attention to the individual officer's assignment preference sheet—usually referred to as the April Fool sheet, as it had once been due for submission on April 1. The Foreign Service is a government bureaucracy, and personnel assignments are made on the basis of a good number of criteria, beginning with the "Needs of the Service," what jobs are open, and the selective human behavior of people in small, intimate organizations. Clearly, the more senior one became, the more that individual qualifications such as language, special skills, and "corridor reputation," combined with whom you knew, became more pertinent factors. Even after the reforms, reorganization, and expansion of the early 1950s, the Foreign Service remained a small organization of three thousand–plus officers that prided itself on being an elite professional group. Writing and speaking skills, foreign language and area experience, personal traits, and how you did in your last tour were what went into corridor reputations. Administration and management were not highly appreciated skills, as diplomacy was considered an art not a skill. While today this attitude is not politically correct, it is still alive and well in today's Foreign Service, albeit somewhat under cover. In any case, as I obviously didn't have much of a corridor reputation yet, Nairobi was as good a starting place as any.

It was a very Foreign Service sort of place for many reasons, and a good introduction to my career. My colleagues were friendly and cooperative, willing to help out a new boy. (Except that I did get into the black book of the consul general out of innocence and for reasons I still think superficial.) But Nairobi was important for another reason: it's where I met my wife, Aida. Later we married in Washington DC, in April 1963 when I was studying Spanish en route to Nuevo Laredo. Over the years at various posts, people would casually ask how we met—with an unstated insinuation about my distinctly provincial Detroit origins and her much more glamorous Iranian-Armenian persona and nickname as the Persian Princess. This has always given me the opportunity to respond, with deliberate Foreign Service casualness, "Why, at a cocktail party in Nairobi."

After the Spanish language classes, my new wife and my still jazzy Sunbeam Alpine sports car went off to spend two years issuing (and refusing) visas on the Texas-Mexico border. It was not the most desirable of professional opportunities—I had not joined the Foreign Service to end up on the U.S. border. Unhappy as I was, I was also a "good soldier" and served my consular tour with only moderate grumbling (no serious effort to buck the system). In many respects, it was not a bad two years. I certainly learned a lot about consular work and never disdained it afterwards. In fact, consular work on the border provided me with some of my best Foreign Service stories. This is true for many FSOs. After all, how many people have had the opportunity to negotiate the release of an American citizen being held captive in a brothel?

From Nuevo Laredo we went off to Angola, where I did consular and administrative work for less than a year, then on to Zambia as the head (and only American staffer) of the Economic-Commercial Section, followed by a return to Washington as the Kenya desk officer. Desk officer is not an official term or title—I believe the official phrase is country officer—but it is the traditional term, and one much respected in foreign offices and other organizations that deal in international affairs. While relatively junior (except for the senior officer on a very big country desk like the USSR in the old days), the desk officer occupies a central position in all that is happening between the United States and "his/her" country. Desk officers are in the middle of whatever is going on, and the professional satisfactions are generally enormous.

It is a conventional attitude among FSOs that Washington duty is onerous and distasteful, as real diplomacy is practiced and lived in the "field." Washington assignments are required but never sought. In reality, Washington assignments are often sought for professional and personal reasons. But just as army officers glory in the appellation "mud soldiers," so, too, do FSOs like to identify themselves as diplomats and not State Department officials. After all, Washington is full of civil servants (a lesser breed), but FSOs are diplomats (a definitely higher class of elite public servants). A sense of historic ownership of the foreign field is part of the reason that FSOs resent the growing presence of others (political appointees, CIA officers, Treasury representatives, DEA agents, and so forth), intruding on the historically sacred grounds of embassies and consulates and messing around like bulls in the china shop of diplomacy.

I did not go directly from Zambia to the Office of East African Affairs, but instead went on a six-month detour to the Foreign Service Institute for its relatively new six-month course in economics. On the basis of my Nairobi tour, I was now slotted as an economic-commercial specialist. This was before the creation of the current system of formal career specialties, or "cones"; such specializations existed but were somewhat informal. Nevertheless, there was a well-established pecking order: political, economic, consular, administrative. With Zambia under my belt, I was now inducted into the substantive or "real diplomat" part of the community (political, and economic), though not branded with the most prestigious label (political officer).

FSI's economic course was the first, and quite possibly still is, the only serious substantive course at FSI, whose catalogue consists mostly of language programs and a potpourri of short so-called tradecraft courses covering how to issue visas and perform administrative tasks. There are a number of courses in foreign cultures and political developments, but these are usually quite short—days or a few weeks rather than months—and fairly superficial.

The economic course was quite different: six months of full-time study intended to provide the equivalent of an undergraduate major of thirty-plus academic hours. The faculty were professional academics, not FSOs or civil servants on temporary duty. The class hours were long and the study requirements heavy. The economic course was initiated in the mid- or late-1960s to meet an increasing need for FSOs with basic economic literacy, a quality in short supply among the mostly humanities-trained recruits to the Foreign Service. Since the department believed in the importance of economic matters in contemporary diplomacy and could not manage to recruit sufficient numbers of new officers with the requisite background, it decided to provide the background by means of an in-service training program. I cannot speak to what improvement this program has made in the design and implementation of American foreign and economic policy over the past thirty-some years—there are too many variables and too many cooks—but FSI's economic course continues to be given today and has earned a reputation as being solid, serious, and professional.

For various reasons, I was no more than an average student. Still, I remember the experience with gratitude as it provided the necessary foundational background for the work I did throughout my career. For many years, I was an economic-commercial officer, which is different from being an economist. Even when I was not functioning in the economic or commercial field, the background and intellectual orientation of the FSI course enriched my perspective of contemporary developments wherever I was by ensuring that I always included an economic perspective. This was true for many of my fellow students. In both significantly increasing general economic literacy in the professional diplomatic service and providing the first steps in the development of professional Foreign Service economists, the course has been and continues to be an enormous success.

Kenya desk officer was a good job, and I thoroughly enjoyed it. But what with the economics course and all, I was getting restless to return overseas. Although by now I was more or less an "Africanist"—three posts and one assignment in the Africa Bureau—a chance to go to Europe was too enticing to turn down. It was not Paris or London or Rome, however, but Brussels, as an economic officer. Brussels turned out to be our one European assignment, which may be one reason why we remember it with such fondness. But maybe not. My wife was a native-level French speaker, and I had at least a Foreign Service Institute foundation. In any case, we found ourselves thoroughly at home in Belgium.

Of course, Brussels was not Paris—every young American's dream. But while the city was desirable, our Paris embassy did not have a particularly good reputation for junior officers in the Foreign Service of that day—too big and bureaucratic. Also Brussels was beginning to make the claim (admittedly exaggerated!) that it was the Capitol of Europe as the site of NATO and the European Economic Community (which later expanded into today's European Union). Although Brussels had often been compared unfavorably with Paris, we were excited by the assignment and found it very much to our liking, replete with congenial fellow diplomats and superb dining establishments. We had a lovely 1930s Art Deco apartment in the city center, a lovable Yorkie puppy, and many friends. For three years our life resembled diplomacy in the movies (think Gary Grant and Audrey Hepburn).

When a journalist friend proposed that we attend the annual high society horse race in Brussels (a copy of the one prominently portrayed in "My Fair Lady") I jumped at the idea. So we rented the appropriate costume (the grey long coat, white tie, and high hat also prominently displayed in "My Fair Lady") and off we went. Our wives sensibly declined.

After three delightful years Africa called again, but this time via a posting as a principal officer, albeit of a small consulate (four officers, a total of five American staff) in Lubumbashi. Those with a military background will appreciate the satisfaction of being in command. Zaire, *née* the Congo before it returned later to the name of Congo, is a very large and important country in Africa. At that time it was only a few years past a tumultuous and violent history following the achievement of independence from Belgium in 1960. Lubumbashi was the capital of Shaba Province (formerly Katanga), which by itself was the size of many quite respectably sized countries and which contained the world's third largest copper industry. It was far from the embassy in Kinshasa, where my boss, the ambassador, was located. American diplomats had played major roles in the history of the 1960s, and in Lubumbashi I would be following in the footsteps of some distinguished colleagues. I hoped that my incumbency would also contain an opportunity to shine.

Fate decreed that my time in Lubumbashi was to be cut relatively short. After eighteen months I was recalled to Washington to fill the position of deputy office director of Central African Affairs. Clearly I had performed well enough to satisfy my superiors in Washington or they wouldn't have called me home to what was a good career job. Still, I had to admit that my tenure in Zaire had turned out, in one major respect, like my other African posts. Although I did not realize it at the time, Lubumbashi was to be another round in what turned out to be the defining characteristic of my diplomatic career. Somehow, I always seemed to arrive after historic events and then leave before the next round.

Substantively, the main lesson I took away from these years was that history plays a dominant role in determining culture, and that culture pretty much determines everything else. Why was Kenya, with its British colonial history and particular collection of local peoples, like the Kikuyu and Luo, different from neighboring Tanzania—not to mention Somalia to the north and Ethiopia to the northwest? Nuevo Laredo presented a daily illustration of the mixture and tension of different cultures. Angola and Zambia were to offer slightly different pictures, not out of focus but focused differently. Experience in Belgium, Portuguese West Africa, and Sri Lanka only confirmed this impression, or insight, if I can be so pretentious.

Due to arrive in Lubumbashi in mid-August 1974, I spent one of my last weeks in Europe in Wiesbaden. I had been pursuing, in a more or less desultory fashion, a master's degree in economics at the University of Oklahoma's Wiesbaden center and had one course left to complete. At the end of a beautiful Friday in late August I drove my green Fiat Spyder from Brussels across Luxembourg down the Rhine to Wiesbaden, spent a week in class there, and then returned driving along the Rhine, across the Palatinate to Belgium, and back to Brussels. All with the top down. I felt like the "American in Europe," as in the 1930s novel.

For want of a better term, I used to think of the time before Lubumbashi as my apprenticeship years. I was pretty much a subordinate, doing professional work but always under someone else's direction. Arriving in Lubumbashi after a short stopover in Kinshasa for briefings and a call on the ambassador, I entered into a new phase of my career and my life. Though in a bureaucracy one is always working under somebody's direction, from the middle levels up one has the responsibility of leading and directing down. Not everyone does this with grace and competence. Lubumbashi became my opportunity to find out if I could do it with grace and competence.

After Lubumbashi I always served in some sort of supervisory position, in what the private sector calls middle management. Or, to ponder the warning that John Heimann gave me: One day you will overhear one of your junior officers (those in their twenties on their first or second tour) refer to you as "the Old Man." When that happens, he said, merely smile and accept that you are in a new stage of your life.

On that Friday evening in August 1974, at forty years of age, I became the American consul in Lubumbashi, the most senior representative of the United States of America for over five hundred miles in every direction.

4

Nairobi, Nuevo Laredo, Luanda

Returning to 1959, I arrived at my first foreign posting just before the Christmas holidays. Although not an embassy, the consulate general in Nairobi was a reasonably sized post for Africa in those days, with only about a dozen or so American officers plus other American staff, but it was quite high profile. Kenya and Nairobi were well-known and even glamorous places—what with Hemingway and the movies and all.

Besides the consul general, we had a deputy principal officer, two FSOs in the economic/commercial section, one or two in the consular section, a Central Intelligence Agency section, a labor/political officer, an administrative officer, and a communications section. Rounding us off were the U.S. Information Service (USIS) and the U.S. Agency for International Development (USAID) missions. My direct boss during most of my tour was Margaret McClellan. Interestingly, both senior economic officers during this assignment were women, with service dating back to World War II.

I arrived in December 1959, and my two years in Nairobi were thoroughly enjoyable. I had my first new car, a white Sunbeam Alpine sports car, and a new wardrobe that included my first dinner jacket. The wardrobe had been purchased at "No-Label Louie's"—a plain-pipe-rack furniture outlet located at G and Ninth Streets northwest in Washington. The actual name of the store was "Louie's," but we added the qualifier because the suit jackets had no labels. A lower-cost provider of Brooks Brothers styles, Louie's is now well established under its own name of

Jos. A. Bank. From Louie's we spread out into the world, readily recognizable as Americans in the State Department summer "uniform" of the wash-and-wear cotton poplin suit. This was before Europeans themselves took to wearing brush cuts, blue jeans, and button-down shirts. In those days they sneered at such. If I remember correctly, the summer suits cost $22.50 and winter-weight wool suits upwards of $40.

Nairobi was a surprisingly cosmopolitan and international city, flowering in the last days of the British Raj before independence in 1963. The rigid, three-tiered colonial social structure (Europeans, which included Japanese; Asians, largely the resident Indian population; and natives, or Africans) was beginning to break down. Shortly before I arrived, our consul general had removed the "European" and "African" signs from our restrooms. I have not participated in many historical moments in my career, but I was present at the Equator Club (black tie required on Saturday nights unless your White Hunter vouched that you had neglected to bring it on safari) when the rising African politician Tom Mboya broke the color bar. As it happened, Mboya and the other man in his party wore black tie.

My tour in Kenya coincided with those last years of British colonial rule, and we were all busily trying to adapt and predict. The rush to identify and meet the soon-to-be leaders of a new country was a special interest of the foreign diplomats and journalists in town. A major American undertaking was the so-called Kennedy Airlifts, which transported hundreds of young Africans to the United States for university educations. Although I was an economic/commercial officer, all of us occasionally pitched in to process the rush of visa business. Among that crowd was a young Luo named Barack Hussein Obama, but if I processed his visa application I don't remember.

Kenya was unique as a colony, being the only European colony in Africa, and probably in the world, where the unofficial, private settlers came from a higher social class in the home country than the officials in Government House. As was constantly noted with great satisfaction by British Ken-

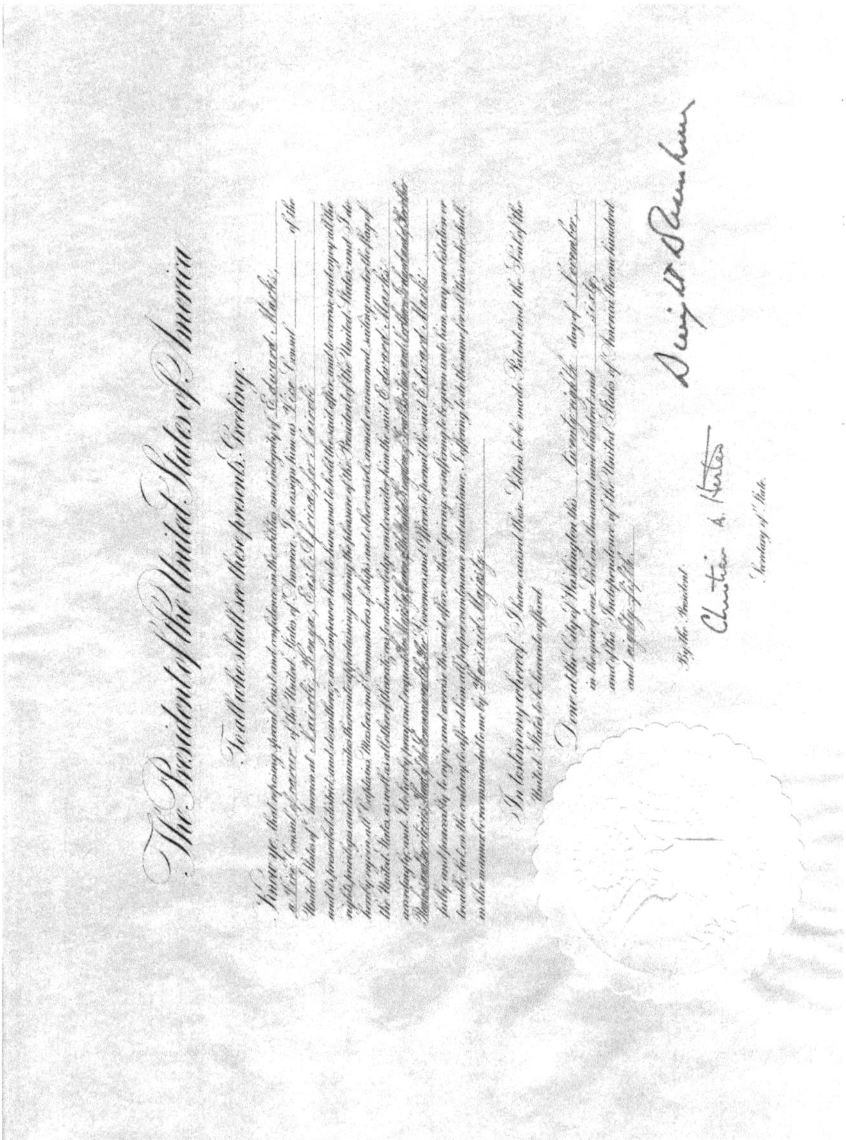
The President of the United States of America

To all who shall see these presents, Greeting:

Fig. 2. Author's commission as the Vice Consul of the United States in the British Colony of Kenya. Author's collection.

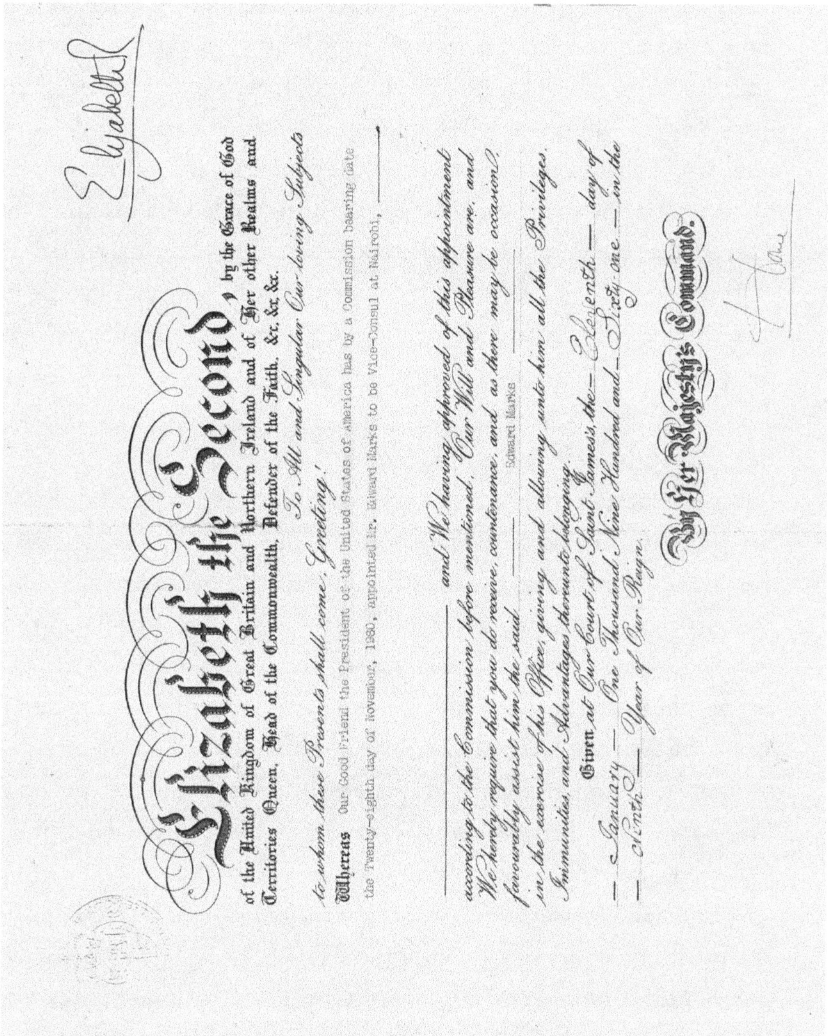

Elizabeth R

Elizabeth the Second, by the Grace of God of the United Kingdom of Great Britain and Northern Ireland and of Her other Realms and Territories Queen, Head of the Commonwealth, Defender of the Faith, &c. &c. &c.

To All and Singular Our loving Subjects to whom these Presents shall come, Greeting!

Whereas Our Good Friend the President of the United States of America has by a Commission bearing date the Twenty-eighth day of November, 1960, appointed Mr. Edward Marks to be Vice-Consul at Nairobi,

and We having approved of this appointment according to the Commission before mentioned, Our Will and Pleasure are, and We hereby require that you do receive, countenance, and as there may be occasion favourably assist him the said Edward Marks in the exercise of his Office, giving and allowing unto him all the Privileges, Immunities, and Advantages thereunto belonging.

Given at Our Court of Saint James's the Eleventh day of January One Thousand Nine Hundred and Sixty-one in the Ninth Year of Our Reign.

By Her Majesty's Command.

Fig. 3. English government authorization (exequatur) to serve as a U.S. vice consul in Kenya, with signature by Queen Elizabeth. Author's collection.

yans, "Kenya was settled by the Officers' Mess, Rhodesia by other ranks." The romantic reputation of Karen Blixen and the White Highlands of *Out of Africa* fame was cherished. That social class attitude, interestingly, remained a characteristic of independent Kenya. This class consciousness, this arrogance of the English county gentry class, was picked up by Black Kenyans who persisted after independence in wearing Saville Row suits, while their peers around Africa experimented with various forms of "authentic" African garments. The Kenyans tended to look down on their African neighbors as country cousins.

This was the beginning of my learning that history plays a role in determining culture, and that culture pretty much determines everything else.

In actuality, Nairobi was a much more complicated place behind the European façade, covering a complex world of Indians and Africans nervously interacting as the prospect of independence became closer every day. Nairobi was the most important city between Cairo and Johannesburg, with a population of about 350,000, of whom fifty or sixty thousand were Europeans or Asians, a large consular community, and the regional headquarters for many airlines, banks, and other international firms. The drama of the Mau Mau Rebellion was only half a dozen years in the past. The "wind of change" forecast by British prime minister Harold Macmillan contrasted with the governor-general of Kenya's description of Jomo Kenyatta as a "leader into darkness and death."

Nairobi and its romantic mystique attracted journalists, academics, and other onlookers from all over the world, coming to watch African independence unfold and European colonialism collapse. Enthusiasm and optimism ran high. Apart from the grumpy colonists now packing their bags, almost all assumed that independence would produce an African renaissance marked by democracy and rapid economic development. Later, I realized that the majority of journalists and academics interested in Africa were emotionally committed to African success to a considerable degree. They were essentially Western liberals trying in some way to atone for the sins of the colonial period. Most Western diplomats, especially we Americans, went along with this mood.

Colonial social life in Nairobi remained active. I wore black tie more often than I ever did again. (In retrospect, the usual scene after dessert at dinner parties of a row of tuxedoed gentlemen "visiting Africa" in the garden while the ladies used the bathrooms, was really funny.)

While I did not go on any actual hunting safaris, I did get around the country some and even spent Christmas Eve 1961 in a blizzard at fifteen thousand feet on Mount Kenya. Work was interesting, and my boss and the other officers were supportive and helpful. I thought I learned a lot and performed reasonably well. Unfortunately, for various reasons I got crossways with the consul general, a development which I thought then—and still believe—was due more to his character flaws than any youthful follies of mine. His view of me, however, did not do my career prospects any good. His reviewing officer's statement on my annual efficiency report kept me in my very junior grade of FSO-7 a couple years longer than warranted, and probably contributed to my next and decidedly unglamorous assignment as vice consul in Nuevo Laredo, Mexico.

Still, Nairobi was my first post, where I continued to learn about the responsibilities that go with a public position, however junior, and thus why diplomats are generally conservative in manner and behavior.

Nairobi was especially important for another reason. I met my future wife at one of the innumerable cocktail parties and receptions, which also produced my best Foreign Service line, mentioned earlier.

From Nairobi I went to Nuevo Laredo on the Texas-Mexico border. It turned out to be an interesting interlude, with added exposure to the cross-cultural world, although I grumbled from beginning to end. I had not joined the Foreign Service to spend two years on the U.S. border, especially as I had grown up on one. Nevertheless, two years passed quite pleasantly in Los Dos Laredos. In its bicultural environment, almost everyone had family on both sides of the border, social life was cross-border, and we ate Tex-Mex food before it became common in the rest of the States. All this was before the drug wars of a later era completely changed the atmosphere.

It was a real cultural border, a frontier between two cultures in a way that the Canadian border certainly was not. Two distinct cultures came up against each other, although not strictly at the border itself but in a roughly defined area just north of the border. From Nuevo Laredo south, the country was Mexico in every respect. North, in Laredo and in a fuzzy area spreading as far as San Antonio, there was a cultural mix where people said things like "*parkear su carro*," ate Tex-Mex food, and spoke English (mostly) with a heavy dose of Spanish words, not to mention accent. The language as well as the food was Tex-Mex.

The U.S. Air Force base outside of Laredo was a pilot-training base, with many foreign students. They included a number from Iran, whom Aida invited to our house for "home-cooked" Persian meals. I often wonder what happened to them.

Nuevo Laredo produced some of my best Foreign Service consular stories, as is common among Foreign Service people. Securing the release of a U.S. citizen held in a Mexican brothel, mentioned earlier, was one of the best. Others were usually less amusing, albeit interesting.

The consulate in Nuevo Laredo sits at the Texas-Mexico border. Prostitution and what we consider underage drinking are legal, or at least acceptable and certainly readily available in Mexican border towns like Nuevo Laredo. A good number of young (and old) men and boys from all over Texas hopped into their cars on Friday nights and roared down to spend some time in the bars and cantinas and brothels of Mexico. Needless to say, that crowd included many of the servicemen stationed at the numerous military bases in Texas.

Given this activity, and people being people, we thus had a constant stream of applications for immigrant visas by Mexican spouses of U.S.-citizen husbands. At this point, Section 212(a)12 of the Immigration and Naturalization Act often reared its head. That section referred to immoral background or intentions, the possession of which precluded receipt of any visa to enter the United States, most especially immigrant visas for permanent residence.

Now, prostitution may be considered an immoral activity in the U.S., but not so much in Mexico. But because of public health concerns, Mexican prostitutes registered by the local authorities and regularly inspected by public health officials. This available source of information gave U.S. consular officers a ready way of dealing with a delicate problem: how to separate the sheep from the goats, so to speak, in this category of visa applicants; in other words, how to identify any visa applicant ineligible under this provision of the law. The problem was complicated because many applicants were eligible. So, being bureaucrats and human beings (the two categories are not mutually exclusive), we used a rule of thumb set by a long line of predecessors: We assumed that the Mexican spouse of a Mexican-American would not fall under Section 212(a)12 on the presumption that Mexican-American men would not go down to Mexico to marry prostitutes, and eligibility was thus assumed.

However, an Anglo-American with a new Mexican wife was a different story (unless, say, the American spouse in question was a well-known lawyer from San Antonio and the Mexican spouse a daughter of a well-known Mexican banking family). Checking with the always cooperative Mexican public health officials on the obvious cases—and they really were obvious—produced a positive identification nine times out of ten. Consequently, such an applicant was ineligible for a visa. Even though the applicant was now the legitimate wife of an American citizen, the immigration law prevented her entry.

Often that would not be the end of the story. American immigration law in fact recognizes the possibilities for reform and redemption. If the applicant swears that she has reformed (easily enough done) and the sponsoring spouse signs a request for a waiver of ineligibility on the grounds of reform, the law provides for a waiver and the visa can be issued. The process took about six months although the key requirement—admission of the charge—was obviously a delicate if not traumatic event.

The actual visa interview would take place in the visa officer's private office away from the public reception area. As the applicant was being interviewed, the husband, usually present, waited outside. If the applicant had been identified as a prostitute I would have to inform her that her visa application was denied. I then would explain the option available to her and that it was up to her to explain to her husband why. If she would admit the charge, her husband could apply for a waiver. This action required the husband to acknowledge his wife's background on the exemption application form. The emotional implications of this act are obvious. For some, those accepting and essentially comfortable with the wife's previous employment, the event was at most a bit embarrassing, although we made every effort to keep it low-key and "in-house," so to speak, involving only the two participants involved.

Getting a woman to admit she is or has been a prostitute, then having her go out and tell her husband was a bit daunting, at least for this new, young, and innocent FSO. The whole process was a vivid introduction into people's complicated lives.

I saw many different reactions in my two years with this responsibility. Believe it or not, there were those who were either so naive or so witless that they did not understand the situation in which they had met their beloved. After all, the Mexican cantina can be a rather jolly place, and some of these young Anglo men were true innocents. Reactions varied, from a shrug of the shoulders to high dudgeon and refusal to accept the charge. Three cases stand out in my memory.

The first arose when I arrived at post. The young lady had been interviewed, found ineligible under 212(a)12, had applied for and received her INS waiver, and all that remained was for me to issue the visa. An unusual aspect of the case was that her husband was an air force lieutenant—unusual in that almost always the spouses in this situation were enlisted men or the civilian equivalent. When the young woman came into my office, I almost fell off my chair. She was young, lovely, and elegant, well dressed in the style of that time and place in a linen summer frock, white high-heeled pumps, and matching handbag. Her English was correct and fluent, with an attractive Mexican accent. She could have passed easily as the daughter of one of Nuevo Laredo's best families. Yet she was only nineteen and had spent the last five years or so working in the brothels up and down the border. She obviously had innate class and taste and was clearly brighter than her husband. She broke down in tears when I gave her the visa. (This was when I learned to keep a box of tissue in my desk drawer.) I often wonder what became of them, but I felt that wherever they went and whatever they did, she would, in the language of the day, be an asset.

A second case was of a completely different kind. The young wife, not to tiptoe around the bush, was almost a central casting image of a Mexican prostitute. Her husband was a young man from San Antonio with an Italian last name. During the wife's interview, the husband, his central casting image of an Italian-American mother, and several other family members waited outside. The mother's attitude was not exactly joyous. The applicant denied the charge, although the identification of her as a "working girl" was unequivocal, so I had to deny the visa. I explained the waiver procedure to her. I am not sure how she explained the visa refusal when she went out to the family, but the mother seemed somehow gratified, and they all left talking loudly and never came back.

The next case was a real tearjerker, involving a horny-handed construction contractor from Galveston. He was quite well-to-do and a real diamond in the rough. He had met his lady love in one of the towns along the border. She was not beautiful, not elegant, not young, and had seven children in tow from at least three fathers. He wanted to take care of her and the children, but she could not get a U.S. immigration visa, even with an INS waiver, because Mexican law would not permit her to take the children out of the country without permission from the father, or rather fathers. This was not possible as she was not even sure who they were, much less where to find them. She was therefore stuck in Nuevo Laredo, where her American husband (they had gotten married) had set her up in a nice house, although he had already built a house for them in Galveston.

He came down every weekend in his Cadillac and tried to get her through the Mexican system. We in the consulate were rooting for them and were prepared to process the visas but could not do so without passports for the children, which they could not get. (I do not remember why, but we could not get a passport waiver.) It was a tragic situation. Our sympathies were so engaged that, in fact, we kept hinting (illegally and unprofessionally) to him that he ought to get the visa for his wife and then slip the kids across some night, but he would not. He insisted on doing things legally, and therefore remained trapped. It was almost a soap opera but with real people. It was unresolved when I left Nuevo Laredo.

Other visa stories involved the adventures of various types of American tourists, like rescuing a guy who thought he was Jesus Christ from jail and driving him across the bridge to the railway station on the U.S. side. By and large the Mexican authorities did not make a lot of trouble for Americans, especially the kids who got into trouble. The Mexican police would grab and book them for a quick fine and then let them go. Tourism was too important to the local economy.

I only had one tricky American citizen situation in my two years in Nuevo Laredo. It involved a tourist of the type who does not usually get into trouble on the border—a doctor, lawyer, or some such—who had been involved in a car accident. This sort of incident was usually sorted out quickly and rarely involved the consulate. But this particular individual had become aggressive with the police and others, and they had tossed him into jail. He was very unhappy. I could have gotten him out right away, upon his promise not to leave town until the accident charges were sorted out the next day, probably to include a fine. But I could see by his body language that he had no intention of keeping that promise, which would have left me holding the bag. The Mexican authorities would clearly have settled for a fine, as they had no real desire to keep him in jail, but he was very much into that indignant American mode; "Who do they think they are? They can't put me in jail, I am an American citizen, etc." Soon enough, the Mexican police shrugged their shoulders and settled for a fine, but he did spend some hours in a Mexican jail.

Another thing I learned on the border and in visa work is the real cultural gap between the official and the applicant, the foreigner, in this case Mexican, who was merely trying to travel across a border for one reason or another. Many were what we now call economic migrants or refugees. For the sophisticated or middle-class applicant, the process is polite and understandable. To the economic migrant, however, the consular officer is this foreigner—this rich and powerful "Gringo"—talking about ideas that are as complicated as the doctrine of the Trinity. This was especially true of the category of "bona fide nonimmigrant," a key concept in U.S. immigration law (and one almost impossible to administer as it requires reading the applicant's mind and future intentions). To the applicant, you are talking gibberish. It was not a language problem; in fact, my Spanish became quite good. As all who have had to do it know, trying to explain the concept of the bona fide nonimmigrant in any language is almost as difficult as explaining the theory of the Big Bang.

I learned that the consular officer and the applicant were often two different worlds in conflict. It wasn't quite as stark as Kafka's world, perhaps, but in a situation where the applicant is essentially seeking to change his life, speaking to the incomprehensible official world was an art form. Were they really lying? In the truest sense, yes, of course. To the applicant, however, we are arbitrary officials who need to be placated because we hold the key to passage across the border. What is it you want to know? Whatever it is he will tell you. They don't care because your concerns are not about anything that has any meaning or reality to them. What is important is to get across the border. All in all, it was an interesting exposure to cross-cultural interaction and cross-cultural misunderstanding.

But time passed and the Personnel Assignments Office reappeared in my life. My wife and I went back to Africa, to the consulate general in the Portuguese colony of Angola—another small, off-the-beaten-path consular post. Only four American officers at the post, and we all pitched in with the various tasks, although I did most of the consular and administrative work. Along the way I passed through the Foreign Institute language school to have my Spanish modified into Portuguese. This process was quite successful, although later experience and the passage of time produced a linguistic mixture called "Portunol."

Despite the by-now widespread assumption that the "wind of change" would soon produce independence all over Africa, the Portuguese resisted. They were still unwilling to accept the change. Portuguese officials were quite aware of developments elsewhere in Africa but repeated constantly the theme that they were the first into Africa and would be the last out. I learned a lot about the Portuguese in Luanda. They are a very stubborn people, and I became very fond of them.

The Portuguese view of history was self-centered. In 1965 they still had no intention of giving way to the "wind of change," having retitled Angola as an "overseas province" and therefore not a "colony." The permanent population, including Africans, were all legally Portuguese citizens.

This was still the Portugal of Salazar, and Portuguese Angola was a classic settler colony cut off from the wider world. Luanda was a lovely town, all red-tiled roofs and Mediterranean looking, some of it dating from the early days of the Portuguese presence in the fifteenth century. The city lies on a little bay, with magnificent beaches on both the bay and ocean sides and a marvelous old fort at the head, overlooking the ocean on one side and the city on the other. There were only a few Portuguese international flights a week from Lisbon and Kinshasa (Congo). One of the favorite social events of the week was going out to the airport to see the planes and people come and go.

Despite the pretended legal situation, Angola was obviously a colony. There were five hundred thousand residents of pure Portuguese origin (some resident for many generations) among a total population of five or so million that included quite a few mestizos, people of mixed Portuguese and African families, and the two groups constituted a robust settler community embedded in a more classic "colony." The Portuguese pride themselves on not being racist, although in fact it was only a relatively short time since they had extended citizenship to all residents and eliminated the distinction between *indigene* and *civilizado*. However, they were clearly free of the more obvious and extreme racial attitudes, including sexual, of most European colonials. Yet one heard from time to time the tacky but very Portuguese "witticism"—"God made the white man, the Devil made the black man, and the Portuguese made the mestizo."

And the Portuguese are stubborn, a trait illustrated by an incident in the global war between the Portuguese and the Dutch in the early seventeenth century. The Dutch tried to take over Portugal's global empire—global because it included holdings in Asia, Africa, and Latin America. A Dutch fleet took Luanda from the Portuguese in 1610, but the defeated garrison did not surrender, retreating into the hinterland, with the Dutch following them. A series of skirmishes ensued until the Portuguese, with some native allies, finally held at a place called Massangano, about 110 miles inland from the coast. There they built a fortress and a church, a really elegant structure that is still standing. They held out and waited for relief, these sixty or seventy Portuguese in the middle of Africa, and relief did come—seven or eight years later. Now I call that stubborn.

Given that history, I could understand—without accepting—the boasts the Portuguese officials and colonials would repeat in those days, rejecting the "wind of change" and those anticolonial attacks they were receiving from many quarters: "*Nos, so nos!*" (Us, us alone!) and "We were the first in Africa, we will be the last to leave!"

A funny place. Angola, as Portugal itself was not an open, democratic society. Yet in one sense you had equality of treatment. The political environment, the role of the political police, and limitations on discussion and behavior in Luanda were no worse than they were in Portugal itself. We didn't find that bit of hypocrisy found in the French and British colonies, with democracy at home and autocracy in the colony. Angolans and Portuguese were equal before the law and the political powers, all at the bottom.

In Angola, while most senior people in the government and in the commercial and professional classes were "white" Portuguese, there were also significant numbers of mestizos and a few token Africans. The peasant class was essentially African, but the working class in the cities and small towns included "white" Portuguese, mestizos, and Africans. For instance, there were Portuguese cab drivers in Luanda. The racial question was blurred and not as clear as it had been, for instance, in Kenya.

Recent history also played a role. Independence in the Congo (later renamed Zaire) in 1960–61 had been pretty nasty, and later got even worse. For the Portuguese, the Belgian Congo was an example of what not to do. They interpreted that recent history as confirmation that they were right to stay and continue to impart civilization over time. They felt they were better at the civilizing mission because they claimed to be devoid of racial hang-ups, unlike the other European colonizers. They had been in Africa longer, they said, understood it better, with a mixed racial society themselves, and were therefore able to build a society in Angola that could survive. Or so they said.

A greater danger to Lisbon's rule was the possibility of a Rhodesian-type independence by the local elite. Many in the important mestizo community were in sympathy with the Portuguese "white" settlers. Lisbon therefore not only had to worry about an African independence movement; it had to watch out for a Rhodesian-style "UDI" (Unilateral Declaration of Independence), with the local whites taking over control and declaring themselves independent. There was real interest in that option among the local whites, and it could have become a real possibility if the African rebellion in 1960–61 had not required Lisbon to send a large number of metropolitan troops to Angola. By the time the Rhodesians had set the example, fifty thousand Portuguese soldiers in Angola made it no longer a realistic possibility. That is, if the temptation to go that route did not infect the metropolitan troops—a development not beyond the realm of possibility.

I wrote a memo on the subject, arguing that the change in Angola would occur as a result of developments in Lisbon, when a post-Salazar government would cast off the "overseas provinces." And that is exactly what happened. Up to the time of the revolution in Lisbon, Portuguese control in Angola was not effectively challenged.

It was in Luanda that I began to develop the view that there was not much real difference between the various European colonial systems in Africa. The British always claimed that they were the only ones who knew how to properly run and develop a colony, while the French said the same thing. Both the English and the French—officials, academics, journalists, and colonists themselves—also held the opinion that the Belgians, on the other hand, were terrible and the Portuguese even worse. I later decided that that was largely nonsense spouted by colonial office apologists and that there was really not much difference between colonies. Differences did exist, but they arose from whether or not a specific colony was run by and for settlers or by an administrative system.

Our little consulate general was relatively cut off from the world. Telegrams were transmitted through the international telegraph system. We used to obtain our classified pouches by making our own weekly courier runs by airplane to Kinshasa, and surface pouches were received via U.S. flag freighter. We would seal the outgoing pouches (canvas mail bags), carry them down to the port, and hand them over to the captain of a U.S. flag freighter. Really old fashioned, and very charming. In fact, Luanda was for me a replay of a conversation I had listened to a few years previously. Three or four young officers were sitting around the old DACOR (formerly Diplomatic and Consular Officers Retired) house a few years before our first tours. We were listening to an about-to-retire FSO spout the old litany about how soft the Service was now. His theme song was, "When I was a vice consul in Tegucigalpa in 1932 . . ." Well, Luanda was my Tegucigalpa.

My colleagues were solid, responsible, intelligent professionals, well grounded in the basic work of diplomacy. I learned a lot from them. They helped me with my writing (drafting in Foreign Service talk), and they helped me learn about context.

One of the consulate officers was CIA under State Department cover. A standing joke among the consular corps was the observable fact that only two consular officers in Luanda had their own "personal" Land Rovers. One was our "vice consul for visas." The other one was a South African vice consul who lived across the street from us and used to do his week-end gardening in what looked suspiciously like military fatigue pants and army boots. But Luanda was a small community, really a goldfish bowl for us foreigners, and I suspect both our "spies" were under instructions not to take chances. They were quite circumspect. Some years later I was amused to see a newspaper report of my neighbor's appointment as chief of staff of the South African army. Also some years later, a South African diplomat whom I had known in Nairobi told me that when he visited Luanda after I had left, he discovered that it was accepted knowledge that the American CIA person in the American ConGen was Ed Marks. I wasn't quite sure how to take that.

We Americans, and other foreigners, were therefore in a time warp. The "wind of change" was now rampaging through Africa, including the other Portuguese colonies, while life in Luanda pursued a peaceful, almost somnolent pace. Many a day was spent on the beaches of the sheltering bay, sunning and swimming and enjoying fresh seafood and Portuguese *vinho verde*. The mood was supported by poor communications, as we were cut off from the world in a manner much different from today: no TV or direct telegraphic traffic, much less email or Skype. In addition, Angola was part of the Southern African holdout region, and South Africa had a very big presence.

What with the dual pressures arising from our NATO military interest in Lisbon and the South African economic and political involvement, we were out of sync with the wind of change. Actually, few in Washington cared much about Angola, and we just did not feel or sense much Washington pressure about independence, such as had been evident in Nairobi a few years earlier. The Americans and most of the foreign consular communities in Luanda, apart from the South Africans, certainly thought independence was in the cards, tried to maintain and establish contacts outside of the official and colonial communities, and tried to report on the evolving situation—but at that time the evolution towards independence was moving rather slowly.

One story illustrates this atmosphere. Our deputy principal officer

(DPO), Bob Flenner, spoke excellent Portuguese, had been in Angola about four years, and knew many people up and down the social scale. One good friend was a member of a prominent nationalist, anti-Lisbon local mestizo family. Tio (uncle) Ernesto, as everyone called him, had been involved in various antigovernment activities at one time or another but was now back in Angola. Frankly, he was a genial drunkard, and the Portuguese authorities had obviously decided he was not much of a threat.

Tio Ernesto dropped by the consulate general one day, and we—Tio Ernesto, Bob, and I—were sitting around the office chatting. When Tio Ernesto heard about my colleague's impending transfer, he became quite excited and said, "No, you can't leave us. You know us, you understand Angola, you sympathize with us, and you cannot leave us. I am going to send a cable to President Johnson saying that you cannot go, you must stay here because you understand us and we need you." Tio Ernesto asked if he could use the telephone to send a telegram to Washington, dialed a number and the ensuing conversation (loosely translated) went something like this:

"Ola, Joao, this is Ernesto. I want to send a telegram through to Washington to the American president about our good friend in the American consulate who they want to send away from Angola. I don't want him to go, and I want that telegram to go through and I want you to make sure it isn't stopped. Okay?"

Tio Ernesto then hung up and explained. "That was Captain [So and So], the secret police officer who handles my case. I want to make sure that my telegram to President Johnson is sent." He then picked up the phone again and called the telegraph office and dictated a cable to ask President Johnson to keep our DPO in Angola "because he is understanding and sympathetic to the people of Angola." We laughed and Tio Ernesto wandered off, weaving his way down the corridor. But damned if two or three weeks later a request didn't come from the department to provide a reply to the telegram, which the White House had bucked over to the State Department for action!

Essentially, we assumed that independence was coming, even if the possibility did not look promising at that moment. We tried to make contacts across racial and political lines as best we could, and we had reasonable success. The Portuguese did not run a very tight political or social ship, and we reported how they were handling the economy and political developments. Basically, they were standing pat, thinking (or hoping) that they could ride out the storm. We didn't think so, but we also felt that the change would not occur very soon and would not happen independently in Angola. The Portuguese were too solidly implanted, with the large Portuguese and mestizo populations.

In their provincial way, the overall official tone and actions (limited as they were) we adopted were a good example of the complex and competing interests that so often affect U.S. foreign policy. Specifically, in this case, our relations with South Africa and our security relations with Lisbon, a member of NATO, were higher priority than the impending independence in Angola.

But there was also the question of our general pro-independence Africa policy and, specifically, the Congo, which obtained independence in 1960–61. The experience had been pretty nasty, and later got even worse. The Portuguese had interpreted the problems in the Congo as confirmation for their policy.

An interesting point of fact: while the Portuguese had close official ties to South Africa, it was well known that they intensely disliked each other. You can imagine the South African, especially the Afrikaner, attitude towards those "funny little Mediterranean people," mostly interbred with Africans as well. But, given political developments and geography, they were now allies and partners. On the one hand, the Portuguese felt the Belgian reaction, the way they had managed the Congo and then scuttled and left, was a bad example, while on the other hand, they felt the South Africans weren't doing it right either because of their racial bias. They claimed that they had the right balance between the two.

Therefore, as diplomats do, we in the consulate general accommodated ourselves to the local situation. We certainly didn't defend the Portuguese position, and we talked quite openly about changes occurring all over Africa. We certainly tried to extend our contacts beyond the official community, including the opposition, but it was a limited involvement because there weren't many of them around. The exception, if you will, were the Portuguese version of "parlor pinks," who were in fact even invited to the Governor General's house for official parties and could socialize with us. We obviously weren't meeting any African militants in the bush. We were on the leading edge locally, but certainly not in advance of it. It was the sort of position often taken by diplomats, one determined by events and policy but which contributes to the public disdain for diplomats. A disdain based on lack of understanding, but nevertheless prevalent in an age of mass communication.

We were operating with a Portuguese colonial administration that was quite willing to deal with us, at least on consular and commercial questions. Although we technically came under the authority of Embassy Lisbon, as Angola in Portuguese terms was an "overseas province," in fact we operated as an independent post reporting directly to the African Bureau.

To back up a bit, the rebellion that had broken out in Angola in 1960 had been pretty bloody during the first year, and in a period lasting until early 1961 the situation looked truly dangerous for continued colonial rule. When the rebellion began, the Portuguese had few troops in the country, and those almost panicked and broke. After a crucial incident in a northern town, however, where the civilian residents fought and won a battle against the insurgents, Salazar decided to hold firm and rushed troops to Angola. By the time I got there in mid-1965, the armed rebellion had been essentially defeated. Holden Roberto was the best-known leader of rebels, but he was physically out of the country, mostly in Zaire, and armed insurgents no longer posed a threat.

There is no point in recounting the ebb and flow of this colonial war, but it was interesting to note that in 1965 the Portuguese had approximately fifty thousand troops in Angola, with the security situation well under control. At the same time in the much, much smaller country of Guinea-Bissau (Portuguese West Africa), they were losing a similar war with the same number of troops. Angola, however, was a much larger territory, with friendly (to the Portuguese) neighbors on its southern borders with South-West Africa and South Africa. But Guinea-Bissau was completely surrounded by newly independent African countries— Guinea (Conakry) and Senegal.

In the middle sixties Angola was quiet. The sunbathing and food were excellent, the economy was starting to boom, and the Portuguese were in firm control.

This was the situation we were trying to monitor, and we had to report that the wind of change was not yet blowing in Angola. In Southern Africa the Portuguese, South Africans, and Rhodesians were holding out against African independence.

The consulate general in Luanda was an independent post, as was Nairobi, reporting directly to the Africa Bureau. But it was a smaller and less prestigious post than Nairobi and in Lisbon faced a different and more demanding attitude than had existed in London. This was partially due to the character of the U.S. ambassador in Lisbon, George Anderson, a conservative retired admiral. He was focused on NATO and Portugal's membership in it and was supportive of the Portuguese government's attitude towards its "overseas provinces." His attitude reflected the general viewpoint of the European bureau in the State Department and the military security—NATO crowd, which influenced our policy towards Angola and which was much more ambiguous about independence in Angola than elsewhere in Africa. We in the consulate general were pretty much imbued with the African Bureau attitude, but we had to watch our step vis-à-vis Embassy Lisbon.

We didn't get many visitors in Luanda in those days—it was a very out-of-the-way place. But one day a traveling group from the National War College came through for a visit of a few days. Such an overseas tour was traditional for War College students. (I later participated in one myself.) We arranged the usual events for official visitors, including a one-day bus tour "up-country." The itinerary also included a Portuguese military briefing. It was a classic military briefing event, maps and all. As the visit control officer, I was with them and sat in the back row.

As the Portuguese had not heard about service unification, there were separate army, then air force, and finally navy briefings. It had been largely an army war, so the army, with all the requisite charts and young captains with pointers, described how they had won the war. Then the air force did the same sort of briefing, showing how air power and mobility had been the real key factors. The navy gave its best, but they had a tough case to make. As we were leaving, I heard two of our NWC students commenting that it was "a pretty good briefing. Just the way we do it at Fort Leavenworth." There was little or no comment about political aspects or the implications of guerrilla war, and no reference to Vietnam.

One of the amusing aspects of Portuguese society under Salazar was the passion for anti-Salazar jokes common among government and military officials. Travelers returning from Lisbon would be expected to bring back the latest such jokes. I was quite friendly with an air force lieutenant colonel, who swore that his mother had been Salazar's secretary for many years and had, as one of her jobs, the responsibility for keeping up to date Salazar's own joke book of anti-Salazar jokes. For instance, when the new bridge over the Tagus River in Lisbon was opened, the formal bridge opening by Salazar illustrated the difference between an accident and a catastrophe: the former was when Salazar tripped and fell into the river, the latter when he was fished out.

I had only been in Luanda for about eleven months when I received a direct transfer to Lusaka, Zambia, to replace Hank Cohen, the regional labor and economic officer for the Central African Federation. (This was only the first time that Hank, an old friend, did me a favor.) This occurred in August 1966, when I was acting as the Luanda consulate general's communications officer, that is, code clerk. The ConGen had two communicators, one male from State Department and one female from the CIA. They were both young and unattached and soon after arrival at post were shacking up together. One day in July Consul General

Harvey Summ called me into his office. He was jumping up and down and laughing himself silly. Between roars of laughter he said, "Our two communicators want to get married, and they can't wait to get married here in Luanda, because there is a six-month waiting list, and they cannot wait six months as she is pregnant. They are going to South Africa to get married." This would leave us without our classified telegraphic capability for several weeks. I was given a quick course in how to run the code machine

At that time our rather unsophisticated communications system called for cables to be sent through the commercial telegraph system after we had run them through our code machines. We did the same process in reverse for incoming classified messages. For three days I filled the floor of the code room with telegraphic tape. I couldn't decode a message to save my life, until I discovered that the major problem was the irregular electrical system in town. If I waited until noon when everybody in town went off to lunch, the electrical current stabilized and the code machines worked.

The second message I broke successfully was a cable from the department to the consul general stating that a replacement officer was needed in Lusaka. The Central African Federation had broken up and the incumbent economic officer was being transferred. I had been recommended, and the Africa Bureau wanted to know what the consul general thought about it. I thought it was a good idea, as Luanda, though lovely, was a little boring. The consul general okayed the proposition, and I left Luanda about a month later.

My stay in Luanda had been short, and even shorter for my wife, as she had gone directly from the U.S. to Tehran to visit her parents for a long visit. But I believed I had learned a lot and developed a real fondness for Portuguese wine and food, and for the Portuguese themselves.

5

Zambia

I went directly from Luanda to Lusaka as second secretary of embassy, economic/commercial officer. The embassy was smallish compared to many and had only been in business a couple of years. Nevertheless, there was a nice new custom-built chancery and an enthusiastic and young-ish, Kennedy-appointed political ambassador, Robert Good. (While I disapprove of political ambassadors in theory and in practice, some of them are quite nice people.) I was the only economic officer and so, with my local Zambian commercial assistant, constituted the embassy's total economic/commercial section. In fact, the only full-time State Department reporting officer, as there was not a State Department political officer. In addition, there were the usual other agency representatives, including from AID and USIA.

Aida had an opportunity to teach French at the International School. I was in my third African country, but this time a year or so after independence.

In the great drama of modern history, Lusaka was a backwater; yet at the time it lay at the crossroads of two historical developments. The "winds of change" were blowing in full force as the European colonial system in Africa unraveled, and we were in the midst of the Cold War. The two processes were intertwined everywhere, and Zambia was one of the ground zeros for both. One immediately noticeable condition in Lusaka was gas rationing (as a member of the diplomatic corps I received ten gallons a month).

As Northern Rhodesia, Zambia had been part of the Federation of Rhodesia and Nyasaland, a British colonial creation similar to the East African Community. Zambia had copper mines, Nyasaland (later Malawi) had good agriculture, and Southern Rhodesia (later Rhodesia, then Zimbabwe) had six hundred thousand mostly British settlers and self-government. Northern Rhodesia produced much of the wealth of the federation, and Southern Rhodesia lived off of it, or so the Africans thought. As the Zambians used to put it, the federation was like a cow with the mouth (and the copper mines) in Northern Rhodesia, but the stomach in Southern Rhodesia.

With the movement towards independence, the African leaders in Nyasaland and Northern Rhodesia were interested in governance by majority rule—the last thing Rhodesian whites wanted. With the federation dissolved, Rhodesia's white-dominated government under Ian Smith went for what they called a "Unilateral Declaration of Independence," claiming to repeat the United States experience. Few other governments accepted this initiative, especially the British, and the so-called UDI crisis went on for some years. This created a serious problem for Zambia, as its major rail and road links to the outside world ran through Rhodesia, especially as the country's secondary links ran through Zaire (still called Congo-Kinshasa at that time) and were threatened by the political turmoil in that country.

Zambia's president, Kenneth Kaunda, was one of Africa's new leaders and modeled himself on Tanzania's popular Julius Nyerere. As Zambia did not have a single dominant tribe, and Kaunda was not a member of any of the local tribes (he came from people who lived in neighboring countries), he was personally free from the obsessive tribalism that afflicted so many African leaders. Kaunda was of the generation of African leaders later referred to as Africa's "Big Men," leaders who stayed in power for long periods.

Though not as ideologically militant as some, Ghana's Kwame Nkrumah had finally alienated even some of his most fervent admirers with his extravagance (political and financial). Kenya's Jomo Kenyatta turned out to be too "old-fashioned" to earn the admiration of the Western political "groupies." Nyerere was everyone's favorite, having translated some Shakespeare into Swahili, although his persistent and cheerful espousal of socialism (albeit "African socialism") caused heartburn in some circles.

Kaunda appeared to follow Julius Nyerere, Guinea's Sekou Touré, and others by enunciating a formal philosophy he called "humanism." Purportedly based on the needs of human beings, it was not particularly rigorous intellectually, but it did include the sine qua non of all Third World political theory: the need for a command economic system to remedy the injustices of the colonial era and produce economic development. Although the "socialist" label caused some consternation in the West, especially in the United States, colonial economic systems had been, by and large, command economies and the newly independent African governments were essentially just taking them over. They called themselves socialists, intending to keep the profits in the hands of the government and distribute them locally.

Kaunda introduced his humanism and proceeded to implement it by nationalizing the whole economy, including the copper mines. Interestingly, he tried to extend his influence internationally by sponsoring the creation of an international copper producers' organization, to replicate what the oil producers had done. Soon after I arrived, Kaunda hosted a conference in Lusaka that included the world's major copper-producing countries, Chile, Zaire, and Peru, but not the United States. The project didn't work out, but the conference gave me a chance to resurrect my Mexican-learned Spanish with the Chileans and Peruvians—a very Foreign Service experience.

Kaunda appeared to have Nyerere's good traits without the explicit socialist label; "humanism" sounded pretty good, even if no one could figure out exactly what it meant. All in all, he appeared to be the most promising African leader to Western eyes, especially to Americans like my academic ambassador.

And the world's eyes were focused on Zambia because of the new political dividing line solidifying in Southern Africa. By 1966 the first major wave of the independence movement in Africa was over. The "winds of change" had arrived but were now stalled in Southern Africa, along the northern borders of Angola, Rhodesia, and Mozambique. Facing them were the so-called frontline states: Zambia, Malawi, and Tanzania, with Zambia as the spearhead. The newly independent African governments therefore had to wrestle with the problems of independence while in direct contact with the apartheid system in South Africa. Kaunda was the guy on the front lines. Although this was a popular position for Kaunda and Zambia, it was also a difficult one. With the cutting of the traditional transportation and communication links south, Kaunda had to find new access to the outside world in order to export his copper and bring in necessary imports such as fuel and spare parts.

Much of this conflict took place in public discourse; and it was interesting to watch Kaunda perform. He had an interesting habit that caused some of us to be slightly cynical. Often at an emotional point in a speech, Kaunda's eyes would begin to get moist, and he would pull a handkerchief out of the sleeve of his safari-type jacket. Some Westerners cried with him, while others tried to keep a straight face. He was far from being a bad leader, although his performance in office was mixed. His centralized command economic system was pretty much a failure, but he never became a serious tyrant. He was eventually removed from office in 1991 by an honest election—not that common an event in Africa.

A four-sided political competition prevailed in Central and Southern Africa: the West, including the former colonial powers; the Communist Bloc; the African nonaligned countries; and the regimes of the Southern Redoubt. The situation became even more complicated as it became clear even to the most passionate cold warriors that the Chinese and Russians were in competition with each other. The Chinese were at the height of their puritanical period, so the Chinese mission people in Lusaka ran around in their little Mao hats, waving their little red Mao books. (I still have my copy, but I had to get it through an intermediary, as the young man handing them out at the Chinese booth at a trade fair wouldn't even acknowledge my existence, much less give me a copy.)

Lusaka, like many capital cities in the Third World, was abuzz with these developments, and we in the embassy had a sense of being in the front lines of U.S. foreign policy amid great events of history.

Zambia sat in the center of what was the Southern African economic structure built in colonial days, based on an elaborate railway system that crossed Zambia as it linked the east and west coasts of Central and Southern Africa. Copper was an important element of that structure, and together Zambia and Zaire probably produced about 40 percent of the world's copper. Actually, they share the same copper deposit, with the border of the two countries running right through the middle of the deposit. The transportation structure east and south was cut because of Rhodesia and UDI, while the outlets east through Zaire and Angola were not reliable. (This was the period of the Simba Rebellion in Zaire [then still Congo] and the attempted breakaway of Katanga.)

The effective cutting of these links created a de facto blockade for Zambia. The Zambians faced serious problems: how do they get their copper out, and how do they get necessary imports—especially fuel to run the modern economy, including the copper mines—in.

All this was taking place in the regional interplay, which in turn was playing out within the wider context of the global Cold War. While we were terribly enamored of the emancipation of African countries from colonial rule for its own sake, we could never forget that Africa was also one of the regions in which the Soviets were aggressively trying to expand their presence and influence in Africa, as were the Chinese. How to separate our concern for Africa from our concern for the so-called Communist threat posed an interesting diplomatic question, especially as the civil rights movement in the States and the resulting growth of African Americans' interest in Africa was an increasingly influential factor in U.S. foreign policy.

The Soviets were busy trying to cultivate the Africans by playing on the inevitable anticolonial attitudes of the new governments. Stomping around with small checkbooks and soft words, they presented themselves as the alternative to the old colonial powers. They expressed sympathy for the new regimes and offered them an alternative development model, some military training, and academic scholarships—and they carried on lots of intelligence activities and subversion, or so our CIA colleagues kept telling us. Essentially, the Soviets encouraged the Zambian instinct to participate in the Non-Aligned Movement, which was generally anti-Western in orientation. It was difficult for some of us to figure out why the Soviets should bother; after all, what were the connections to any Soviet national interest? But we put it down to the exhilaration of the global competition—a motive much like our own.

The Chinese meanwhile were busily trumpeting Mao's Great Leap Forward. At first, we thought of them as part of the Russian-led Communist bloc, but it became increasingly obvious that they were playing their own game in competition with the Soviets for influence. Whether or not the Chinese were allied with the Soviets, their activities in East and Central Africa really shook up the head offices of the Western powers. The Chinese were playing a large role in the Non-Aligned Movement. No one else was willing to build the railway, certainly no one in the West. And the next thing you knew hundreds, even thousands, of Chinese showed up in Dar es Salaam and started building the Tanzam Railway.

The U.S. opposition to Rhodesian UDI was important. Soviet policy was pretty much the same, but the amount of tea they could provide to go with sympathy was limited—although their rhetoric was more out-spoken. Their open support of the African National Congress (ANC), the South African independence movement, was greatly appreciated all over Africa. The Soviets' main problem was their inability to provide much concrete assistance in dealing with the Rhodesians and South Africans. The Soviets were not in a position to offer serious financial or military assistance. But, with the Chinese bellying up to the table with big chips—namely, the railway—we became doubly excited. In reaction we probably overplayed the Communist threat. The Africans felt, I think rightfully, that only the West could eventually help them the most. The British still had a residual responsibility for Rhodesia, and they had the levers and the entrée that could help resolve the problems, which they eventually did.

The Chinese offer of the railroad was a major bid that greatly excited the Western powers. Different people on our side had different motivations: our Africanists could concentrate on supporting Kaunda and his new government, antiracists and idealists could fight against apartheid in Rhodesia and South Africa, and cold warriors in the CIA and the Department of Defense could focus on stopping the Communist tide. They all contributed to a general policy of support for Zambia.

Meanwhile, the country was being cut off from its supplies of fuel and was suffering from its inability to export its copper. To help, the U.S. and the UK set up an airlift of cargo planes—mostly C-130s—flying from the Zambian copper belt to Dar es Salaam and to Kinshasa. They brought in rubber containers of fuel and flew out copper on pallets. Talk about expensive! Some stuff also dribbled in and out through the Congo and Tanzania on the dirt road. None of this was economical, but it demonstrated political support for this brave and beleaguered African country facing up to the apartheid regime to the south. The airlift went on for about a year, ending sometime in 1967. It was most dramatic—shades of the Berlin Airlift!—and we all got a charge out of it.

The longer-term Western counter to the railroad was the proposal to hard-surface the existing dirt road from Dar es Salaam to Kitwe in the Zambian copper belt. The Western countries floated a lot of economic arguments that the Chinese railway was a bad idea and argued that "tarmacking" the highway would be quicker and more cost-efficient. When fully provided with a hard, all-weather surface, it could be used to support a fleet of heavy trucks to bring in fuel and carry out copper. We pushed ahead with this idea.

The economic arguments went back and forth. The advantage of the road proposal was that it could be significantly improved faster and cheaper. The key point was that the road would be ours and could preempt the Chinese invasion. Clearly, the politics of the Cold War were driving our interest.

Significant trade no longer existed across the Rhodesian border, and we diplomats in Lusaka were forbidden by our governments to even visit Rhodesia. Meanwhile, the idea of building the hard-surface road continued to be discussed among potential Western donors, focusing on how many kilometers each participant would build. The United States for quite a while did not actually commit itself to participating in this project, although the African Bureau was very enthusiastic. The problems were funds and a general lack of interest at home.

We hadn't yet committed ourselves when Vice President Hubert Humphrey announced he was making a trip to Africa. The announcement of the trip to tour Africa produced the usual bureaucratic fight over where he would go, which capitals he would visit. Our ambassador argued he must visit Zambia to show the U.S. flag in support of African nationalism, show moral support for a frontline state and opposition to apartheid, and demonstrate moral and political support for a moderate African leader. The decision was eventually made that he would stop in Lusaka, although it turned out to be only a four-and-a-half-hour airport stop. It wasn't much more than a touch-and-go, but it enabled the vice president to drive into town, lunch with Kenneth Kaunda, and give a speech.

The next big question for Embassy Lusaka was what the vice president would say and do while he was in Lusaka. Presidents and vice presidents do not like to make public appearances in foreign countries without saying something newsworthy. I don't remember where the idea came from, but someone came up with the brilliant suggestion that the vice president could announce a U.S. government decision to finance a significant section of the Tanzam highway—three hundred kilometers, I believe. All of a sudden, the bureaucratic objections to the funding were overcome and the financing was approved. The vice president duly arrived, made a press statement supporting African nationalism and independence and announcing our contribution to the Tanzam Highway as evidence of our commitment. From then on we started referring to the highway—informally and in-house—as Hubert's Highway. I believe the *Economist* also picked up that term (possibly from me as I was a friend of the *Economist* stringer in Lusaka).

Despite the casual manner in which this decision was made, it could be justified given the context: we were in competition with the Soviet bloc and/or the Chinese for influence, supporting independence for majority-rule African governments, and opposing the apartheid principles of South Africa. But these are political arguments, not an economic development rationale, and that raises the long-standing debate as to whether economic aid funds are primarily political or developmental (or both). The economic support of Zambia can easily be justified as the use of development money in support of U.S. foreign policy and objectives, as identified by the administration.

Most of the rest of our economic assistance programs in Zambia at the time, as in most other African countries, had a more obvious development character, such as education and agriculture. Even though the Tanzam Highway project was overtly political, one could argue that this country could not survive if it could not import or export; and if it couldn't survive, then long-term development concerns were irrelevant. In retrospect, I would describe much of our economic assistance at that time and in that place as a form of trauma medicine—the economic equivalent to what happens in a hospital emergency center. Yes, it was political, but its purpose was to assist a newly independent government to take hold, to make the transition to independence. Long-term economic development concerns were and are important, but had to take second place for the moment. As the years went by, our economic assistance continued to be politically motivated for the most part, and we never did figure out an effective economic development policy in Africa— USAID experts and public diplomacy programs notwithstanding. The argument continues today.

When I left Zambia at the end of 1969, the political situation in and with Rhodesia had not been resolved, but the airlift had been over for some time. Traffic was moving regularly in both directions over the mostly hard-surfaced, not completely finished Tanzam road. The Tanzam railway was still under construction and had not yet reached Zambia. Now, in the early years of the twenty-first century, both are essentially decayed relics.

It was difficult to tell how well—or badly—things were going, as the country was still operating on the momentum and investment of the colonial period. We could begin to see the beginning of British disinvestment in the copper industry, and some nervousness among the commercial farmers (largely British or Boer), although their property had not yet been touched. Kaunda had high hopes for his international copper producers' organization, hopes that proved illusory, but he was essentially focused on the struggle with white-ruled Rhodesia.

Zambia was newly independent and most of the preindependence white (or, as they said, European) farmer and business communities were still around, the largest number working in the copper companies. They constituted a relatively large European technical and skilled worker class, unusual in Africa except for South Africa. The colonial social structure was still in evidence, especially up north in the mining towns.

The local version of apartheid was finished, although in some back rooms and at some dinner parties racist remarks were occasionally still voiced. The formal colonial social structure was dying, although most social life remained segregated, despite persistent efforts, especially by diplomats, to invite Africans. But it was not easy, for several reasons. The Africans themselves had problems mixing in the European or British manner due to a lack of common background. So much of the intercourse was a bit forced, artificial, and formal, and African social life by and large did not include "Europeans." Personally, I had even less opportunity for contact with Africans than those on the political side, as there were as yet few Africans in the commercial sector or even in the economic departments of the government. I did hire and trained an African commercial assistant, and that was a bit of a breakthrough, but I was still largely dealing with expatriates.

But with independence, in Lusaka Africans were filling the ministerial positions and starting to move further into the government and mining company bureaucracies. Africans probably had as much of a problem reaching out as we did. They were only in their third or fourth year of taking over a society that had been completely in the hands of white expatriates (and some Indian middlemen). Only a comparatively small group of Africans had the education and experience commensurate with the responsibilities they were now assuming.

Kaunda's humanism philosophy was, as one might imagine, long on general statements and short on specifics, but it contained a lot about the rights of the individual human being. At the same time, he was moving slowly towards a one-party system, but in a gentle way. He had moved much faster on the economic side, nationalizing much of the economy. The copper companies were an obvious target, but so was much of the private sector. There is an interesting aspect to this development, which was not uncommon in Africa. To a considerable degree the local Greek community played the "outcast elite" role of the small merchant, the role played by Indians in East Africa and Lebanese in West Africa. (I later discovered that Greeks and an even more important community of Sephardic Jews from Rhodes had performed the same economic function a few hundred miles north in the Congo.)

This led to one local Greek businessman's special role. He had been a Kaunda supporter in the early days of the freedom struggle in the 1950s, lending Kaunda money, sympathy, and presumably advice. This did not make him especially popular in British colonial society. After independence this man became prominent as Kaunda's economic advisor, although he did not hold a government position, and he began to be socially quite popular among the remaining British expatriates and the expanded diplomatic community. It was under his guidance that Kaunda implemented a bureaucratization of the whole monetary economy: organizing everything down to the Lusaka supermarkets into a collection of bureaucratic bodies, which in turn were integrated into a single government-owned commercial company of which the Greek merchant became the head. He was suspected of doing extremely well personally out of this arrangement, although we had no proof of it. The British expatriates were scathing about this man—his motivations, his honesty, and his alleged profits—but still sent him social invitations.

Into this changing situation came the visit to Zambia of Senator Edward Brooke (R-MA), America's sole Black senator at the time and a delightful gentleman, naturally interested in Africa. In 1968 an elaborate trip around Africa was arranged for him, heavily promoted by the administration for obvious reasons. When Brooke came to Zambia, the ambassador gave a big reception in his honor. During that party a senior African minister commented to one of the embassy staff that while the party was quite nice, he was interested in meeting our Black senator. "Where is he? I don't see him." Despite repeated efforts to point out Senator Brooke, whose complexion was not very dark, the minister kept repeating, "Where, where?" Looking right at a small group surrounding the senator, the minister said, "Which one in the group? I don't see him." All in all, Senator Brooke's success was modest, but the visit was a good public relations effort. Again, this was the sort of thing being done at that time.

While this and a few other incidents, such as the Humphrey Highway affair, did not quite get into Evelyn Waugh country, they came close, although a mix-up at the British Embassy might qualify. This was when a letter to the foreign secretary in London was placed in an envelope addressed to the Zambian minister of foreign affairs, while the letter intended for the minister was sent to the foreign secretary. Still, there was that sense of being on the front line of the Cold War and of history in the making, though we may have been fooling ourselves. The 1960s qualified as an eventful historic period, in which Africa may have played a relatively marginal part. But still, it was invigorating.

At that time the Cold War was in full flood, but some of us were more fervent Cold Warriors than others. President Kennedy's admonition "Ask not what your country can do for you," was in everyone's mind. Some of us, I will say, were less than fully enthusiastic about the virtues of centralized planning and nationalization that were all the rage among most newly independent governments. Since these new governments were fervently touting centralized planning, opposition to that approach tended to place one in the exploitative capitalist camp, among the white settlers.

So, we tended to go along with African political attitudes a bit more than we probably should have done. A degree of patronization prevailed among American and European supporters of the decolonization process, by and large liberals of various persuasions. Conservatives, on the other hand, still tended to bemoan decolonization and express support for Rhodesian UDI and to "understand" the justification of the apartheid regime in South Africa and the Portuguese argument for the maintenance of their "overseas provinces."

We did raise some of these concerns in our reporting from Embassy Lusaka. We discussed extensively the complex transition problems of a complicated industry like copper, which was heavily dependent on Western technology and investment. The key question was how to manage the transition so that it produced wealth for the newly independent nation and its African population without killing the golden goose. Unfortunately, that is exactly what happened.

From our foreign policy perspective, as an embassy and as a government, we did not do too badly, at least in the short run—if one accepts the legitimacy of the Cold War as a foreign policy priority and the tactical needs arising from that assumption. We resisted bloc expansionism reasonably successfully. The Tanzam highway was a good enough development project at the time, as it served both U.S. and Zambian needs. Whether we were successful in the long run, and more particularly in terms of African development, I would have to note that the history of Africa in the ensuing forty years has been rather depressing. But I don't assume that what we did or did not do was the crucial determinant of that recent history. Africa would probably have followed the path it has followed regardless of what we did.

In terms of personal education, I was starting to appreciate more fully the role of culture and of history and politics in determining culture. National borders emphasize this matter, as the U.S.-Mexican border had demonstrated. After all, Nuevo (new) Laredo is a Mexican city, while Laredo, Texas (the original settlement), is American, because politics (and war) had rearranged national identities and consequently culture. In fact, all along the Mexican border Tex-Mex is a cultural phenomenon, merging the two cultures. In Laredo, Texas, and Nuevo Laredo, Mexico, the motto is *Los Dos Laredos*, referring to a mixed community, mixed in languages and families as well as cuisine. (My experience was long ago, and recent history with the rise of the drug problem, the drug cartels, and the immigrant waves may have produced a different and less inviting environment.)

Zambia had a similar situation, although I did not fully realize it until my later tours in Belgium and Zaire. The Zambian and Zairian (and now once again Congolese) copper belt towns exploited the same mineral-rich terrain and were inhabited by similar ethnic peoples. But an international boundary established only about one hundred years ago had created two somewhat different cultures as well as nationalities. While underlying African cultures continued, the educated and leadership classes now had different cultural and political attitudes. In Zambia people drank beer and spoke English as the official language; in Zaire they drank wine and spoke French. And these habits, not more than two or three generations old, will no doubt persist into the future.

And so my Zambian tour came to an end. Lusaka was my first full-time reporting job, a classic diplomatic function. I had excellent supervisors in William Edmondson, the deputy chief of mission, and Ambassador Robert Good. Both were intelligent and open-minded, though different in style and approach. The ambassador was a liberal arts academic and political appointee, while the DCM was a pure professional—a balanced, solid, and sympathetic supervisor, colleague, and friend. I was still having trouble with my drafting, and he worked patiently with me—an effort I remember with gratitude today.

6

The Belgian World

It was back to Washington as the Kenya desk officer, after a six-month economic course at the Foreign Service Institute. We bought our first house, in the low-rent part of Bethesda. Aida got a job at the Embassy of Guinea-Conakry, and we settled into the life of minor bureaucrats in Washington. More about all that later.

After three years in Washington on the East African desk, I became restless to return overseas. Although by now I was an "Africanist," more or less, with three posts and one assignment in the Africa Bureau, the chance to go to Europe in 1971 was too enticing to turn down. It was not Paris or London or Rome, however, but Brussels, as economic officer. Brussels turned out to be our only European assignment, which may be one reason we remember it with such fondness. But maybe not. My wife was a native-level French speaker and so took to Brussels like a duck to water, and I had at least a Foreign Service Institute language school foundation. In the event, we found ourselves thoroughly at home in Belgium.

As noted in chapter 3, Brussels is a city much maligned, one that cannot really compare with Paris, but as Mark Twain I believe pointed out, neither can any other city. They are all sui generis and attractive or not in their own right. Brussels turned out to be livable and enjoyable. While maybe not actually the capital of Europe, as its seat of the European Community and NATO encouraged the Belgian tourist office to proclaim, it was and is a comfortable European city, with all that phrase implies. I noticed that despite the gibes about Brussels and "little Belgium," the city was full of diplomats, European civil servants, and business executives who showed no inclination to leave. Good salaries certainly contributed to this attitude. But, as was commonly said by us temporary Brussellois, Brussels is a much better place to live in than to visit. In any case, we had a lovely apartment in the center of the city, a rambunctious Yorkie pup named Maximillian (Max to his friends), and lots of Belgian and other friends. Aida took up formal training in cooking, and we had three years of access to Belgium's deservedly well-known restaurants.

Again, blessed as I was with an excellent and supportive supervisor, Edwin Crowley, and congenial colleagues, the work environment was a happy one. The bilateral embassy, as we called the embassy to Belgium, distinct from the other American embassies—to the European Community and to NATO—was in the center of the city and within walking distance from my apartment.

There was nothing special about the work, mostly general economic reporting and bilateral contacts on matters such as civil aviation access and rights. The Belgians were trying to expand their national airlines' access into the United States and wanted to add landing rights in Chicago. The U.S. government (USG) was not prepared to let the Belgians into Chicago, for capacity and other considerations, but were prepared to offer Atlanta. The Belgians, however, were insistent and as it turned out short-sighted. Atlanta in the following years turned into a major world airport, and the Belgians missed the chance to get in on the ground floor. That decision may not have been crucial, but it is worth noting that SABENA (Societé Anonyme Belge d'Exploitation de la Navigation Aérienne), Belgian's former national airline, no longer exists. Another and more noteworthy event was the oil crisis, as the Middle East oil producers in OPEC turned down the spigots and jumped the price. The resulting crisis was exciting, as a high-powered team came in from Washington to work with our European friends to deal with the problem. As often happens, however, the Washington team ran the show, and we in Embassy Brussels served as bureaucratic handmaidens.

But I did get some personal benefit out of the crisis. I spent much of that period writing reports (telegrams) on the state of the petroleum industry in Belgium and how the government was responding to the crisis. Belgium was far from being a major player in this developing situation, but Belgium was where I was posted and so I did the necessary. About a year after the crisis ended, I was faced with the need to produce a master's thesis for the distance-learning course I was pursuing at the University of Oklahoma. Having no subject in mind, I was reminded by a colleague that my yearlong reporting effort on the petroleum crisis might constitute the necessary material. Most of the reporting had been unclassified, so there was no security problem. There may or may not have been an ethical problem from an academic perspective, but I ignored that possibility, arranged all the year's telegrams on the subject in a sequence, did some heavy editing and rewriting, and "*Voilà*," I had my master's thesis. Not a seminal paper in the economic field, to be sure, but then I was under no illusion I was going to compete with John Maynard Keynes or Larry Summers. It was sufficient, and I received my master's degree in economics from the U of O.

In addition to its many attractions and pleasures, Belgium offered a revealing insight into the age-old problem of cultural and political conflict. The country is divided between the French-speaking Walloons and the Flemish, who speak Flemish Dutch. The conflict is old, and it dominates the internal life and politics of the country. My time in Belgium was a crucial period, as the tension began to heat up and a book entitled *La Guerre des Belges* (The war of the Belgians) openly discussed the increasingly testy mood as the economic balance began to shift to the advantage of the Flemish.

It was and remains a situation complicated by history, culture, economics, and, most importantly, language. It replicated situations I had seen in Kenya, Mexico, and Zambia—the persistence of conflict determined by cultural history, with language as the most visible and obvious bone of contention. Flemings were increasingly refusing to speak French, the official language of the Kingdom of Belgium since its establishment in 1832, and the Walloons were continuing to express Francophone arrogance. Everything now had to be language-identified, from political parties to symphony orchestras. (The small—1 percent—German language community also had official status, but pretty much tried to stay out of the way of the major contestants.)

Foreigners, who constituted a large number in Brussels since it became the "capital of Europe," watched all this with some bemusement. As the saying goes, all of us have sufficient fortitude to bear the misfortunes of others. In one sense, the squabbling confirms the long-standing condescending attitude many Europeans harbored towards Belgium in general and Brussels in particular. Americans have less of this attitude, if only because we are not convinced that Europeans in general have that much to be condescending about, given the history of the twentieth century. Also, Belgians generally do not share the French and British superior attitude towards Americans and so quickly earn American sympathy. Belgians, both language communities and especially the residents of Brussels, are open and relaxed about foreigners, taking them as they come and not prone to the little snide remarks that Americans seem to provoke in places like Paris and London.

After a while, and with the guidance of some local friends, I finally learned why this linguistic frontier existed—why these two "peoples," genetically quite similar to each other, speak different languages and insist on different cultures. The answer was quite simply a matter of history. Today's situation in Belgium, and to some degree in Luxembourg and the Rhineland, is simply the heritage of the Roman Empire, whose northern frontier ran through these parts. Aachen, or Aix-la-Chapelle, was the northern headquarters of the Roman Empire, and the frontier ran along what is now the Rhine Valley and across the Ardennes along the River Scheldt more or less, pretty much cutting across what are now Belgium and Holland. So, the Walloons speak a Romance language while the Flemings have stuck with a Teutonic tongue—yet both eat *waterzooi*, cook with beer, and enjoy *pomme frites*, mussels, and *gaufres* (waffles).

SPQR (The Senate and People of Rome) still influences our world after seventeen hundred years.

A more current and in-house example of the role of borders in human affairs could be seen in the existence and relationship between the three American embassies in Brussels: the bilateral embassy to Belgium and the multilateral embassies to the European Community (EC) (now the European Union) and the North Atlantic Treaty Organization (NATO). Having three embassies in one city is an unusual situation, and the relations between them were somewhat frosty. The bilateral ambassador liked to think he was the senior, while the other two knew they were more important. Mostly they circled around each other, keeping their distance, with as little interaction as possible. Interestingly, the staff of the three American embassies did not fraternize much with each other either, unless there had been previous personal contact. This was easy enough, as their "host" audiences were different. The staffs of all three embassies watched this delicate dance of their chiefs of mission with some amusement. Still, it was an illustrative, if not terribly important, example of how "borders" are created and maintained.

As we never returned to Europe on assignment, Belgium remains our "Europe," and we went back often over the years. The only other city in which I felt so at home other than Washington was New York. Both are cities where I feel I return as a former resident, not as a visitor.

After three years in Brussels, it turned out that it was time to return to Africa. By now I was an established member of the Foreign Service community and was pleased when Hank Cohen—not a personnel officer—called me in early 1974 and offered me the position of consul and principal officer in Lubumbashi, Zaire. Lubumbashi, Élisabethville in the former Belgian Congo, was a prime assignment for an officer of my age and rank, and I grabbed the offer.

Arriving in Lubumbashi, after a short stopover in Kinshasa ("Kin La Belle" as the Belgian colonists called it) for briefings and a call on the ambassador, I entered a new phase of my professional career. On a Friday evening in August 1974, at forty years of age, I became the American consul in Lubumbashi, the most senior representative of the United States of America for hundreds of miles in every direction. The Belgian Congo became the Democratic Republic of the Congo in 1960, was renamed the Republic of Zaire in 1971, and renamed again the Democratic Republic of the Congo in 1997. Many of its cities were renamed after independence and have retained those names. Élisabethville became Lubumbashi, and so it remains.

I was back to Africa but this time as a principal officer, albeit of a small (four officers, total of five American staff) consulate. Those with a military background will appreciate the satisfaction of being in command. Zaire is a huge and important country in Africa. At that time, it was only a few years past a tumultuous and violent history following the achievement of independence from Belgium in 1960. Lubumbashi was the capital of Shaba Province (the former Katanga), which by itself was as big as quite respectably sized countries. It contained the world's third largest copper industry and was far from the embassy in Kinshasa where my boss, the ambassador, was located. American diplomats had played major roles in the history of the 1960s, and in Lubumbashi I would be following in the footsteps of some distinguished colleagues. I hoped that my incumbency would also provide an opportunity to shine.

In Lubumbashi I began the personal habit of writing long, discursive, unclassified, annual "Letters from. . . ." These were openly imitative of the famous Janet Flanner's *New Yorker* "Letters from Paris." The temptation to begin doing so came from my status as principal officer; there was no one to say nay and no one to edit, so the letter could be quite individual. (My ambassador in Kinshasa and the Powers That Be in Washington could have told me to shut up, but they never did and in fact appeared to enjoy it.) I sent the first one from Lubumbashi but never did a second, as I was transferred in the middle of my second year. But I renewed the practice later in Cape Verde, Guinea-Bissau, and Colombo. (Much of this book derives from those letters and I hope provides some sense of life as a Foreign Service officer out in the field.)

The mechanics of obtaining the information and opinions contained in a Foreign Service report are usually left out of the report itself, if only because they vary little from post to post. While I don't claim that the working conditions in Zaire in those days were markedly different from those in other Third World countries, discussion of them can provide further insight into the nature of Zaire as a country and society, as well as providing some insight, I hope, into the professional activities of a midlevel working diplomat.

Lubumbashi is Zaire's second most important city, as the center of the country's major economic activity. It is also the second largest urban region (the Copper Belt), located at the country's furthermost fringe, two thousand kilometers from the capital. It is where the airplanes turn around: the end of the line. History and current politics combine to make Lubumbashi a passive dependency of the capital. The Lubumbashi area produces copper and serves as a commercial and light industrial center but otherwise minds its p's and q's. It is a cautious city where, in those days, the only overt manifestations of political life were the apathetic marches of support for President Mobutu, ordered by the regional commissioner at times of national crisis, and the ubiquitous song-and-dance groups extolling the virtue of the president and the Authentic Zairian Revolution. The media were obsequious, and the city lived by rumors. The population blamed the central government for economic difficulties, while also recalling the chaos of the pre-Mobutu era. The students at the university were notable only for the cynicism with which they pursued the diploma that ensured entry into the new, postcolonial elite.

The consulate, now closed, was a one-story colonial cottage, which sat rather complacently in the center of a large, landscaped plot. Outside the consulate windows, the sun shone (most of the time), and the grass was regularly clipped. The consulate's nearest neighbors were the French consulate general, the zoo, and the residence of the regional commissioner for Shaba (in other times, the residence of the vice governor general of Katanga and the president of the Republic of Katanga). Not too far away was the city center, with its somnolent market-town air, somewhat dilapidated but still then appearing neat and clean to visitors from the capital. It was little changed from preindependence days, and a faded sign on the city square still indicated the road to Jadotville (now Likasi). Comparatively few white faces were seen in the city center during the day, and none at night.

The American consulate in Lubumbashi was opened in the late 1940s as a special-interest post. That special interest—minerals—remains and has become even more important with the creation of an independent country and other developments in world politics and economic trends. American political and economic involvement in Zaire had created a vested USG interest in the country, and the consulate was charged with traditional listening-post responsibilities.

Lubumbashi then still had a racially mixed population at the managerial, professional, and commercial level, although the trend toward Africanization was well advanced and moving rapidly. Though the government was composed solely of Zairian nationals, the copper company and other relatively large firms still had significant numbers of foreign (mostly European) personnel, despite recent nationalization measures. The university had a sizeable foreign group. Approximately 10,000 such expatriates (6,500 Belgian; 2,000 French; 500 Italian; 600 Greek) still lived and worked in Shaba Province in 1974.

The American community in Shaba then numbered approximately 450, half of them contract employees working at the new copper project at Tenke-Fungurume or the power project at Kolwezi. The rest were mostly missionaries or Peace Corps Volunteers. Fewer than forty Americans, including the five consulate staff and their families, lived in Lubumbashi itself.

The size of the American community in a country is important for diplomats, because its nationals are the first and most obvious source of local information or intelligence. This was certainly true in Lubumbashi. The Belgian consulate general had the most extensive local involvement because of the still large community of its nationals and the range of their activities and interests. The Japanese consul (who spoke no French, English, or Swahili) was the most divorced from Zaire and appeared to act largely as a Lubumbashi reference point for Japanese transiting en route to or from the Japanese-owned copper mine at Mushosi. He occasionally appeared at local government functions looking resigned and bewildered. The real Japanese representative was the resident copper company manager. The Italian and Greek consuls serviced communities that had once been large and spread throughout the region. As these communities diminished, their consuls' contact with the Zairian local administration dried up noticeably.

The American consulate played a special role in local life because of the massive U.S. involvement in Zaire since independence—championing the central government, opposing the secessionist regimes, and in particular supporting the current regime. While sometimes blaming the United States for decolonization and the resulting chaos, old-time white residents also looked to the consulate for assistance and guidance, whether or not they were U.S. citizens. (Bill Harrop, the American consul in 1967, was widely credited with having saved the white community from massacre by uncontrolled mobs encouraged by a racist governor.) Zairian officials and private individuals recognized the special U.S.-Zairian relationship, with private individuals sometimes implying criticism of the USG for not using that influence to correct errors in current government policy.

Nevertheless, the dominant characteristic of the American consulate in Lubumbashi was its isolation from Zairian life. Zairian officials were generally pleasant, or at least courteous. They were also distant and refused categorically to discuss anything but the weather or any specific item of business. They did not initiate any contact with the consulate except when specifically instructed to do so.

Private Zairians were not much more open, although some did occasionally permit conversation to wander into areas other than the weather. Even they, however, would rarely discuss politics—internal or international. The prevailing atmosphere was one of caution. Zairians were essentially passive vis-à-vis foreigners in general and foreign consuls in particular.

One exception, to some degree, were some Zairian university faculty. Zairian professors had greater exposure to the outside world. They were relatively open with their non-Zairian professional colleagues, although they, too, remained reserved with foreign officials such as consular officers. One has the impression they would have liked to expand personal relations but felt nervous about doing so.

Points of contact with Zairians never seemed to expand into a network of relationships. Every contact with a Zairian had to be separately initiated, and each initiative appeared to start again from scratch. One reason for the apparent failure of initial contacts to breed ongoing and expanding relations was the Zairian apathy towards social relationships with foreigners. Zairian officials appeared to have a "policy" on social relations with foreign consuls. Invitations extended to such officials for an event with a purpose, such as a visit to Lubumbashi or for a national holiday, were usually accepted. Invitations extended without a specific purpose, the classic diplomatic technique for expanding relations with local citizens, made Zairian officials nervous. While they may have accepted the first time, they usually declined thereafter unless the invitation was clearly tied to an "event." Return invitations were nonexistent.

It was important to remember that many senior officials were, in a way, themselves foreigners, posted to Shaba in accordance with the central government policy of assigning officials out of their areas. They, too, were therefore strangers who did not speak the local language and were viewed with some distrust as outsiders. Much of what consulate officers learned about Zairian life came from secondhand sources—the private resident foreign community.

Resident private foreigners had a much wider range of relationships with Zairians. As noted, foreign professors at the university often had excellent professional ties, which extended into social and personal relationships. The best contacts, however, clearly belonged to the "old settlers." A classic love-hate relationship existed between Zairians and the remaining *colons*. Many of these settlers had business ties with Zairian officials and private citizens, who would barely exchange a word with a foreign consul but would wander off for a beer or coffee with a longtime Greek or Italian or Belgian resident and promptly begin to regale him with all the gossip about the regional commissioner's latest property acquisition or instructions from Kinshasa. These resident foreigners, in turn, were open and informative with the consulate, although their information was padded with rumors, embroidered with opinions, prejudices, and cynicism, and often colored by bitterness.

Public information was practically nonexistent in Shaba. The newspapers were laughable, the TV and radio without any credibility. Rumors abounded and, given the almost complete lack of means for confirming or rejecting them, continued to circulate for relatively long periods of time. While little was believed, almost anything was worth listening to and repeating. The most authoritative type was that preceded by the remark, "My brother (cousin, partner, best friend, boss, or another) just returned from Kinshasa and heard from a close friend that . . ."

The consulate's relationship with Shaba's other "government"—the government-owned copper company Gecamines—was much better. Despite an active program of Zairianization (replacing foreigners with Zairians) of its professional and managerial ranks, expatriate personnel still largely ran Gecamines. Mostly Belgians, plus the odd Frenchman, American, Czech, or other at the senior level, they were open to personal and professional contacts with foreign government representatives. Government efforts to limit this sort of contact within the past year, for instance, included instructions from Kinshasa that requests for information such as those from consuls were to be approved by the managing director (a Zairian national) before they could be answered. Shortly after that, Kinshasa prohibited all visits to mining sites and installations without prior approval by the minister of internal affairs. This prohibition most definitely applied to consuls resident in Shaba.

Despite these restrictions, senior Gecamines personnel remained open to contacts with consular officers, at least partially because the Zairian managing director of Gecamines was open to social contact with foreigners and did not appear diligent in enforcing these Kinshasa edicts. Nevertheless, much of the consulate's hard information on Gecamines's operations came from "defectors"—senior expatriate employees about to resign or be fired.

As a result of this typical relationship with the old colonial class, the consulate's monitoring of the copper industry was relatively good. But elsewhere in local society, the consulate awaited developments and was rarely aware in advance of events. One excellent example was the reign of terror imposed on Zairian Lubumbashi citizens in the spring of 1975 by a band of special security agents from Kinshasa. These agents carefully avoided all whites while energetically and indiscriminately harassing Zairians. The reign of terror had been in operation for almost two weeks before the consulate and other foreigners eventually learned of it only as rumors became more insistent and detailed, as second- and third-hand reports began to fit together. During such a period, consulate personnel would be meeting local officials at formal events or in scheduled appointments to deal with specific business, but no mention of ongoing events would be made. For instance, during the week of December 23–27, 1973, tension and firefights at the Angolan-Zairian border at Dilolo caused the Zairian government to airlift close to three hundred soldiers from Lubumbashi to Dilolo by Zairian Air Force C-130s brought in for the purpose. No Zairian official mentioned this airlift, which went on for three days, and the consulate was not aware of it until an American citizen working for Air Zaire told us about it on Friday, December 27. Rumors of the border situation continued to circulate in Lubumbashi, but not one Zairian official would make the least reference nor would they respond to inquiries. Officially, the subject did not exist. In fact, no problems existed officially. It was most frustrating to professionally nosy diplomats.

Nevertheless, problems did exist, and we did eventually become aware of them. The consulate was particularly concerned with Shaba's economic situation and that of Zaire itself. Serious economic problems were many and revolved around the copper industry, whose continued health was vital to the country. Economic and commercial developments over the previous two years had been extremely adverse and posed serious threats to the continued viability of the Mobutu government's policies and international role, if not to the continued existence of the regime itself.

The consulate could and did monitor these trends and found the local situation consistently deteriorating. Life was increasingly hard for the average Zairian, who suffered the repercussions from outside developments and central government policies. We foreign observers were unable to find a single bright spot in the local scene. All was gloom and stagnation, a perspective aggravated by isolation from the broader scene.

As a result, we in the consulate thought our selective view of developments resembled that of the engine-room crew of a large ship. We sat and watched the machinery go round and round and worried about its ability to continue, threatened as it was by lack of maintenance, spare parts, lubrication, and skilled operators. At the same time, no word came from the bridge. Was the captain aware of the engine room's problems? Where was the ship heading? Occasionally, the bridge relayed vague sailing instructions and weather information, but then silence, except for a sort of continuous political Muzak, which descended upon the engine-room crew.

Though I had hoped that this assignment would give me an opportunity to shine in some dramatic way, like some of my predecessors, such an opportunity did not arise. My time in Lubumbashi was cut relatively short after eighteen months, when I was recalled to Washington to fill the position of deputy office director of Central African Affairs. Obviously, my superiors in Washington were pleased enough with my performance or they wouldn't have called me home to what was a better career job.

It is a continuing regret to me that although I had five African posts in the exciting and dramatic period between 1960 and 1980, I was never present when truly dramatic events took place. I left before independence (Kenya) or arrived a couple of years afterward (Zambia, Guinea-Bissau, and Cape

Verde). Countries had revolutions or civil conflicts before I arrived or after (Zaire). Although there were problems and tensions in most of these countries, my tours of assignment turned out to be relatively quiet interregnums. By the time I arrived in Angola, the initial independence uprising had been effectively quelled and would remain so for several years. I arrived in Lubumbashi after the unlamented Mobutu Sese Seko had turned the economy upside down (and in the process changed his name from Joseph Mobutu), and I left several months before the legendary Katanga Gendarmes invaded Shaba Province from their exile in Angola. It was all very frustrating for a young man who had joined the Foreign Service to observe history from close up, and maybe even play a role in it. I finally decided that I was a mirror image of the Li'l Abner character, Joe Btfsplk, who created chaos around him wherever he went. Only I had an opposite effect; I wandered through Africa in a tumultuous and historic period spreading calm and boredom. I once tried, only half-facetiously, to convince the Africa Bureau to send me to the hottest spots they had, promising that my karma would almost immediately calm the raging mobs, like oil on stormy water. They never took me up on my proposal.

Still, Lubumbashi did provide an opportunity to observe another cultural border, or rather two cultural borders. Lubumbashi was the largest of the Zairian "copper towns," small cities built on and around copper mines. They lay in southern Shaba Province in a line roughly parallel to the Zambian border. Just a hop-skip-and-jump away sat the Zambian copper towns. Both sides were essentially mining the same enormous subterranean copper deposit. The inhabitants on both sides belonged to various tribes, but all were indigenous Africans, somewhat mixed up and shuffled around by the African wars of the nineteenth century. And now they were divided by an international border established only a few generations earlier by European colonizers, the Belgians and the British. As already noted, those north of the border were former Belgian subjects, speaking French as the "national" or educated language and drinking wine; those south of the border used English in the same way, while drinking beer. I don't know if this cultural border will last as long as the one in Belgium; only time will tell.

Certainly, language persists as the most obvious manifestation of culture, as another experience in Lubumbashi demonstrated. When I arrived in "Lubum" on a Friday, with my dog but not my wife, who had diverted to visit her family in Tehran, I was settled into my new house and immediately handed an invitation to dinner for the following evening. I soon discovered that my host was the only American businessman in town and, in fact, the only nonofficial American around. The dinner party was small and informal: two couples. another single man, and my deputy. The other men were all local businessmen, Belgians of long residence. After dinner they decided to show me what there was of Lubumbashi night life, so we adjourned to a local bar. It was a pleasant enough place, nothing spectacular, with a respectably sized crowd sitting around chatting and drinking. At one point I decided it was my turn to buy a round of drinks, so I went up to the bar to order. While waiting for my order to be filled, I suddenly realized that the two young men next to me were speaking in Spanish. Surprised at the sound of Spanish in Central Africa, I jumped in with my Mexican version and exchanged a few remarks.

Returning to the table with my new neighbors and friends, I commented on the encounter and all was revealed. The young men at the bar were not speaking Spanish but Ladino—the language of the Sephardic Jewish community expelled from Spain over five hundred years ago. I later learned that the largest element of the local European colonial community consisted of Sephardic Jews, of which one of my dinner hosts and his wife (Solly and Emmy Benetar) were prominent members. Solly's grandfather had left the island of Rhodes in the last years of the nineteenth century for South Africa. Hearing of opportunities in the Belgian Congo, he had walked to the new town of Élisabethville, thereby founding its Sephardic community. All Belgian citizens, this community was dying, along with the overall colonial community, as they moved on to South Africa or Belgium. But in 1974, in the very heart of Africa, a sizeable community of several thousand Jews still spoke Ladino as their home language, five hundred years after leaving the Iberian Peninsula.

Culture really does count, and last.

7

Guinea-Bissau

In early 1976 I left Zaire and returned to the Africa Bureau as deputy director of the Office of Central African Affairs, mostly focused on Zaire. Another home-based assignment, or as some of us called it, back in the Mother Church. Soon chance in the personnel system played a role, and in slightly less than two years we were on the road again. The first U.S. ambassador to the newly independent countries of Cape Verde and Guinea-Bissau, Melissa Wells, was pulled out after only six months and elevated to a senior position at the U.S. Mission to the United Nations in New York, and a scramble to find a replacement for her ensued. When the Africa Bureau's executive director discussed that need with me, I mentioned as casually as I could that I was a Portuguese speaker with experience in Portuguese Africa. Much to my surprise and gratification, I was soon nominated as the new ambassador extraordinary and plenipotentiary to the Republics of Cape Verde and Guinea-Bissau. The title was almost bigger than the two countries combined, which was a sobering thought.

Aida and I arrived in Bissau, the capital city of Guinea-Bissau, in the fall of 1977. The arrival was conducted with a modicum of style, as we were transported from Dakar by the airplane of Embassy Dakar's air attaché—one of the few bits of privileged style I have enjoyed.

We settled into Bissau, although "settling in" is not really accurate, given the truly difficult conditions existing in this poor and newly independent country. The embassy staff, including my predecessor, had up until recently been living in hotel rooms in the city's one rather sad motel/hotel. An ambassadorial "residence" had been found for us, but its limitations were so obvious that we soon moved out when somewhat better accommodations became available. I will pass over this subject briefly by merely noting that the new "ambassadorial residence" was a two-bedroom apartment located on the fifth floor above the chancery— without an elevator. Living above the shop, so to speak. A *Los Angeles Times* reporter, the only American journalist who ever visited us, spent a few days in Bissau and wrote an article asking whether it was worthwhile asking USG officials to serve in such places. And this was after sitting on my balcony, drinking my gin.

After a week or so I flew to Cape Verde to present my credentials to President Aristides Pereira and visit our mission there. Unlike some places with dual ambassadorial accreditation, we had set up two diplomatic missions. The one in Cape Verde's capital, Praia, was headed by a permanent chargé d'affaires, and I was supposed to supervise the post from Bissau with periodic visits. This I did for my three years, providing some variety but little in the way of better creature comforts. Our occasional visits to Dakar, usually when traveling between Praia and Bissau, on the other hand, at least provided hot showers.

When we arrived, Guinea-Bissau was ending its third year of independence and Cape Verde its second. Being accredited to two countries is relatively rare but not unusual. Both countries had been Portuguese colonies and had achieved independence under the leadership of a single movement—the PAIGC (African Party for the Independence of Guinea and Cape Verde). But despite sharing the same political party, they had decided to set up independent countries. The senior man, Aristides Pereira, became president of the party and president of Cape Verde. The next most senior was Luis Cabral, who became vice president of the party and president of Guinea-Bissau. This setup reflected the reality that the leadership of the PAIGC in Guinea-Bissau was largely composed of ethnic Cape Verdeans.

Fig. 4. Author's appointment by President Carter as the U.S. ambassador to the Republic of Cape Verde. Author's collection.

This situation was a central aspect of the basic and unavoidable demographic character of these two new countries. Cape Verde was populated completely by Cape Verdeans, a cohesive society with an essentially Portuguese culture. Guinea-Bissau was a much more mixed society, composed of Cape Verdeans who had immigrated during the long Portuguese colonial rule, a locally created mulatto class, and—for want of a better term—"pure" Africans, with varying degrees of acquired Portuguese culture (up to the status of *assimilados*—detribalized Africans who had achieved full legal status as Portuguese citizens). The Cape Verdean immigrants to Guinea-Bissau during the colonial period had filled many if not most of the colonial government's civil positions and completely dominated the private sector. The reality of this history was reflected in the wry comment that Guinea-Bissau had been colonized by the Cape Verdeans rather than by the Portuguese.

The dominant role of the Cape Verdeans in the colony of Guinea-Bissau translated into a dominant role in the independence movement—the PAIGC—and then into the leadership of the newly independent government in Bissau. As Cape Verdeans, they were thus racially, culturally, and socially similar to the dispossessed Portuguese colonial leadership and racially, culturally, and socially different from the vast majority of the population

We foreigners were not sure how these groups related to each other or how serious any tensions might be, but we increasingly suspected that intergroup tensions were growing. This was especially true in the capital city, where the Cape Verdeans in the government administration and the economic sectors had flourished.

Like most, if not all, political movements of the twentieth century (and maybe most centuries), the PAIGC believed that its political truth was self-evident and that only essentially corrupted personalities would cavil at its pronouncements of policy and goals. This endemic religiosity was enhanced in the case of the PAIGC by the strong feeling of wartime camaraderie shared by most of the leadership. However, that tune changed as time passed. The Guinea-Bissau government leadership soon was unusually frank in admitting that national management was much more difficult than the liberation-struggle derring-do. Their willingness to admit this did not make the problems less onerous or the irritations less irritating. And so—slowly, quietly, and at the time peacefully and in a very relaxed manner—the various disparate elements of the Guinea-Bissau political, social, and economic scene began to reveal their separate natures. Local politics was being invented.

Still, many of the local Cape Verdeans conceived of the rebellion as theirs and reaped the rewards by assuming the leadership roles in Guinea-Bissau as well as more naturally in Cape Verde itself. The contradictions inherent in this situation were beginning to surface, and the implications were becoming the primary topic of the professional gossip of the expatriate community. What were those contradictions and implications?

A loosening of coherence was beginning to take place on several levels and in various sectors. On the broadest level composed of the party-state—which is itself a mystical amalgam of One Party and Two States—one could begin to sense the inevitable strains between the two national governments of Guinea-Bissau and Cape Verde and the mix of institutional loyalty, inertia, careerism, and ideology which the two governments, by their very existence, fostered if not created. The strains were not yet public but were beginning to be sensed by outsiders as the political elite of both governments protested continuously their undying loyalty to the Party and its commitment to unification. This growing tension was obviously tied to the ethnic character of the ruling leadership, all Cape Verdean in Cape Verde and mostly Cape Verdean in Guinea-Bissau.

At the national level in Guinea-Bissau, signs of incipient political fragmentation began to appear. The overriding political ideology was still the Party; its successful struggle for independence—the "*Luta*" (struggle or fight)—and the resulting legitimacy. (Not all senior officials of the government—as compared with the party—were veterans of the struggle, hence the occasional whispered hint that such-and-such an official had been a clandestine member of the party in the colonial days. The party itself tried to withdraw membership cards acquired rapidly on the eve of victory.)

However, as time since independence passed, differing political tendencies or perspectives began to appear among the politically active. First, a group of radical or "Soviet-bloc" adherents, dithering between Soviet and Cuban allies but generally interested in retaining and expanding ties with the Soviets, deplored the new links with the West and were generally desirous of a more radical and ideologically pure governmental policy and orientation.

A not insignificant number of other local leaders were showing signs of a rather liberal cast of mind à la Léopold Senghor or Félix Houphouët-Boigny. Nothing very open, but clear interest in foreign aid (the more the merrier and therefore inevitably Western) and investment, if possible, and a firm conviction that Western European cities were clearly much nicer than their Eastern European counterparts.

The largest group was a bit more difficult to define. Their major orientation was "classic" African nationalism; independence from the Portuguese was the goal, and now the siren call of pure African nationalism surfaced. President Luís Cabral clearly exemplified this viewpoint (although as time passed he showed tendencies toward more liberal leanings).

The majority of foreign observers, both residents and visitors, spent much time gossiping about these matters. The PAIGC had long been the darling of intellectual circles in Western Europe, particularly the Scandinavian countries, along with a clique of academics and journalists. They came periodically for visits, to sit at the feet of various leaders like Commissioner of Economic Development and Planning Vasco Cabral and then return home to write glowing apologias for radical periodicals on the PAIGC-led rural development approach. (Commissioner Cabral's Lisbon café, Communist Party background, personal charm, verbal ability, and ministerial incompetence made him the perfect guru for foreigners.) These treatises had little to do with reality, as the government itself was well aware. A report on foreign economic assistance, prepared by Vasco Cabral's department, was withdrawn and burnt prior to public release, when top leadership discovered that over 70 percent of all development projects were located in the capital city area.

Some change appeared at the annual New Year's Day 1978 ceremony for the diplomatic corps. The four most senior leaders present were the president of the Council of State (Cape Verdean), principal commissioner (African), commissioner for security affairs (African), and commissioner for foreign affairs (*assimilado*). They represented a subtle reorganization at the top level, following the death of the former principal commissioner the previous July. This group represented real political power in the country and thus significant political representation for all the major ethnic groups. However, the bulk of the senior government officials below them (the rest of the commissioners, the senior bureaucrats, and party officials) were largely Cape Verdean.

Such concerns gave some importance to the little affair in November 1978 involving a disaffected former freedom fighter, one Malam Sanha. His effort to infiltrate the country and initiate resistance to the newly independent government was itself of little import. His reputation was poor at best, his connections apparently minimal, his supporters largely disreputable, and his timing—just two months after the most popular African military leader was promoted to prime minister—laughable. Nevertheless, and despite the government's calm and efficient reaction, Sanha's effort did create a frisson of fear.

Being a proper, accredited, modern, progressive liberation movement, the PAIGC fully opposed all forms of racism and special privilege. But ethnic politics began, timidly, to rear its head. While Cabral and Principal Commissioner Nino may have shared a similar political or ideological perspective, there were differences between them of potential import. Cabral was a Cape Verdean and a political leader during the Luta, while Nino was an African and the popular leader of the largely African army. There were rumors that Nino and other Africans were not happy with the predominance of Cape Verdeans in the party and the government.

The Cape Verdean–African difference had always been a potential source of trouble but had been subsumed by a complex net of familial relationships and a strong sense of camaraderie stemming from the long independence struggle. The question being discussed among observers was whether this tension would or could result in a coalescing of Africans into an anti–Cape Verdean movement, creating a divisive racial element in local internal politics.

On the other hand, continued contact with Guinea-Bissau brought us outsiders to a greater awareness of the strength and extent of family ties among the Guinea-Bissauan elite, regardless of color. In fact, we concluded that all—I repeat, all—members of the Guinea-Bissau modern elite were related by family ties. Given the small size of this group, possibly four thousand individuals—including children—most had several ties, both by blood and by marriage. The vast majority of individuals were probably related within the category of third cousin, and the numbers of people with double and triple relationships (such as third cousin through one relative, first cousin through another, related by marriage) were legend.

The local comment that Guinea-Bissau was a family, not a country, was probably literally true with respect to the leadership class. The common word of address in Crioulo, or Creole (the country's lingua franca), was *primo* or cousin. We realized that this meant, literally, that those who did not have a closer tie considered each other at least cousins. This state of affairs is not surprising, given the small size of the population involved, their casual sexual habits (illegitimate births were common and carried little or no social stigma), and the breeding proclivities of local men. The president of Guinea-Bissau, Luís Cabral, recognized somewhere between twenty and thirty siblings, and the minister of justice recognized twenty-four. An embassy officer listened to several senior government officials, including the minister of justice, debate who among their parents' generation deserved the prize as the most productive paterfamilias. They could not agree.

Close linkages of this type had another, less pleasant aspect. As all were related, promotions and assignments had a whiff of nepotism about them. Certainly much of this was unavoidable given the size of the country. Nevertheless, the nomination of President Cabral's divorced wife as ambassador to the Ivory Coast and the appointment of Amilcar Cabral's widow as ambassador to East Germany typified a number of situations that raised some eyebrows.

Although the country is both Catholic and animistic, there is a substantial Muslim population, and some were in the governmental and party elite, such as Minister of Defense Umaro Djalo. Those Muslims who were members of the new leadership class did not appear to be any different from their peers, possibly because they were lapsed Muslims, just as the others were mostly lapsed Catholics.

Nevertheless, while a level of racial awareness did exist and was accompanied by a low level of background tension, it did not surface as a factor of political importance until several years later, after I had left Bissau.

While the government worried about weightier matters, certain attributes of a more relaxed life in a capital began to manifest themselves in this hitherto rather austere little city. The number of foreigners had grown in the previous year, most of them young specialists or volunteers sponsored by the UNDP or bilateral economic assistance programs. The smallish diplomatic corps began to bloom. Most diplomats now had some sort of permanent housing, wives began to reside in Bissau, staffs were being beefed up, and a modest diplomatic social life had begun.

After what seemed an eternity of discomfort—pounding, drilling, sawing, and other assorted inconveniences associated with construction— Embassy Bissau's chancery renovation was completed in September 1979. The dirt floor in the reception room was now covered. By November the dirt, dust, and noise were only a memory, and the dignified calm appropriate to a chancery now settled upon us. During the same period, the drive to find and renovate appropriate housing for embassy staff came to fruition. The embassy now had adequate, if modest, work and living facilities.

I even had a new official car. The car on hand when I arrived was a Ford Torino sedan, not very old but already showing wear in the tropical environment. Then catastrophe struck. A state funeral was held for the recently deceased prime minister at the Presidential Palace in the center of the city. The official guests, including the diplomatic corps, arrived in sequence in their cars. In due course my car pulled up. I exited and began to stride up the steps. But I didn't get very far when it became obvious that my car would not start. My embarrassed driver was frantic but could do little, and finally four sympathetic onlookers stepped forward and pushed the car around the corner and out of sight. When this event was reported to Washington, a decision was made to provide a new vehicle. Eventually a brand-new bronze-colored Chevy Impala arrived. It was one of the largest cars in town, and, when flying its two flags, fully restored the status of my driver among his diplomatic corps peers.

These welcome internal achievements marked the end of another year of improving relations between the Guineans and the United States. The suspicion, to say the least, with which the first official Americans had been greeted in Bissau in 1976 has long since been changed into a relaxed and even warm reception of Americans by local officials and private individuals. The Voice of America reported that the number of letters from listeners in Guinea-Bissau (and Cape Verde) was remarkable, given the size of the country. A USIA-sponsored basketball coach was enthusiastically received, and the second visit by a United States Navy ship was such a great success that the seven-person official delegation invited to luncheon aboard the USS *Trippe* was augmented by seventeen assorted wives, children, and assistants in a holiday mood. (It also provided me with the first and only time I have been piped aboard a U.S. Navy ship, an unforgettable event. For those without navy experience, this means that when an American ambassador reaches the deck, the loudspeaker announces the arrival as "The United States." Few moments can touch that.)

In 1979 the International Visitor program took off, and those members of the Guinea-Bissau cabinet who had not yet traveled were now lined up for their visits to the New World. The U.S. government visitors' program was especially popular in Guinea-Bissau and Cape Verde, as many locals had relatives in the large Portuguese (Cape Verdean) population in the United States. Everybody appeared to have a cousin in New Bedford, Massachusetts.

In November 1978, the wives of most of the resident ambassadors held the first ever charity affair in independent Guinea-Bissau, an international buffet dinner dance under the patronage of the president, who attended with all of his cabinet. The Chinese participated with evident gusto, while the Soviets and Cubans stayed away (to the delight of the Chinese ambassador, who commented that perhaps their absence was explained by their dislike of spending money). The French Embassy and the French Cultural Center, which apparently were not on speaking terms, presented separate displays.

However, on the occasion of the second diplomatic corps social event in Guinea-Bissau, the corps's first annual dinner for the minister of foreign affairs, the Soviet ambassador made up for his prior absence. Having failed to reply to all queries from the Senegalese dean of the diplomatic corps as to whether he would attend, our Soviet colleague showed up at the appointed hour without spouse but with an interpreter and demanded two places at the head table. The dean granted the Russian's right to a head table seat on the grounds of diplomatic precedence but refused all attempts to place the interpreter alongside. The dinner then proceeded more or less normally by local standards; the failure of the city power system shortly after the serving of the first course struck all present as normal. As the dinner was being given in the open air next to the empty swimming pool at the hotel, this provided an opportunity for a charming dinner by moonlight. The corps was quite satisfied with its efforts to introduce diplomatic standards to Bissau, and even the Brazilian ambassador's concern over the possibility of rabies after she was bitten by one of the numerous cats roaming nearby was taken in stride. Lawrence Durrell would have felt right at home.

This somewhat tentative normalcy became clear among the ranks of the governing elite. Increasingly from 1976 through 1979, the foreign observer could watch this class—no other word applies—gingerly come out of its Liberation Movement uniform. Increasingly confident of its political position and of their individual positions, this group of people and their wives (important point) began to surface socially and publicly.

The somewhat austere living habits of the first few years after independence had begun to be replaced; houses were being remodeled; stereos, radios, records, cassettes, and imported drinks and goods were available to the governing elite. Particularly noticeable was the improvement in the style of dress of the feminine members of this class. Increasingly well dressed for evening affairs, the prevalence of chic European-cut jeans and similar apparel now became common in the city streets, offices, and stores. Some aspects of this consumer class rise were potentially disturbing. Special arrangements were apparently available to elites at the new government-owned supermarkets and through the national airline, which weekly imported supplies of foodstuffs and drinks from Dakar. There were reports or rumors of creeping corruption among senior officials—more related to living standards than to bank accounts, it must be said. The habit of official overseas travel had taken root; it was an unusual week when it seemed that at least half of the cabinet was not traveling somewhere in the world. A typical sight at the airport was the returning official or delegation, loaded down with bulging suitcases and carry-on luggage. Only in the most traditional area of new-country ostentation—official cars—had the government been relatively restrained. Here the Swedish connection meant that ministers and other senior officials rode about in Volvos rather than Mercedes: not quite Volkswagens, but still. (It should be noted, however, that the governor of the National Bank insisted on a more traditional international standard and drove a large black Mercedes.)

Still, the craze for champagne (French, of course) among the top governmental and party leadership became embarrassing. At large public affairs, cold bottles of champagne were brought ostentatiously to the prime minister and other senior officials, while the common run of guests (including diplomats and other ministers) had to content themselves with more normal refreshments. The top leadership openly discussed the obvious superiority of champagne and seemed unaware of how blatant and, it might be said, nouveau riche their behavior appeared.

One amusing sign of the times was the sudden popularity of tennis. At least half the cabinet, including the president. the prime minister, and their spouses and children, had taken up the sport. A common sight at the decaying courts in town was the former freedom fighter and liberation movement dignitary dressed in Jimmy Connors–style tennis attire, carrying several rackets under his arm. The number of available courts in town decreased by one-third when the party appropriated the former Chamber of Commerce building together with its tennis court, which was now reserved for the president and a few other senior officials.

What price egalitarianism?

In other words, RHIP (Rank Hath Its Privileges) reared its head and showed signs of picking up speed. The discipline of the liberation struggle days had clearly been relaxed, marked by a definite growth of high living among the country's new leadership class. This was not a surprising development—to the victors belong the spoils—if only because many of the new leaders and particularly their wives came from the old local bourgeois class, many wealthy by local standards. The tourism minister's wife, for instance, was only doing her Lisbon shopping where she had done it all her life.

All this did not yet constitute widespread or serious corruption. If any, was it serious? There were no rumors (or at least only one) of government officials taking kickbacks or receiving other sorts of large-scale payoffs. Government contracts, the most obvious source of corruption, still appeared to be openly (within the government) and honestly concluded. What was going on was a comparatively rapid growth in high living styles for the leadership. As their salaries were modest (about $500 a month for ministers, plus a car, driver, house, and utilities), the question arose as to how they supported their new lifestyle. In some cases, family money (often through the wives' families) may have been a partial answer. But the most obvious answer was the use of official funds and the receipt of friendly assistance from overseas interests. For instance, several leaders had their children in private schools in Portugal, with the bills being paid by Portuguese business friends. On trips many leaders received extensive hospitality, possibly including financial supplements to their government-authorized traveling expenses.

None of this was yet serious, and certainly not yet dangerous to the regime or party discipline. Amilcar Cabral was never an ascetic and left a tradition of enjoying the good things of life. However, these developments in Bissau brought sharp private criticism from Cape Verde president and PAIGC secretary general Aristides Pereira. A much more austere personality, he was reportedly increasingly concerned by what he considered drift and slackness in the Guinea-Bissau government. Pereira ran a tighter ship and sharply limited overseas travel by his senior people.

In any case, these new manners did not appear to have seriously disturbed the general population, at least not in the capital city. Most people appeared to view this development with a combination of mild envy and good-humored cynicism. As the new expansion in elite living style was accompanied by a general atmosphere of relaxation, the ordinary Bissau citizen, who had been after all at least a de facto supporter of the colonial regime, appeared content to let the victors take their ease without much concern.

The government made attempts to share the good times and went in for some holiday cheer. It used new commercial credits from Portugal and Brazil to import a large quantity of consumer goods for the 1979 holiday season, thereby creating at least the facade of prosperity. The end-of-the-year mood was quite jovial and relaxed, and the old custom of holiday festivity—severely subdued since independence—resurfaced with great openness. Two new government-owned supermarkets opened in November, and the small, privately owned shops were full—by Bissau standards—of shaving cream, textiles, children's clothes, toys, and foodstuffs, including wines and liquors. The prices were horrendous by local standards and the pricing puzzling—why should a Portuguese wine cost twice as much in Bissau as in Cape Verde? Nevertheless, the stores were full of shoppers, and not just the government elite. People did have money in their pockets, maybe because there had been little to buy up until then.

What with fully stocked stores, the streets full of people careening around on the numerous bicycles imported during the year, the numerous parties, and the holiday spirit, the mood in Bissau in December 1979 was relaxed and even jovial. Those first few years following independence were marked by the sobriety considered appropriate for serious and self-consciously progressive regimes, but cheerfulness had recently been breaking out. The prior year's carnival was enthusiastically celebrated for the first time in ten years, with a mammoth street parade and many parties. In 1979 Christmas and New Year's signs and symbols were widespread for the first time since independence, modified to read "*Feliz Natal, Camarades*."

8

Guinea-Bissau Politics and Economics

Time had passed since independence, but agricultural production remained especially problematic. The crops were unusually poor for several years, and the hoped-for production of sufficient rice to meet internal needs was not achieved. In January 1978 the government turned openly to the international community for food aid, convoking the resident diplomatic corps in a rather naïve little gathering. Government representatives openly explained the problem and formally asked the assembled diplomats to forward the request for food aid to their governments. The appeal was made to the international community as a whole—otherwise the presence of the representatives of the PLO and the Polisario could have been embarrassing. In any case their presence, plus that of the Cubans, East Germans, Soviets, Egyptians, and Nigerians, proved to be largely ceremonial.

As time passed, the need for a noticeable success became more urgent and more embarrassing in the face of comparatively massive flows of foreign aid. The social and physical damage incurred by the country during the war was, of course, a reasonable excuse as to why self-sufficiency had not yet been achieved in the five years since independence, but it could not be used forever. Independence had not brought the millennium— and everybody fervently denied they really thought it would—but some results should be forthcoming to justify the struggle. Self-sufficiency in rice would represent such an accomplishment, the government had promised it, and the country had been self-sufficient in rice in the colonial days.

Government policies increasingly appeared to be a handicap, however. The farm-to-market system was clearly inadequate, yet the government persisted in implementing a largely state-owned commercial structure. The combination of war-afflicted damages, poor rains, and inefficient, if not actually disincentivizing, government commercial policies had resulted in disturbing reactions by Guinean farmers. In the north many were reported to have shifted their farming activity across the border into southern Senegal in search of Senegal's hard currency and consumer goods. In the south there were reliable reports of farmers limiting their activities to subsistence agriculture on the grounds that crops grown for sale were not worth the effort. (Even if government buyers arrived punctually, there was little to buy with Guinean pesos in the poorly stocked state-owned stores.) Nevertheless, the countryside was sufficiently productive and the population density low enough that real famine was unlikely. The food shortage fell largely on the capital city of Bissau, requiring food aid from the country's friends.

The major industrial and infrastructure projects—the automobile assembly plant and the agora-industry complex at Cumore—reportedly made progress but with few apparent results. For instance, the Citroën assembly plant reportedly began to turn out small numbers of the modernized version of the legendary Deux Chevaux by December 1979, but none ever actually appeared on the streets of Bissau. The new road to the airport was finally finished, but it appeared to serve mainly for the periodic high-speed caravans of official and diplomatic cars making the trip to participate in high-level departures and arrivals— flying their flags, of course. The driver of the American car—a full-size Chevrolet—was inordinately proud that we flew two flags when everyone else only had one.

Many foreign advisors earnestly debated whether any of these projects would ever become economically viable, even though the government continued to point to them with pride, despite the absence of visible results. Some of the less dramatic projects—rice irrigation, secondary-school construction, soil and bug research and control, artisanal fishing, and others—at one point appeared to be moving ahead, but over time even these withered away.

Meanwhile, foreign economic assistance continued to subsidize the government and the country's monetary economy. The Swedes agreed to increase their annual aid to approximately $14 million to compensate for inflation, as did the Dutch. All the other donors at least maintained the generous aid levels of previous years. The annual total, exclusive of Eastern Bloc military assistance, was at least $50 million and possibly as high as $70 million, a fair amount of money for a small country with a population of under three million.

Few of the country's actual problems appeared to be meaningfully addressed. Nothing was resolved, and the country remained poor and undeveloped. The leadership was increasingly preoccupied with the real day-to-day problems of government and increasingly uncertain that they knew what to do with them. On the surface, nevertheless, political life was calm, and no insurmountable problems were on the horizon.

Despite these concerns, the general mood of relaxation and openness reflected the increased confidence of the ruling elite, an interlocking directorate of government and party leaders. Coordinated, not ruled, by President Luis Cabral, the collegial character of the government became more evident. Internal political tensions and rivalries were remarkable only for their absence. At the same time, the ruling elite began to show open evidence of privilege in their general style of living, as the almost priggish austerity of the early independence days became permeated by a growing preoccupation with the present and the problems of everyday life. Guinea-Bissau's elite had discovered that rank hath its privileges—and did not appear to be spurning them. Whether this development would eventually grow into an abuse of power and general corruption was a question for the future. At that moment it was not yet offensive, and the Bissau population at least appeared to accept it with a sort of good-humored cynicism.

In external relations, the Government of Guinea-Bissau (GOGB) had successfully pursued the policy that had slowly taken form over its first three years, combining three essential themes: retain the fraternal links with the Soviets and Cubans, expand ties, particularly economic, with the West, and generally play down rhetoric in pursuit of genuine, low-keyed nonalignment. Relations with the United States continued to improve in all aspects, and the ties between Guinea-Bissau and Senegal became more evident every day, resulting from President Senghor's deliberate policy of rapprochement.

The Chinese were present in Bissau with a largish embassy but somehow never seemed to play a noticeable role. I always assumed they were essentially watching the Russians, and maybe us. Although polite enough when we ran across each other, usually at government events, they were essentially standoffish. Then one day at an event for diplomatic wives, a crowd of Chinese women, led by the Chinese ambassador's wife, surrounded Aida with excited conversation, of which she could only get one word—recognition. The word had just come through that China and the United States had established formal recognition. The Chinese ladies then hustled Aida onto a waiting government helicopter—she thought she was being kidnapped—and stayed with her throughout the day's events. After that, we were rather friendly, exchanging hospitality (a long and boring movie at the Chinese embassy about the Chinese FBI fighting political criminals, for instance) and enthusiastic greetings at public events.

To celebrate the event, we held a reception at our apartment for the two missions—American and Chinese—plus a few friends. After a time, I noticed the Chinese ambassador standing by the window with an obvious air of wanting to go home. He caught the eye of his wife and gave one of those conjugal signals about leaving. However, she was sitting on the couch, energetically chatting away with several women and dismissed his signal with a curt negative nod. He appeared to sigh and wandered off to get another drink, where I joined him.

Relations with the North Korean ambassador also illustrated the peculiar character of diplomatic life. At a local protocol event (President Cabral departing on a foreign trip), the Russian chargé d'affaires (in the absence of his ambassador) had broken diplomatic protocol by inserting himself in front of several ambassadors, including the North Korean, who was visibly furious. My closest friend in Bissau, Portuguese ambassador Antonio Oliviera Pinto da France, and I decided we could have some fun with this. We used the next monthly diplomatic corps luncheon to make solemn statements bemoaning junior officers' lack of appropriate respect and discipline, as in failing to respect diplomatic norms and protocol, and called on the assembled chiefs of mission to ensure that their staffs were properly instructed. Everyone present knew whom we were referring to. After Antonio finished his remarks, in a deliberately exaggerated florid Latin style, the North Korean ambassador jumped in with a fervent support for our remarks. And he wasn't kidding, as we were. He had always been rather cool to me, but after that event he evinced a general relaxation of attitude and even allowed me to bum the occasional cigarette. (I was in the process of giving up smoking.)

The collective belt-loosening was equally apparent in Guinea-Bissau's increasingly restrained political style. Although a one-party state—legally and actually—the prevailing mood was a form of political laissez faire. Despite the official rhetoric about the need for discipline—"*A luta continua,*" or "the struggle goes on"—in actual fact the party and government leadership (same people) showed all the signs of old hounds turning around on themselves prior to settling down for a good nap.

The party was organized formally by the principles of democratic centralism—with emphasis on centralism. The government was organized along similar principles—with the National Assembly replacing the Party Congress—led by a double-headed organizational monster composed of a Council of State, whose president was the chief of state, and a council of commissioners or ministers, headed by a principal commissioner or prime minister. Most senior personalities wore two or more hats, party and government. The true organization was thus much more informal and collegial, particularly as the president and deputy secretary general of the party, Luis Cabral, acted as board chairman rather than dominant leader.

Cabral's prominent but not predominant role stemmed both from his history and his personal characteristics. Although a founding father of the

PAIGC, he was, after all, only Amilcar Cabral's younger brother and had never played a prominent military role. In addition, he lacked the drive and the arrogance and probably the desire to play the maximum leader.

A sense of comradeship still pervaded the top leadership; in some respects, any meeting—formal or informal, or even merely accidental—somewhat resembled a chapter meeting of American Legion vets from World War II. Confident in their cause, proud of their success, and full of good feeling for every buddy from the old days, the GOGB leadership was relaxed about themselves, their colleagues, and their future.

As implied previously, President Luis Cabral directed but did not control this process. He was well liked and respected in the party and in the country, but he was not a dominant leader and needed to constantly convince his colleagues and adjust to their views. Apart from everything else, he had to always be aware of the latent tensions between those of Cape Verdean origin and pure Black Africans. Cabral appeared to perform this coordination task quite well.

The principal commissioner (prime minister), João Bernardo "Nino" Vieira, had been elevated to this rank in mid-1978, following the death of the country's first chief of government in a car accident. Nino had a reputation as the country's most formidable military leader and a stern disciplinarian. It was rumored, and hoped by some, that in his new position he would take hold of the day-to-day administration of the government and bring some order into the house, but Nino had failed to do so. In fact, there was an increasing suspicion that his lack of formal education and general sophistication were proving to be handicaps too large for him to surmount. There were those who said he was merely getting ready and soon would exert himself. Similar comments were made about other ministers, giving rise to occasional rumors of a government reshuffle.

Certainly, almost all members of the government, either openly or by implication, gave the impression that the harsh realities of governing a poor country were more daunting than they had imagined in the heady days of the independence struggle. The old slogans appeared increasingly irrelevant. The more serious ministers appeared to be burying their uneasiness with the situation by active involvement in their daily tasks, but on an individual, uncoordinated basis. Some government reorganization did seem to be in the wind, but the still-strong fraternal ties of the liberation struggle placed severe limitations on the extent to which senior personalities could be removed from office.

In this atmosphere, every government minister pursued his own policies, more or less. There was remarkably little governmental discipline at the highest levels, which inevitably reflected down through the bureaucracy. Five years after independence, this allegedly socialist government had yet to produce an economic development plan, despite the efforts of the commissioner of planning and economic development, Vasco Cabral. The other ministers went on their merry way, ignoring Vasco Cabral and his efforts to centralize government economic activity. Their opposition to Vasco was political (he was a rather romantic radical), practical (he was a terrible administrator and manager), personal (each was building his own fief), and quite effective.

There seemed to be a widespread realization among the leadership that they must abandon their earlier dreams of rapid change under a regime of strict austerity, and that the realities of their situation and their country required more modest plans and achievements. An interesting decision released one December announced that all taxicabs belonging to the government-owned monopoly would be sold to individual drivers. Government officials admitted that the bureaucrat–taxi driver had been a complete failure and that they were returning the industry to the private sector. Considering the persistent stories of problems in the administration of state-owned commercial activities, foreign observers wondered whether the taxi reversion was not a straw in the wind.

Most foreign observers and experts, for all the obvious reasons, bemoaned this lack of government discipline and central control. Certainly, several projects then under way probably deserved criticism. With each minister pursuing his own policies, except for those who did not appear to be doing anything but enjoying the limited fruits of victory in this poor country, the criteria applied to development projects varied with each minister's personal interpretation of the government's overall development strategy. As that strategy had never been specifically defined, each minister was pretty much on his own, limited only by what he could get foreign donors to finance.

Nevertheless, this situation—so regrettable in the eyes of professional development experts—may have had its advantages. First, it was part of a political atmosphere remarkably free of tension and competition. Each leader was secure in his position and obviously felt no need to conspire against others. The country's political life was thus quite free of plotting and squabbling. President Cabral was the president and chief of state but directed a collegial form of government, and his colleagues were clearly that—colleagues. As a result, the political rumor mill in Bissau was dull and the resident diplomatic corps generally quite bored with local politics. Five years may not be long in the life of a new country, but rampant political ambition had so far been avoided in Guinea-Bissau, and this in a reasonably open system without the inhibiting influence of a strong dominant leader.

The situation was not without its beneficial effects on the country's human rights situation. Although a one-party state, the lack of internal political tensions within the party contributed to a loose and easy style of government. The presence of a security policy, though, meant that overly aggressive criticism of the party and the government was not permitted. On the other hand, people were quite free in their private lives and discussions, where comment about and criticism of the government were common. There was little feel of oppressive political rule.

The only political prisoners kept in custody, apart from one or two leaders of the African commandos organized by the Portuguese prior to independence, were the twenty or so individuals connected with an abortive armed uprising in late 1978. These prisoners were tried and the leaders condemned to death, but the leadership was apparently unable to bring itself to implement the death sentence, even though one of the alleged leaders had already previously benefited from a death sentence commutation. The reluctance to inflict harsh penalties had been seen in the then-recent handling of the death sentence imposed on two young men charged with rape of minor children. One rapist, himself a minor, had his sentence commuted by a review authority to fifteen years' imprisonment. The other, charged with rape of a two-year-old and a nine-year old, had his death sentence confirmed by the Council of State at a special meeting.

Finally, it was a moot point whether this style of reined government leadership was harmful to the process of economic development. Certainly, the record of other poor new countries, all equipped with maximum leaders and detailed economic development plans, was not encouraging. Perhaps Guinea-Bissau's more eclectic approach, adopted however inadvertently, may in the long run prove more effective by permitting greater experimentation and step-by-step development.

The year 1979 ended with a flurry of highly publicized meetings and speeches on the state of the nation. The Third Guinea-Bissau and Cape Verde Intergovernmental Conference was held in Cape Verde and, to no one's surprise, announced that the process of unification of the two countries was proceeding apace. A new executive secretariat was created to backstop the conference, and a schedule of mixed commission meetings was announced for 1980 to further ever-closer coordination and cooperation between the two governments. The personalities appointed to fill the newly created positions to implement the stepped-up policies, however, only convinced us outsiders that the commitment remained more rhetorical than real.

The Guinea-Bissau National Council of the PAIGC met as usual in December 1979 to review the year with pride and reveal with confidence the plans for the coming year. They mainly revolved around a renewed drive to recruit and train more and better party members and officials. The Council of State also met in December. Nothing was announced about its deliberations, except the decision to uphold the death sentence on the convicted rapist.

Presumably, the Council also approved the subject and tone of the final event of the year—the president's reception of the diplomatic corps, government and party officials, and other notables in the Palace of the Republic on December 29. That event had been moved from early January to late December and somewhat altered in composition and character. Whereas in the previous year only the dean of the corps and the president addressed the reception, this time the principal commissioner (prime minister) and the secretary general of the National Trade Union preceded the dean. The dean, the principal commissioner, and the secretary-general all spoke briefly and in generalities and concluded by offering their best wishes and hopes for a happy and prosperous new year to the president, his new wife, and the people of Guinea-Bissau.

President Cabral then replied with a long—very long—discourse, in the form of a review of the developments of the past year and a summary of the current state of the nation. His essential message was that, while enormous problems and tasks faced the nation, a certain amount of progress and development had occurred and should be recognized with pride. He announced that priority areas for the coming year would be agriculture, fisheries, and natural resources. The president spoke with even less recourse to ideological language and to traditional PAIGC slogans than in the past—a tendency we had been observing for several years now. Only at the very end did he even refer to international developments and foreign affairs, and half of his comments on the external world expressed gratitude to the members of the international community who had contributed so much assistance to Guinea-Bissau. Cabral's reference to international developments was a brief and perfunctory reiteration of the PAIGC's and GOGB's continued opposition to "colonialism, imperialism, Zionism, and racism." No specific countries, movements, or individuals were named.

Following the conclusion of the president's speech, the diplomatic corps was invited to pass through a reception line composed of the president and several of his senior colleagues, at the end of which we found ourselves outside of the hall without the glass of champagne with which we had been rewarded in previous years.

Life in Guinea-Bissau continued without any marked changes into 1980, the year I left, upon my transfer to the National War College in Washington. Foreign economic assistance continued steadily and grew despite mounting absorption problems. The numbers of foreign experts, advisors, volunteers, and what have you were daily more obvious in the streets of Bissau. At the end of June, the first American volunteers arrived—eleven from Crossroads Africa.

The country's major development projects continued to move ahead. While some faced criticism, it was clear that even the most pessimistic judgments fell far short of saying that the government had yet made any truly serious or catastrophic mistakes. A negative virtue, possibly, but the persistent tendency to show caution continued to serve this new country—at least for the moment.

External relations also jogged along, with no sharp breaks or significant new developments. Even Senegal's decision to close its embassy in Bissau, along with twenty-two others around the world, was a surprise but would probably not materially affect the steady growth of ties between the two countries. Dakar is Bissau's obvious regional entrepôt, and the Bissauans appeared perfectly content for it to be so. Otherwise, the government's low-key approach to foreign affairs continued.

The balancing act of choosing between the old liberation-struggle ties and the new realities (and often preferences) calling for ever-closer relations with the West remained the centerpiece of Guinea-Bissau's foreign policy. The Bissauans appeared so comfortable and satisfied with this policy that probably only an enormous shock would change it. (That would soon happen, but not on my watch.)

The year 1980, before I left, was marked by a local event in many ways typical of life in Bissau in those days. On June 12 President Cabral held his long-promised fishing trip for the diplomatic corps in Bissau. By special plane and helicopter, the diplomats flew to the island of Bubaque for an evening party. The next day, clutching cameras, sunhats, and—in the case of the Chinese ambassador and his interpreter—umbrellas, the diplomats filed onto the regular inter-island ferry specially leased for a day on the water, to include fishing. The North Korean won the ambassadorial competition for the first fish (prize of twenty kilos of shrimp), and a good time was had by most (a few were seasick).

At about one o'clock, the ferry approached a most beautiful and romantic stretch of beach on the ocean side of the island, where a beach buffet awaited the corps. Suddenly, the mood changed as the ferry encountered high waves. Efforts to offload the passengers—diplomats, ministers, protocol officers, wives, girlfriends, and children—were supervised by an increasingly distraught president, as his personally laid plans ran into trouble. The transfer into small boats became chaotic, and soon the beach area was littered with water-soaked diplomats who had thrown themselves, or were thrown, into the surf. The president's smaller yacht became trapped on the beach by the surf, and the gallant efforts of a large number of more or less sober dips and VIPs to push it off failed. Despite the actual danger, the mood was essentially festive, the transfer having been implemented with enthusiasm, if not much professionalism.

Dramatic individual scenes included that of the Chinese ambassador and his interpreter wading ashore in baggy, striped boxer shorts, still carrying their umbrellas; the Soviet ambassador climbing down the side of the ferry boat in his undersized orange briefs; the American ambassador's wife being thrown into the waiting arms of the commander of the Guinea-Bissau Navy as he stood chest high in the surf; the foreign minister's wife walking up and down the beach in the confusion, alternately shaking her head and roaring with laughter; and finally, the five-foot-two, brush-cut French chargé d'affaires standing ankle deep in the surf, chortling with glee as he filmed the whole two-hour debacle on his Super 8 camera. Soon labeled by some as "The Longest Day," the landing of the diplomatic corps on Bubaque Island's Bruce Beach passed into local legend. And the largely amateur crowd who starred in it anxiously awaited the first public showing of the film of the event—which of course never happened.

9

Cape Verde

As noted, I was accredited as ambassador to both Guinea-Bissau and Cape Verde, while residing in Bissau. Our small embassy in Bissau (eight Americans) was matched by a similar establishment in Praia, the capital of Cape Verde. The Praia embassy was headed by Chargé d'affaires Howard McGowan, except when I was physically present there. Together with our locally hired staff, everyone was busy, as in Bissau, with the problems of opening an American embassy, albeit a small one, in a difficult environment.

I soon began periodic visits to Cape Verde for upwards of a week at a time, usually separated by several months. To be honest, there wasn't much of anything dramatic or fast-breaking going on in either country. As in Bissau, the challenges were not violent or even political, but generally centered on the perceptual shortage of everything usually considered desirable for everyday life. We, however, in both the Bissau and Praia embassies were better off than the local inhabitants, as we had recourse to outside supplies.

The visitor who arrived in Cape Verde in those days was struck first by its barrenness: ten years of drought had reduced the country's ten volcanic islands to a state of nature strongly resembling pictures of the moon. Brown was the dominant color, and the isolated spots of green were almost shocking in their vividness. Most visitors reacted with a feeling of depression, followed by a real sense of pity and admiration for the inhabitants of the islands. The inevitable question was—but how do they survive? The answer was—barely, and largely with help from the expatriate Cape Verdean communities and from foreign aid.

Next one was struck by the realization that, except in a geographic sense, Cape Verde was not an African country. It was a small, poor Portuguese province, adrift off the coast of Africa. The Cape Verdean peasant may be no better educated nor in any sense richer than his counterpart on the coast of Africa, but he is not an African; he does not belong to the tribal cultures that, with local variations, exist from one end of Africa to the other. Cape Verde has a distinctive culture of its own, rich in music, literature, and a whole bag of cultural identification and memories. But this culture is clearly a regional or provincial version of the broader Portuguese culture and differs no more from the "norm" than the various provinces of metropolitan Portugal itself.

However, geography is determinant, and Cape Verde as a political and economic nation-state had taken its place on the international scene as an African country. It talked African politically and tied its economic future to West African regional economics. It is difficult to see how it could do otherwise.

There is another link to the African continent peculiar to Cape Verde. As noted earlier, Portuguese West Africa, now the Republic of Guinea-Bissau, has often been described as having been a Cape Verdean rather than a metropolitan colony. The administrative and commercial sectors of the colony were heavily staffed by Cape Verdeans, who had obeyed the economic imperative of the islands to emigrate. It was from within this group that the independence movement arose, and the independence of both Guinea-Bissau and Cape Verde was won by an ethnic Cape Verdean rebellion fought on the African mainland in the name of both countries.

At that moment, however, independence had brought relatively little change in Cape Verde. As a country, as a culture, and as an identity, Cape Verde existed prior to independence. A large amount of foreign economic assistance was forthcoming, but it probably did not then exceed the economic flow from Portugal in the final years of the colonial period. To the average Cape Verdeans, life was unchanged, as their status and

personal sense of identity remained the same. However, outside influences were beginning to play a role forbidden by the colonial regime,
and the international environment in which Cape Verde now lived was
dramatically different.

Although isolated geographically and, until recently, politically and
culturally, Cape Verde nevertheless also had a long tradition of family
connections with the outside world. The islands' traditional poverty had
created a national vocation for immigration. There were, and probably
still are, more Cape Verdeans residing outside the islands than within.
Dakar alone had a Cape Verdean community larger than that of the
capital city of Praia. There are large communities in Portugal and Holland, not to mention the largest of all in the United States. There were
sizeable numbers of Cape Verdeans in Angola and Guinea-Bissau until
independence caused many to return to Cape Verde or to Lisbon. Many
worked as seamen on European merchant ships and as household help
in Western European households. Most of these expatriates, an early version of Europe's "guest worker" communities, retained extremely close
ties with their mother country. Their remittances of funds to families at
home have always been a major source of the islands' income.

America's Cape Verdean community is somewhat different, as the
country long ago became a permanent emigration destination. The
American Cape Verdeans (the largest element of the so-called Portuguese
community of New England) originally came from the Cape Verdean
islands of Fogo and Brava, with Brava becoming almost completely
depopulated as the old tradition of returning to Cape Verde to live out
one's final days died out. Certainly, independence and the passing of the
old timers contributed to this, but another factor had been the Ameri-
canization of the second and third generations. In any case, Brava exuded
a lonely atmosphere with its numerous deserted houses built for their
old age by emigrants to the United States now left empty.

The differing overseas emigration destinations of the various islands
reflected the still-significant regionalism of the different Cape Verde

islands. Cape Verdeans identify themselves by their islands as much as by anything else. There is even a local version of the New York–Washington competition. Although Praia is now almost as large as the major port of Mindelo on São Vicente Island, the evident prosperity and (comparative) sophistication of Mindelo create a strong feeling of superiority on the part of the Mindelense. Mindelo was and still is the home of the old merchant and seafaring classes and was the center of conservative opposition to the PAIGC and the idea of independence. The new government viewed Mindelo with some suspicion, even though the majority of the current leadership are themselves Mindelense. As the true capital of Cape Verde in the colonial days, even though Praia was the administrative center, Mindelo was where the Cape Verdean elite was largely formed. Some of that elite became the leaders of the independence movement.

The "Portugueseness" of Cape Verde was also evident in the government's operational style, such as the preoccupation with official documents. Although the current postindependence national dress was a citified form of safari suit, Cape Verdean delegations boarding airplanes for Europe were resplendent in three-piece suits from Lisbon. (Having been burnt once or twice, Cape Verdean reception committees meeting Senegalese delegations at the airport were now also well turned out in suits, white shirts, and dark ties.)

The oratorical style of the leadership in both Cape Verde and Guinea-Bissau was an interesting mix of three cultures: Latin, African, and leftist. The result was a prodigious prolixity. Cape Verdean president Pereira's speech to the Third Party Congress in Bissau in November 1978 lasted over nine hours. Guinea-Bissau President Cabral's later speech to the Guinea-Bissau National Assembly topped that at twelve and one-half hours, spread over two days. (My close friend, the Portuguese ambassador to Bissau, and I made a pact to last it out, trying not to giggle openly as various dignitaries attempted to sneak out unobserved as the hours dragged on.)

There is an old saying that Portugal is a family, not a country. This is even truer of Cape Verde, whose extended family includes the overseas communities. It sometimes seems that everyone has a relative in the United States, from the president of the Republic to the embassy chauffeur. Following Cape Verdean prime minister Pedro Pires's speech at Boston University during a visit to the United States, every member of his delegation asked permission to visit relatives. One of the prime minister's closest advisors, a radical young party type, walked up to the prime minister in his hotel room and, with a big grin on his face, asked permission to "go home for dinner." His father lives in Boston.

There was an active small-town social life in Praia, but one from which foreigners were largely excluded. The new leadership was sufficiently Cape Verdean to follow the local tradition of extramarital liaisons, and some of the most senior ministers installed young ladies in their own or other houses.

The level of literacy was reasonably high by African standards, with an estimated 20 percent literacy rate. Although Cape Verdean women were still kept in their place in the Latin tradition, there were in fact many quite sophisticated and well-educated women in the islands. Curiously, women—mostly Cape Verdean—played a larger and more prominent public and social role in Guinea-Bissau than in Cape Verde. This was probably merely another manifestation of Cape Verde's essentially old-fashioned Portuguese cultural style.

In sum, Cape Verde is a unique little country. Although all former African colonies presented a facade dating from their former metropolis (croissants in Brazzaville, steak and kidney pie in Lusaka), Cape Verde remained profoundly Portuguese—but Portuguese of a previous generation, despite the fashionable political rhetoric.

Surrounded by seawater, the islands are a virtual desert, though the new independent government had vague ambitions of fostering tourism and commercial fishing. The country in perspective is a mixture of centuries-long political and cultural isolation with an equally long tradition of humble working-class emigration for work. It is European in background, but with traditions from a Europe that no longer exists, and located in Africa with the implication of this geography. And finally, its location makes it a potentially important strategic location for military use by a major power. All in all, it would seem the new government of the old country of Cape Verde found itself with a puzzling and difficult set of problems and concerns. As they are a nice people—tenacious, hard-working, and serious—one can only wish them the best of luck.

Cape Verdeans in general and the government in particular were clearly pleased by the opening of the United States Embassy. With only a moderate amount of pushing, the government agreed to meet our desperate housing needs by building four new houses for our use. Designed by the one local architect, Lisbon-trained thirty years earlier, the houses were a bit bizarre and soon became one of the sights of Praia. (We had to do something to mask them.)

The early leadership in both Guinea-Bissau and Cape Verde were largely Cape Verdean in ethnic and cultural background, and the single political party that ruled both countries was formally committed to unification. This commitment appeared increasingly illusory as time passed and, given the fundamental cultural differences between them—not to mention practical problems relating to geographic distance and institutional inertia—may have always been an unrealistic dream. Divorce eventually occurred.

The Cape Verdean government's political attitudes were still very much in a formative stage in the early years of independence. Most of the senior leadership, and certainly President Pereira, were essentially moderate men, though wedded to Third World "progressive" views. The minister of defense, Silvino da Luz, appeared to be the standard bearer of a poorly defined, reportedly more radical younger group. We did not really know much about them, but da Luz himself seemed more clearly oriented towards close ties with the Soviet Union.

As 1978 passed into 1979, the dominant tone seemed to be one of drift, both politically and economically. The government leadership just seemed to relax and enjoy their current life of comparative ease—after all the years of exile and insurgency.

The dominant consideration was the eleven-year drought, which not only affected government policies but drained both public and official morale. The international community continued to be generous, and both emergency food assistance and development aid ran at a high level. Whether or not development assistance, largely devoted to agriculture, is in fact a meaningful development strategy in a country like Cape Verde remains an open argument; but the GOCV persisted in pursuing it. Unfortunately, few of the development projects had yet produced much in the way of visible progress, and there were growing signs of impatience with the government's development record, both within the leadership elite and the general public. A different approach was beginning to be considered but was not seriously implemented until long after I left. (This approach, to attempt to emulate Singapore on a modest scale, proved successful. By the early years of the twenty-first century Cape Verde was noted for both democratic political stability and impressive economic growth.)

In those early days of independence, however, the government of Cape Verde began to show signs of institutional insecurity. Both bureaucratic procedures and security controls continued to expand. The undercurrent of competition between Prime Minister Pedro Pires and Minister of Defense Silvino da Luz was an open secret, with Pires having further consolidated his position as the president's man and da Luz having had a bad year in several ways. The Soviet Union intensified its efforts to expand its influence during 1979, with only mixed results. Its military assistance program to the new Cape Verde armed forces moved smoothly ahead, but sharp rebuffs met all efforts to build on the program.

The general population continued to adjust itself to PAIGC rule, although with no marked enthusiasm. The leadership continued to struggle with the problems of development, bureaucracy, and government, finding them difficult and probably insoluble in the short run. Ideologically, the party and the government continued to modify their revolutionary ideology while pursuing efforts to obtain greater control over, and instill greater discipline in, the country. Most important, the rains failed again, and the drought remained the major preoccupation in Cape Verde. In 1979 the rains came early and in quantity, and the corn crop promised to be the best in years, almost a return to "normal." Then, in October, the rains failed to return, and the corn withered and died. Net corn production for the year was zero, although some minor crops such as beans turned out reasonably well.

The drought took an increasing toll on Cape Verde's public and governmental morale. Fatigue appeared to afflict the whole society, and glimpses of frustration appeared in the attitude of the most senior government officials. What to do? Numerous development projects were under way, designed to lessen Cape Verde's dependence on fickle rain—from digging wells for underground water through reforestation to water desalination—but these would take time and a heavy commitment. Cape Verde's goal was to duplicate somehow the Las Palmas success, by a combination of techniques to restructure the microclimate of the islands, build a water reservoir system, and exploit underground and mountain caverns, thereby producing relative stability in water supply and thus crop production.

Foreign donors—the United States, Holland, the Federal Republic of Germany, France, the United Nations Development Fund—were financing and conducting these projects, plus a few other donors on smaller projects. Like most governments of newly independent underdeveloped countries, the government of Cape Verde was loath to refuse any offers of assistance and was therefore, by virtue of both conviction and opportunity, launched into ambitious development schemes. Doubts persisted about this approach, however, among some government officials and foreign experts. Can in fact these methods bring about a meaningful result and, if so, when?

Visitors to the Island of Fogo were impressed by the West German–sponsored show farm, with its rows of vegetables and fruit flourishing in the middle of a desert. The project depended on a sophisticated and expensive dam and irrigation system, completely subsidized by the Germans. It is doubtful whether any crops produced could cover the costs involved, which mostly required hard currency. Due to inadequate planning and transportation, much of the produce was beyond the means of the local population.

Similar questions were asked about other projects. With money, almost anything could be done, but would it be worthwhile? Or were we, with the best of intentions, merely playing development games for our own satisfaction, while preparing further disillusionment for Cape Verdeans when the foreign subsidies ceased and the projects proved unviable? Other doubts existed. Some questioned whether the agricultural production could ever prove truly significant, given the amount of arable land in these small islands, available water notwithstanding. These critics argued that it was a fundamental error to orient Cape Verdean development towards agriculture, which could never provide sufficient income or food for the country.

These doubts were easy to voice but not based on any more sober analysis than the most optimistic agricultural plans. In any case, the GOCV was committed to agriculture, the foreign donors were "willing," and the projects were moving ahead. Certainly, the USAID-financed project for rural works construction of small dams and catchments in the mountainous center of Santiago had already proven of value, as evidenced by the increase in bean and other food crop production in 1979, despite the failure of the rains. Perhaps the argument about this aspect of Cape Verde's development was a false one, between those who believed agriculture must do everything, and those who doubted whether it could do anything. After all, in a country the size of Cape Verde, even the assured production of several thousand tons of green beans, a dietary staple, is of importance to both the economy and the well-being of the population.

Inflation, perhaps 30 percent, continued as well, with no relief in sight. Though the government granted a 25–33 percent salary increase to government workers (including those on public works projects), public grumbling over the inflation rate continued, with the GOCV virtually powerless to control this imported inflation.

Another development was the creeping growth in bureaucracy and accompanying bureaucratic procedures, with the increasing necessity of presenting properly completed, stamped, and approved official forms for any activity. The government had even reinstituted the old colonial passport check system with registration at hotels. While the government liked to call itself a socialist regime (small "s," and definitely not Marxist-Leninist), this increase in bureaucratic machinery and procedures probably was motivated more by traditional Cape Verdean (read provincial Portuguese) mores than by any new ideology or approach to government administration. Cape Verdean society and culture retained a strong sense of nineteenth century formality, as reflected in the operational style of the independent Cape Verde government, just as it had been in the colonial Portuguese regime.

This increase in bureaucracy probably also reflected a basic insecurity in the government. As noted elsewhere, the ruling PAIGC assumed control of Cape Verde in 1975, following the Portuguese revolution, under very special conditions. The Portuguese military officers who assumed control in Cape Verde immediately after the revolution were, like their colleagues in Portugal, Angola, and Mozambique, fervently radical. They consciously abetted the assumption of authority by the comparatively small band of PAIGC leaders (possibly less than one hundred) who flew over from Guinea-Bissau accompanied by slightly more than one thousand Guinea-Bissau soldiers of the PAIGC. Many observers, and not only those opposed to independence for Cape Verde, seriously doubted whether the PAIGC itself could have won an election or independence from Portugal. In any case, no such elections were held, and the PAIGC established itself in power. That the leadership was aware of its fragile hold on public support was clear, although they would perish before admitting it, and this understanding is a partial explanation for the government's persistent sense of unease and insecurity, and overreaction to transient civil unrest.

This attitude, plus the resistance to further Soviet military influence and other issues, appeared to have somewhat adversely affected the position of Minister of Defense Silvino da Luz, isolating him even further from his ministerial colleagues. Meanwhile, Prime Minister Pedro Pires continued to build his political base in the party and the government bureaucracy. President Pereira remained unchallenged, and internal political maneuvering concentrated on the question of his succession. Rumors resurfaced at the end of the year that Pereira was considering retirement within the next few years. His health continued to bother him, and he had an air of fatigue, in the opinion of several observers. Any hint that President Pereira was ill or might retire in the near future only heightened interest in the smoldering struggle between Pedro Pires and Silvino da Luz. The government pursued policies largely in compliance with Pereira's ideas and wishes; but equally obvious was a noticeable lack of enthusiasm, extending even to opposition, among some other members of the party and government elite. At the same time, many members of the elite and of the general public shared (often from different perspectives) a sense of impatience with the government's lack of apparent progress in developing the country.

Numerous critical political questions, such as party-government relations, succession to President Pereira, the desirable degree of public discipline, relations between party faithful and technicians, were therefore open and burning questions for internal maneuver and debate. A growing, if muted, feeling of insecurity and tension in Cape Verde markedly contrasted to the relaxed atmosphere prevailing in its sister country, Guinea-Bissau.

Nevertheless, nuances did strike the outside observer. The expulsion of the radicals and the continued rise in importance of nonparty senior officials (bureaucrats and technocrats), the steady drive of Pedro Pires to build a strong solid political base, and the hesitant but nevertheless significant internal reaction to Soviet pressure led one to conclude that the government was continuing along the path of relative moderation that had been evident since soon after independence. The same ambiguous character persisted with respect to foreign affairs. The use of Sal International Airport as the major transit point for Cuban traffic to and from Angola continued and may even have been significantly expanded during the latter part of the year. As many as three flights a day had been counted transiting Sal between Cuba and Angola. At the same time, Sal was a regular stop for South African Airways en route from London to Cape Town. President Pereira firmly rejected efforts to get the South African traffic stopped.

The president was deeply saddened by the death of his old friend and colleague, Agostinho Neto of Angola. Aware that his influence and that of the PAIGC with Angola's ruling party, the MPLA, was on a steady decline, now hastened by Neto's death, Pereira occupied himself with a last-ditch effort to influence developments in Angola, directed towards insuring the unified MPLA's continuation of Neto's policies. Pereira was obviously concerned about the dangers of dissension, as various Angolan leaders struggled for power.

Government leaders' concern was also at least partially responsible for its ambiguous attitude towards the expatriate Cape Verde communities, particularly the largest one located in the United States. Essentially, the government did not trust these communities and thereby alternated attempts to woo them with flashes of mistrust.

The Soviet Union continued its full-court press in Cape Verde during 1979, actively implementing and expanding the military assistance program it initiated in 1977. All indications were that the Soviet effort, which began well, had run into obstacles, being limited to providing equipment, training, and some military advisors to the army and navy. The Soviet desire to provide airplanes and possibly aircrews had been turned down. A subsequent offer to provide air surveillance for Cape Verde's national waters was deflected, and the recent proposal, made the previous December, to build an Aeroflot aircrew hotel at the international airport on Sal Island was also rejected. There are reliable reports that a Soviet admiral showed up unannounced the previous August and made a strong pitch for some form of basing rights; the admiral was sent packing.

The Soviet effort appeared to have run into natural resistance—reinforced, it must be admitted, by discreet action by Senegal and a number of Western countries (the United States included). Certainly, one of the year's most interesting developments was the opening of a large Senegalese embassy, staffed by seven diplomatic officers and headed by an active ambassador with close personal relations to Senegal's president Léopold Senghor. This was followed by a neat finesse, whereby the Senegalese and the French offered to watch over Cape Verde's territorial waters by extending French Air Force patrols out of Dakar. This idea neatly precluded any further pressure by the Soviets to provide the same service.

This episode reflected the blossoming of Cape Verdean relations with Senegal, under the stimulus of a deepening personal relationship between their respective presidents. Pereira and President Senghor hit it off well personally and were deliberately building political and institutional links between their two countries. Senghor seemed to be encouraging the GOCV to establish its distance from the Soviets and limit their options, while the Cape Verdeans were encouraging Senghor to accept the MPLA government in Angola. The amount of travel between Praia and Dakar by officials of the two countries was becoming impressive. (Cape Verdeans were always traveling to Dakar anyway, if only to visit family, but the traffic was now more official and two-way.)

Early in 1979 a dramatic political event occurred—the expulsion of a number of young "radicals" categorized as "Trotskyites" from government and party positions. (Those expelled were publicly charged with being "Trotskyites" disloyal to the PAIGC; privately, government sources informed us that the "radicals" had been in close contact with and receiving funds from the Soviets. We left it to others to resolve this interesting ideological tangle.)

Cape Verde and Guinea-Bissau continued their public adherence towards the eventual unity of the two countries. However, outside observers increasingly believed that the effort lacked substance. The appointment of two well-known but ineffectual Guinea-Bissau personalities—one a minister known as the town drunk, the other the figurehead of the women's movement—to head a newly created unity organization only confirmed that skepticism. Nevertheless, the special relationship persisted, based on family, history, and war comradeship among the leaders.

Meanwhile, the international community continued to look favorably on Cape Verde and quickly met the government's request for food aid following the failure of the corn crop. But the long-term effect on the morale of a people and a government—particularly a new and ticklish one—of annual reminders that it was on the public dole were well marked. Although the country had a balance-of-payments equilibrium (if not a surplus) due to emigrants' remittances, since independence it had fed its people largely on international charity. While other countries were in the same boat, such a situation can lead to the demoralization of the society's leadership, as is often seen in other nations.

But that's not what happened. For various reasons, in the ensuing years Cape Verde became one of Africa's most successful countries, building a stable, democratic political system and achieving remarkable economic success. But that all happened years after my 1980 departure, when my assignment had run its course.

Fig. 5. (*top*) Visiting Arab dhow in Mombasa harbor, 1961. Author's collection.

Fig. 6. Crossing a stream in western Kenya tea country, when
touring by Land Rover and foot, 1962. Author's collection.

IRANIANS MEET — Second Lt. Mohammed Alikhani Jamshid (center) of the Iranian Air Force discusses his newly-won Silver Wings with Mr. and Mrs. Edward Marks at the Silver Wings coffee for LAFB pilot training class 64-F. Marks is the American Vice-Consul to Nuevo Laredo. Mrs. Marks and Jamshid are both from Tehran, Iran.

Fig. 7. Hosting Iranian Air Force student in Nuevo Laredo, 1963. Author's collection.

Fig. 8. Aida and Max in Parc Royale, Brussels, 1972.
Author's collection.

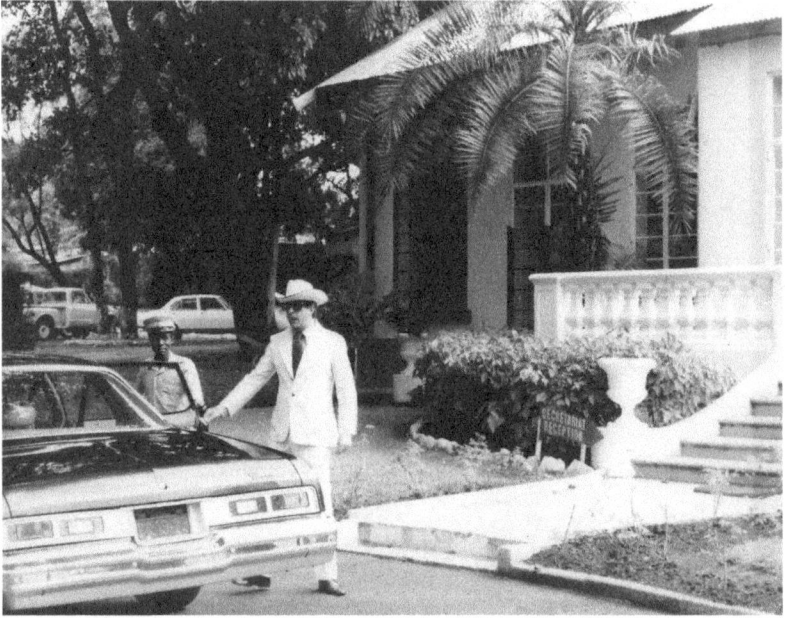

Fig. 9. Author going to make official call on local authorities in
Lubumbashi, 1974. Author's collection.

Fig. 10. (*opposite top*) Painting of U.S. consulate Lubumbashi by
Zairian painter Tshibumba Kanda Matulu, 1974.
Purchased by author and donated to the African art collection of the
Smithsonian Museum in Washington DC. Author's collection.

Fig. 11. U.S. embassy, Bissau, 1978. Office on the ground
floor, staff apartments on floors 3–5, with the author (shown
on balcony) living on the top floor. Author's collection.

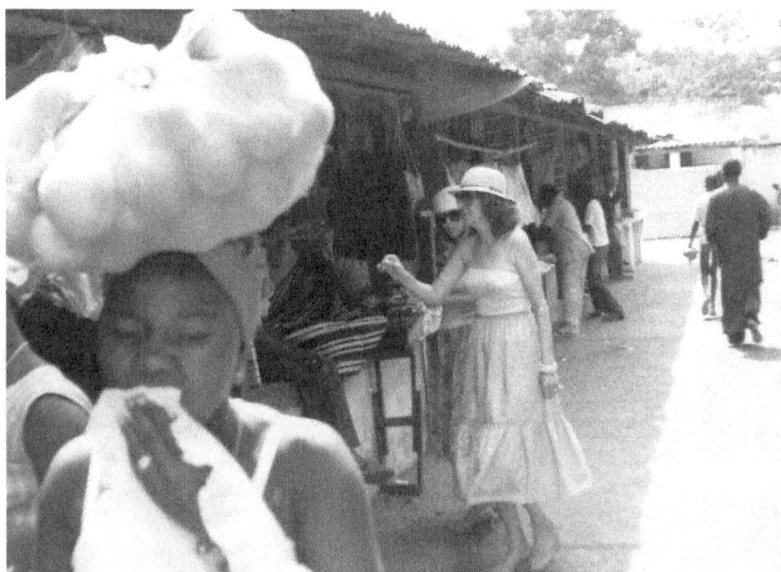

Fig. 12. Aida shopping in Bissau market, 1979. Author's collection.

Fig. 13. (*top*) Aida and author with Guinea-Bissau president Luis Cabral onboard presidential boat during fishing trip for diplomatic corps, 1979. Author's collection.

Fig. 14. Guinea-Bissau president Luis Cabral supervising offloading of diplomats in rough surf after fishing trip, 1979. Author's collection.

Fig. 15. (*top*) Diplomatic lineup at airport for departure/arrival ceremonies for dignitaries, 1979. Russian ambassador, as Dean of the Diplomatic Corps, is in first place; Author is in fifth place. Author's collection.

Fig. 16. Aida in midst of Mardi Gras street celebration in Praia, 1978. Author's collection.

Fig. 17. Author giving prizes on sports day at Colombo
girls' school, 1988. Author's collection.

Fig. 18. (*top*) Author and Arjun Diraniyagala with his 1914 Pipe about to go on a Sunday morning drive around Colombo, 1988. Author's collection.

Fig. 19. Aida and author and the restored 1959 Jaguar, in front of the Galle Fac Hotel in Colombo, 1989. Author's collection.

10

Fort McNair

I was not immediately posted to an ongoing assignment upon leaving Africa in the summer of 1980. Instead, I became a student at the National War College at Fort McNair in Washington. This was a standard enough assignment for someone of my rank.

The class of 1981 arrived at the National War College in early August, as is the custom. We drifted into the old building at the end of the Fort McNair peninsula and, with only minimal confusion, worked our way through the various registration lines. By noon we had completed the initial paperwork, found our desks, met our committee comrades, and finished for the day. It was an auspicious beginning.

Three-quarters of the class were military officers. The other forty were civilians and more of a mixed bag, with the dozen State Department Foreign Service officers comprising the only other identifiable tribe. The mood was much as one would expect of a group of Americans of that age and background—a mixture of new post and new school. For this student, at least, there was also the mixed feeling of diffidence, respect, disdain, and amusement of the former draftee now mixing professionally and socially with gaggles of colonels. After twenty-one years, one still remembers one's serial number (US52428657).

Fort Lesley J. McNair is a lovely old army post, built in a more gracious era and gently transformed over the years into a scenic site in the heart of the nation's capital. The resident troops consist of an honor company of the Old Guard one sees occasionally in Revolutionary War dress. However, they only occupy (and that discreetly) the lower post, near the entrance and the commissary. The main sweep of the post is dominated by the row of generals' houses, officers' club, tennis courts, a nine-hole golf course, the nondescript 1950s-built Industrial College of the Armed Forces, and—the crown of the establishment—the pre–World War I National War College.

Time is important to buildings; it can lend character if not beauty if some strength is built in to start with. The old State-Navy-War building next to the White House is a good example of this process. So is the National War College building, beautifully maintained and shining on its lovely site, with the backdrop of the Potomac River. Truth be told, it is a funny-looking building—somewhat post-Victorian, but not yet Art Nouveau, and certainly not modern or contemporary. It is difficult to say what style the architect was constructing in brick and mortar, but it certainly does make some sort of statement. It is prominent, dominates its site, and has been around long enough to acquire a patina. Built before World War I, it stands solidly and promises to do so for many more years. It was obviously expensive, with fancy brickwork and marble and a vaulting three-story center hall. Nothing at all like what we would build nowadays. Still, it stands and serves after seventy-five years, demonstrating the validity of the old cliché about the true value of quality goods.

The students also like it. Its gravitas lends dignity to the college and its program and to each student's very presence.

We were a student body of 160, split four ways between the army, the sea services (navy, Marines, and Coast Guard), the air force, and civilians. The military students had an average age of slightly over forty; we civilians averaged a few years older. For the military in particular, selection for the college clearly had a fairly special meaning: it represented a notable career passage, ending the long years of the "subaltern's" life. Though most of these officers had come from responsible and important jobs, a whiff of the junior officer still hung about them. How much of this retained youth was military and how much contemporary American was difficult to tell.

In any case, arrival at the War College meant that an important ticket was being punched. While selection for senior training is not a guarantee of eventual elevation to the ranks of the mighty, it does separate those who are still in the running from those who are not. In any case, selection is the assumed right of the regular cadre and goes with the silver leaves and eagles on the shoulders.

For us civilians, immersion in the military atmosphere was a bracing and amusing experience. Not that the military environment was arduous; the military were on holiday and the general air was of a long weekend at the Officers' Club. We watched and weighed our military colleagues (presumably as did they with us) and matched our prejudices, preconceptions, and twenty-year-old memories against current reality. By the end of the year we had modified our opinions—somewhat. We also came to a few conclusions. In my case, I agreed with the observations of a friend and colleague who had passed through the college a few years earlier. He decided that the air force types were quick and clever but narrow and gadget-obsessed, the navy types provincial and self-absorbed, the Marines quirky and often intellectual, and the army the most mature and most like us. He did not mention the Coast Guard, but the two in our class were universally admired for their qualities and their general style of being worthwhile adults.

The Marines were the most impressive, the most unchanged from old images. The opposite of trendy, they moved through life with ears attuned to the Corps's drummer—and that drummer still beat the old refrain. On the birthday of the Corps they held a noontime ceremony in the great central hall of the War College. The rest of us, plus faculty and staff, stood around in clusters and hung over the circling balconies to watch. The Marines—some twenty from the War College and the Industrial College across the street—marched in dress blues to the reverberating sound of their own red-coated drum and bugle corps and proceeded to stand tall and salute and honor their friends, their Corps, their country, and themselves—and all in tones and words few present-day Americans can hear without a supercilious smile. But we listened that day and were touched. The Marines performed an old-fashioned ceremony with perfect aplomb, armored by their innocence and their self-confidence. They made it clear that they knew who they were and were satisfied with the knowledge.

For a brief moment, a number of gentlemen who pride themselves on their worldly-wise sophistication had wistful eyes and a few regrets.

The civilians in the class were a mixed bag. Some were Department of Defense civilian employees, quite at home at Fort McNair. Others were stray individuals from a wide spectrum of government agencies, with varying pretenses of legitimate interest in foreign affairs and national security questions—OMB, Treasury, FBI, NSA. There were also a number of openly declared CIA officers, whose exoticism wore off quickly.

The largest single civilian group was the contingent of Foreign Service officers—a dozen from State, three from USIA, some light-cover CIA types, and one from USAID—a veritable flock of FSOs. From the very first day it was clear that no stranger creature existed in the eyes of the average military officer than the professional American diplomat. What manner of beast were we? A vision of limp-wristed cookie pushers passed through their mind's eye, a vision soon to become confused with a growing respect for the average FSO's verbal fluency and obviously easy command of subjects in the curriculum. The military expected that we would know about things like protocol and balance of payments and diplomatic notes, but they could never quite get over our presumption to deal—with no noticeable sense of inferiority—with strategic and military issues.

As the year passed, the military view of their diplomatic classmates seemed to settle into a mixture of limited awe and amiable scorn. When push came to shove in many a discussion, the diplomat usually wanted to seek a solution or an arrangement to deal with the problem posed; not for them were the "surgical uses of military power" or the mobilization of national resources. (I speak of most of the FSOs; one or two made an effort to meet the military on their own ground, both in sports and in the seminars.) In the end, this preference for political, that is, verbal, solutions differentiated most of the diplomats from most of the military. Once understood, this difference was quite acceptable. We all had differing roles to play in the security machinery of the United States government, and understanding that was one of the reasons we were at Fort McNair.

It would be interesting, very interesting, to know what they really thought of us. However, despite the current fashion for telling all, it is probably best that we all retained some modest illusions.

But what did we do all year, from August to early June? Despite the grumbling—some of it the reaction of deprived workaholics and some of it of the "methinks he doth protest too much" variety—we mostly enjoyed ourselves. For many it was a chance to spend a great deal of time with our families; others found themselves finally with enough hobbies or sports, both private and school-sponsored. Some just relaxed and enjoyed their "gentlemen's year." Some did all of the above while working out or adjusting to personal problems and crises so common to this particular age group.

Despite advance information—the War College after all was not a new institution and all of us had friends and colleagues who had attended in previous years—we arrived at Fort McNair somewhat unsure of what we would be doing from day to day. That uncertainty is partially due to the changing nature of the college and the other senior military schools, as successive commandants and presidents of the National Defense University sought to place a personal mark on the institution for personal or career reasons.

We arrived and found an elaborately prepared program, doled out to us in weekly schedules outlining a mixture of seminar discussions, lectures of various types, obligatory and elective courses, occasional films, voluntary activities such as trips, and blocks of free time cunningly described as research and study. At various times during the year, and particularly near the end, there were exercises and role-playing activities. In addition, I hasten to add, there were rather heavy reading requirements, which fed into the desire of many to use the year to finally catch up on their reading. The required reading at first was disconcerting if not daunting.

However, some at least soon learned to take it in stride and dip into it for what seemed worthwhile, while at the same time doing some of that long promised private reading. All in all, a tasty enough menu, which rarely required more than twenty-five hours a week of physical presence at Fort McNair—a gourmet menu for reasonably successful adult professionals rather than a gourmand feast for ambitious young graduate students.

Within a few weeks we learned that the curriculum at the National War College was fairly far advanced along a relaxation curve; work requirements and the guest lecturer program had been more rigorous at some time in the recent past but had been progressively relaxed in accordance with the theory that overprogramming was disadvantageous for this type and level of professional adult education. We made self-satisfied and critical remarks about the highly structured program that had been installed a few years previously at the Navy War College. Within a few months, however, an ongoing if desultory debate began as to the ideal War College curriculum. Many felt that the existing program was a waste of time, others that it concentrated on the wrong subjects or presented the wrong emphasis. Some wanted more lecturers; others wanted fewer. While the program had a highly structured formal appearance, probably for image purposes for Congress, the senior brass, and the media, most of us found that in fact we could pretty much go our own way.

For instance, the almost overwhelming sense of military organization that pervaded the school and the program was soon discovered, particularly by the civilian students, to be somewhat of a facade. At first, we worried about being on time and being in place. Soon we learned that all we had to do was drift; the system was so organized that numerous warnings and announcements kept one in place without any individual effort. It was very comforting.

The legendary lecture program of the War College soon turned out to be a bit of a disappointment. Certainly, a number of famous figures did show up during the course of the year. Several, however, turned out to be Golden Oldies—well known figures of years ago. Most of the speakers were second- and third-ranking officials (military and civilian) and second- or third-rate academics. Neither the secretary of state or the secretary of defense showed up; and since we had a change of administration in the middle of the year, four different individuals were available for these roles. We did get one national security advisor, making his swan song with a carefully prepared apologia. The service chiefs showed up but were not terribly inspirational or exciting. We had the impression that the creation of the National Defense University a few years before had dimmed the reputation of the National War College and that the country's major movers and shakers were no longer interested in taking the time to appear at Fort McNair. By the end of the year, we had almost unanimously agreed that the NDU was a useless bureaucratic institution that was smothering the War College.

On the other hand, we also had the impression that a cautious bureaucratic attitude was inhibiting the speakers' program, and that the current stars on the public scene were just not being invited. It was difficult for us to believe that American senators and representatives would not respond to invitations; and major-league journalists and academics are not known for their shyness. With a few exceptions, however, major contemporary figures were absent from the lecture program.

We spent a good deal of time over the year discussing the purpose of the War College and what its curriculum should be. All pretty much agreed that the formal subject of the year—National Security Policy—was appropriate if one wanted a formal program. But some did not agree that a formal program was the appropriate way for professionals to spend the year. An alternative view held that some form of a sabbatical would be the most useful: a time for personal reflection and individual study, a temporary withdrawal from the obligations of bureaucratic or military life, and yes, even an opportunity to loaf. Laziness was clearly not a characteristic of this group, and a little idling time might well prove profitable in the long run.

We never came to any sort of consensus, although most would probably agree that the year spent at the War College ought to lean towards personal development and education rather than formal training. Unfortunately, training lends itself better to programming, budget justifications, and Hill briefings, so the bureaucratic instinct leaned in that direction.

It is unlikely that the War College will ever regain the individual sense of identity that it reportedly had years ago, when the traditions of the Old Army and the Old Navy were still strong. Some suggest that the War College be turned into a general's course, with the students being either those having one star or having been formally selected for flag rank. The suggestion makes sense, as grade inflation has certainly diminished the importance and prestige of colonels and naval captains. At the same time, the college could become more clearly and authoritatively a multiservice school. At one time general officer meant just that, an officer responsible and presumably competent to command mixed forces. Over time forces have become so diverse and technical this is no longer true, and some thought should be given to introducing senior officers to multiservice command. Many believe that the interservice rivalry and bickering endemic in the Pentagon has gotten out of hand. While the War College with its mixed service student body does in fact dilute such rivalry, its students are in contemporary terms too young and too junior. As they return to their organizations, the mold fits over them once again.

If it is truly desired to recreate a senior military school with a distinctive character and long-term influence, it will probably be necessary to finesse the personnel systems, current commanders, and current members of Congress. One way to do that might be to change the rank and method of selection of the commandant. Instead of a successful two-star commandant with a career yet to pursue, working for a three-star NDU president who may or may not have a career left, we should isolate the War College from the career structure. This could be simply done by appointing as commandant the second most successful senior military officer, that is, the one who lost the competition for chairman of the Joint Chiefs of Staff. Instead of commanding the armed forces today, he would be offered the opportunity to form its leadership. He should be offered a fixed five-year term of office. There are few serious professionals who would decline the offer.

What the school was all about or what it should be was a subject of continual discussion throughout the year. As it was a military school, the military officers in particular soon adopted a fierce loyalty to it. Attendance clearly represented an important point in their professional life, and not merely because it offered the hope of further advancement. Although American society is essentially commercial in character, there remain isolated sectors such as the military—and yes, the Foreign Service—which guard a feeling, however illusory, that one's work has a meaning beyond providing sustenance. The professional military still by and large retain a sense of commitment and loyalty to their calling. Attendance at the War College in itself represents a sign or mark of achievement, of recognition by and among one's peers.

As such, identity with and loyalty to the college came quickly and resulted in fierce indignation near the end of the year when rumors of further change in the War College's status vis-à-vis the National Defense University came trickling down. Apparently well-founded stories began to circulate that the NDU intended to move the War College out of its lovely old building and into some sort of underground monstrosity, and then move into the more picturesque location itself. Apart from the outlandishness of the proposed new construction, and the lack of any demonstrated need for it, the blatant NDU self-aggrandizement of the proposal lit fires of indignation throughout the student body and among the alumni. The proposal reportedly died in the following academic year, although it was unclear that it did so because of its inherent unfitness to live. Or perhaps because the new NDU president had different dreams of glory, as there are stories of a tightened-up and more "rigorous" curriculum in support of a more sharply defined and "useful" program. Anyway, we huffed and puffed, indignant about possible change even before we became alumni. Nostalgia comes more quickly in one's forties.

We never did come to a consensus about the ideal program. The arguments raged back and forth between those who wanted a rigorous intellectual program and those who wanted a hundred flowers to bloom. Certainly, from the civilian point of view the hundred flowers approach was the most appealing. None of us were seriously seeking to be qualified as senior military staff officers. We wanted, by and large, a serious exposure to military attitudes, theory, and thinking as they impact directly on most of our professional concerns. But there was an imbalance between our backgrounds and interests and those of our military colleagues. We, especially the State Department, CIA, and other foreign affairs agency people, were generally well acquainted with the major thrust of the program content, which was designed primarily to bring technically trained military officers up to some sort of generalist level. The War College existed to make policy planners out of infantry colonels, jet jockeys, and ship handlers, not to make leaders of men out of diplomats and other assorted civilians.

As a rule, the foreign affairs agency civilians became part of the educational experience for the military teachers, assistants to the regular faculty. More articulate, generally, than our military colleagues, we had to be careful not to dominate the seminar discussions or the question-and-answer periods. (We were not always successful, nor, to be honest, did we always try that hard.) One rarely finds such a large and captive audience for one's favorite stories and policy prejudices. I, for one, for the very first time, almost talked myself out. This is a good place to thank my military classmates for their patience and good humor.

The military, however, were at Fort McNair to become at least novice policy planners. The intellectual and professional background they brought with them was not auspicious; it had a natural bent towards problem solution. Unfortunately, grand strategy is not about solving problems; it is about living with them. Even when in agreement on the occasional necessity for the use of military force, the military and the diplomats at the War College meant essentially different things. In general, the military saw the use of military force in a given situation as the option of choice for solving the policy problem posed. Diplomats, on the other hand, tended to see the use of force as a necessary expedient to avoid further loss or to move the issue onto another plane or into another time. Troops become chips for the diplomats, and the military can hardly be blamed for a disinclination to look at themselves in that manner.

Still and all, we got along quite well, and the personal contacts made across the professional and organizational boundaries were real and may themselves have been sufficient justification for the year. Most of the students had between ten and fifteen years of service left, and those years would be spent at senior levels of responsibility. The ties and sense of camaraderie that the college created between military and civilians in the foreign affairs field must certainly contribute to the efficiency of the republic's foreign policy machinery.

Is it worth it to the taxpayer? An interesting question and obviously an impossible one to answer. Are military bands worth the expense? More important, are armies?

We were ostensibly at Fort McNair as the result of personnel management decisions. The school year is a traditional part of the military system adopted from the Germans, whose general staff corps and schools were the martial fashion leaders of the nineteenth century. The inclusion of civilian students was a post–World War II innovation reflecting the general American instinct to gild every lily.

It certainly was a pleasant year, by and large, and had already come to occupy a warm spot producing cozy memories in the minds of most of us. In one sense it was a reward rather than a task, and maybe in that form it fulfilled its purpose best. It is not terribly easy to pursue the classic public service careers in contemporary America. The standards and rewards are out of touch with our twenty-first century. The independent nation-state was the creation of previous centuries, managed by aristocratic and bourgeois classes living by a set of rules no longer considered relevant. Some modern nation-states have attempted to deal with the problem by going all the way, turning the nation itself into one vast bureaucracy so that public careers are not differentiated from other activities. But the industrialized and democratic countries are still trying to operate societies composed of mixed private and public sectors, while diluting the psychic and social rewards offered to those who serve in the public sector. What, in other words, is going to replace *noblesse oblige?*

Maybe something will, possibly at the same time something replaces or seriously alters the nation-state. Meanwhile, those who practice the old professions try to live up to the old traditions. We went to Fort McNair and learned about National Security Policy and the Game of Nations. It was a form of rap session, where we reinforced each other's belief in the worth of our ideals and the value of our goals.

11

Colombo

The year at the War College was followed by some months of desultory activity. I was not assigned to a specific job but hung around the corridors, as we say. I spent a few months in a liaison job—something to do with someone's idea about liaising with state governments—but that didn't turn out to be lasting. Then I was nominated as a deputy director of the State Department's Office for Combatting Terrorism, as detailed in chapter 16. This turned out to be both demanding and satisfying, although it was years before 9/11 and the rise of terrorism to the top of our national priority list.

After three years in that job and one on detail as a senior foreign affairs fellow at the Center for Strategic and International Studies (also in chapter 16), the time came to move abroad again. The best job that came my way was that of deputy chief of mission in Colombo, Sri Lanka—working for Ambassador James Spain, a friend and a most distinguished diplomat.

My wife and I arrived at Katunayake Airport in the evening, after a long flight from Hong Kong via Singapore. The new international terminal was still under construction, but even the best of airport terminals look a bit sad at night unless they are full of bustling crowds. The man I was replacing met us there, so we loaded up the baggage and headed into Colombo—our new post and home.

The drive took almost an hour, which is something given that the distance was only about twelve miles. The road we took was narrow, lined with shops, bullocks, shrines, and people, and more like a Third

World High Street than the usual airport highway. New as we were to South Asia, the drive from the airport in some respects formed our initial impression of Colombo, and it was not reassuring. We had hoped for more glamour and development from this shift to Asia after years in Africa. We arrived essentially by back roads, confirming that Colombo was not exactly Hong Kong or Paris. Later I remembered to bring other new people in via the center of town along the ocean. Tired as we were, however, we could see that our new house was quite nice. After a long voyage we were home again—in the way of the Foreign Service.

The overwhelming impression of Colombo gained during the first weeks was that of a frantic social whirl. At first, we thought the luncheons, cocktail receptions, and dinners were due to our arrival and an unusually large turnover of the mission staff. However, as time passed it became clear that the pace of social life in Colombo was always fast. Sri Lankans, it seems, love to give and go to parties. They almost always accept invitations, arrive on time (no Third World casualness about time here), and, interestingly, extend invitations at a faster rate than they accept them. Fellow diplomats will understand the significance of this last statement; how much time have we all spent in numerous capitals trying to entice the local citizenry to (a) accept our hospitality, (b) thereby acknowledging our existence, and (c) providing satisfaction by reciprocating. Oh, the joy in a diplomat's breast when a local dignitary invites him to come and break bread.

This gratification was ever-present in Sri Lanka. The Sri Lankan pleasure in a busy social round is not specifically directed towards diplomats and other foreigners. They behave this way amongst themselves. They like cocktail parties and dinners; they like to eat, they like to drink, and they like to talk and gossip; they like the warmth and bustle of social intercourse. They see no reason why foreigners in their midst should not participate.

Different circles could be identified. The crowd at the Asia Society representative's house was not by and large the same one would find at a prominent businessman's soiree, but everybody seemed to like sending and receiving invitations to lunches, receptions, dinners, banquets, and balls. The steady flow of invitations began immediately upon our arrival in July of 1986. All this socializing soon created another problem. Our social debt mounted rapidly, and we panicked at the thought of how to repay it. Even after our newness wore off, it only abated marginally and that was more than compensated for by our own contribution to the relaxed and jovial socializing of Colombo.

And so the invitations flowed in. Every night it seemed—and often was—that we went to somebody's house to meet new people and exchange names and cards—an exchange that soon resulted in another invitation. All very nice of course, if eventually tiring. But local socializing had a saving characteristic. By and large, after a brisk evening of socializing dinner ends with coffee, possibly a quick pousse-cafe, and then quick goodnights with everybody home by ten thirty or so. No late-night Latin dinners.

The social aspect of the diplomatic life is a real part of it and, to most outsiders, the most striking. In fact, the social character of the diplomat's life is probably the oldest cliché about diplomacy. (There is the story of the visiting American in London at the turn of the century who approached the American ambassador at a reception and commented that he supposed the diplomatic life was probably easy on the head but murder on the feet. The ambassador, reflecting the usual impatience of most diplomats with this type of wit, replied that it depended on which extremity one was most accustomed to using.)

Nevertheless, and at the risk of confirming the cliché, I decided to add up the number of social events in which I had participated during the twelve months of 1987. (There were only forty-five weeks to count, as five weeks of vacation outside the island and two weeks of riots in the streets of Colombo cut seven weeks out of my social calendar.) It turns out that I either gave or attended approximately 277 social events during the (modified) year. We gave 41 luncheons, 21 dinner parties, and another half-dozen events (one wedding for a junior colleague, American community receptions, and so on). I attended 40 luncheons, 65 dinner parties or banquets, 76 receptions, and 31 miscellaneous events having a social cast (despite other purposes). My wife did not attend this entire list (she especially liked to leave the large official receptions to me); but she did go to a number of events on her own, not herein listed. This produced an average number of 6.3 social events per week, slightly under one a day. As Saturdays and Sundays tended, in general, to be light social days, with most people retreating into private life, the average during the week was obviously higher. Maybe that is why my memory is of even busier activity than the figures indicate. Still, it was a busy enough schedule and does justify somewhat the image most people have of diplomats.

Sri Lankan society was, and probably still is, organized around political, economic, professional, social, and other organizations—from the Rotary to the Girl Guides. These groups hold affairs all the time: annual meetings, monthly meetings, award ceremonies, "Miss Sri Lanka" competitions, orphanage foundation laying, dam christenings, and so on. It seems impossible to hold any of these affairs without the presence of at least one chief guest, usually a senior government official, most often a cabinet minister. The newspapers and television news programs are never free of the familiar faces of senior politicos opening art exhibits and lighting the traditional oil lamps. President J. R. Jayewardene himself was an active participant in his day and actually appeared to enjoy it.

Officials at all levels were easily available and open for discussion, although at the very highest levels a concern for protocol limited initiatives. This concern existed even with respect to the main opposition party, whose two highest officials were available for calls only by chiefs of mission. Sri Lankans are voluble conversationalists, and in certain circles politics are the main source of discussion. Conversation was as open as access.

For instance, in one of my early calls on a cabinet minister, following the usual few minutes of introduction and "How do you like Colombo" questions, the minister moved into a detailed discussion of local politics and developments. Although a government minister, he did not hesitate to comment critically on the government's policies or its leader, becoming increasingly critical as the moments passed. After about an hour it was time to go. As I said my goodbyes and expressed my appreciation for his time, the minister suddenly looked puzzled and said, "By the way, whom did you say you were with?" Not that he was concerned, you understand; it was just that after some satisfying political gossip, he wondered who I was.

This attitude flowed naturally from two sources. First is the character of Sri Lankan culture, as described above and below. But the second is a natural outgrowth of the country's modern political history.

Sri Lanka was first conquered, or "colonized," by the Portuguese in the sixteenth century, to be replaced by the Dutch in the seventeenth and by the British in the late eighteenth. Under the British indirect rule policy, local government of a kind flourished. Dominion status—to include voting rights for women as well as men—was achieved in 1931, and a robust political and electoral system has been in effect ever since, with several parties vying for electoral success and alternating in office. Full independence was achieved in 1948.

Unfortunately, ethnic politics reared its head, as the minority Tamil population (about 9 percent) became increasingly restive under increasing Sinhalese political and cultural dominance. While to outsiders the Sinhalese-Tamil differences at first appear minimal, it does not take long to realize the strength of the tension, based upon ages-long competition arising from religious, cultural, and "genetic" or racial differences. (The Sinhalese call themselves the "Golden People" and consider the Tamils "blacks.") The contest goes back thousands of years, with a long history of alternating domination. The tension moderated during the colonial period, as both peoples were subjected to third party rule; but independence and electoral politics meant ethnic politics, and the overwhelming Sinhalese majority soon meant overwhelming Sinhalese control of the government. The ostensible cause of the division was language, Sinhalese or Tamil. Soon after independence this issue became the rallying cry, especially for Tamils, and soon major language-based political parties arose. (Cynics noted that the leaders of these two parties had in fact been educated in English and had only imperfect control of the languages for which they raised banners.)

The vast numerical difference between the communities determined the results over the years, and the Tamil community, largely but not exclusively concentrated in the northern Jaffna peninsula, became increasingly alienated and resentful. By the 1980s a violent youthful and radical movement arose—famous later as the Tamil Tigers—and developed into violent rebellion. Political terrorism had arrived in Sri Lanka.

But real and viable democratic politics persisted and was active during my time in Sri Lanka. Parties and partisan politics were actively pursued, and honest elections and a free press were the norm. And so the government minister mentioned above happily engaged me—a foreigner—in political talk similar to what I could have heard in Washington DC.

That the interest and enthusiasm for social life was not restricted to Colombo's social elite—generally referred to as the Colombo 7 crowd—is evidenced by an unusual project. The third in a series of Pradeepa Halls were government-run community reception centers. These are modern reception centers "replete with all facilities for the use of the public to provide inexpensive centers for the holding of private social functions" and available at modest rental fees for the general public. Their sponsorship is at the highest level, that of the prime minister, who was constantly out on the hustings kissing babies. His "Million House" building scheme was generally conceded to be a major source of his political popularity. He avoided becoming involved in dealing with the country's ethnic conflict but instead spent his time building houses for the rural and poor urban population—and providing them with subsidized halls for "private social functions." His desire to become president was well known.

The East—or Asia—has the reputation in the West as being the place of religions. The normal presence of monks in society probably contributes to that impression, especially in contrast to Europe and North America, where the professional religious have increasingly moved away from distinctive clothing. In Sri Lanka a common scene on evening television was a minister paying obeisance to one or more priests while handing them something: a book, an award, an academic notice, title to a piece of land, a position—or a check. While the minister bowed, the priest remained seated and accepted the presentation or gift with easy assurance and a sober, expressionless face, with the onlooker left to wonder who was conning whom.

There is clearly competition between the traditional secular leadership class and the equally traditional clerical leadership class in the Sinhalese community. Up until quite recently, it had been assumed by both local and foreign observers that the clergy could, at minimum, limit or channel secular political activity. Some doubts have arisen whether this remains true. Has the clergy itself become so ostentatiously secular, in contradiction to its traditional image of humility and religious virtue, that it has lost its hold over the largely rural Sinhalese population? Difficult questions, which can only be answered when and if the secular and clerical leadership elites actually come into conflict. There were signs that such an event was becoming imminent in the summer and fall of 1986, but the confrontation never took place. In retrospect it appears that the government outmaneuvered or cowed a less than coherent clerical class.

At least to someone new to South Asia, the presence of the Buddhist monk in the public places of society was striking. This is possibly due to the distinctive orange robe that stands out so dramatically among both Western-dressed crowds in the cities and more traditionally robed people in the countryside. The saffron color of the monkish robe may have been chosen as a symbol of humility, but it appears to have become instead an elite uniform. The monks are ever-present on local television and in the newspapers, so that it appears that no public ceremony of any kind can be conducted without the almost brooding presence of one or more Bikkhus—as they are called.

Several characteristics of the Sri Lankan monk strike the outsider. Although they apparently come almost completely from rural families and milieus, they generally have the sleek, well-fed, confident air of the upper classes. Even more noticeable are the masculine pride and arrogance of the young monks as they walk around the city in small groups, their arrogance combining with a clear sense of specialness and an almost swaggering air. Their position in society, the enormous respect in which they are held, is clearly the cause of this air; few human beings can resist the blandishments of social specialness. To watch a senior and powerful government minister bow and make obeisance to a seated monk while handing him anything from a diploma to a government check, and to watch the monk acknowledge the gesture with a slight nod of the head, is to see an event of obvious significance in local society. To a Western eye a little respect to the cloth is only good manners, even if hypocritical, but few would accept this obligatory role of public subservience. No wonder the young monk walks around with an air of insufferable pride.

Religiosity surfaces often here. When Ambassador Spain was unable to attend the annual ceremony of the Sri Lanka John F. Kennedy Society on November 22, I went along as the official representative. The society had its headquarters at the home of its president/founder, primary activist, and major supporter in Panadura—some twenty miles down the coast. In addition to the society's president, a few of his friends and relatives, and two of us from the embassy, a smallish crowd of about twenty locals was present. American and Sri Lankan flags were displayed (the president of the society is a flag manufacturer and president of the Sri Lankan Flag Association). Photographs of JFK, Robert Kennedy, and Martin Luther King were displayed on a set of three stands, the total effect being that of an altar. The appropriate national anthems were played on a cassette player, and then the local member of Parliament and I distributed food packages to the assembled crowd of devotees (which was perhaps why they showed up).

What was most interesting was the mood of quite sincere devotion, bordering on piety, on the part of the president and several of his associates. This affair was neither commercial nor cynical. It was highly emotional and in fact partook of the religious. As I stood there, while these unkind thoughts passed through my mind, I suddenly remembered a literary model for the situation I was in. In *Flashman in the Great Game*, the hero meets a legendary (and real) early English empire builder, Nicholson, who remarked that he himself had become the object of a religious cult in Calcutta. They had a temple, priests, adherents, and held regular ceremonies. He did not know quite what to make of it. As I did not know quite what to make of this little Kennedy cult, I merely played my role. After the ceremony we went into the host's house and had quite a nice Sri Lankan curry lunch.

Sinhalese family names are long and quite daunting to the newly arrived foreigner: Jayewardene, Athulathmudali, Wickremasinghe, and so on. It takes a while to get used to them, but after a few months it is possible to roll them off the tongue in a knowing way, much to the awe of casual visitors.

One day in our desultory Sinhalese language class (one hour, three times a week), someone asked our teacher (a well-known local author who also served as our guide to local cultural habits) what these names meant, if anything. A fascinating hour passed as she broke these multisyllabic monikers down and explained their origin and sense. It turned out that they were all constructed phrase names of definite meaning. What was even more fascinating is that these names fit into a pattern, and a similar one at that. The pattern is that of the type of titles and class of a landowning political and military elite of a preindustrial feudal society.

The old Sinhala family names are in fact titles reflecting the positions, awards, and honors of a leadership class, like European titles such as the Duke of Manchester or the Warden of the Cinque Ports. Since a land-based feudal aristocracy is exactly a reasonable description of traditional Sinhala society, this observation should come as no surprise.

An amusing touch to this situation was to discover that another parallel with Europe exists in Sri Lanka. After the revolution (the French one, that is), pushy members of the new middle classes and other arrivistes took to adopting the traditional signs of nobility: the "von" in Germany, and the "de" in France. A similar development took place in Ceylon, as it was then known, after the fall of the last Sinhalese royal house with the British overthrow of the Kingdom of Kandy. Soon after, nonaristocratic Sinhalese families began to adopt the old aristocratic Sinhalese family

names. Just as in Europe, the locals knew who the real Old Regime aris-
tocrats were; so my driver's very deep bow to a neighbor who dropped
in for a drink was later explained by the comment that Mahatia (mister)
Deraniyagala was of the old royalty. But to us foreigners a Sennanayake
is a Sennanayake.

Sri Lanka's economic statistics were misleading. The conventional
per capita GNP figures indicated a relatively poor LDC (less developed
country), somewhere in the neighborhood of Haiti and the Sudan. Yet
the important quality-of-life figures—for education and literacy, health,
and average life expectancy—led to a completely different judgment.
Statistically Sri Lanka was a poor country but one with a relatively
well-off population. There was no readily visible grinding poverty of
the kind one spots instantly in India, Central America, and Africa. That
there were poor Sri Lankans was equally obvious, but the definition of
poor was different. A trip through the new settlements of the Mahaweli
District enabled one to note that no one is dressed in rags; the peasant
working in the field finishes his daily work, washes, puts on fresh clothes,
and (often) sits down and reads a newspaper. To be sure, poor areas and
slums existed in Colombo, but nothing like what offends the visitor's
sensibilities on the streets of Bombay and in the barrios of Central and
South America. A change of clothes may not seem much, but it clearly
indicates some surplus and some grace of life above survival.

Tourism was an important element of the Sri Lankan economy, as in
most of the developing countries in the tropical world. It is interesting
to speculate on the hold of the tropics on the twentieth-century imagination. Where once the tropics and the East were places of mystery,
danger, disease, and discomfort, they now are desirable locations for
work and residence (if the allowances are good enough) and certainly
increasingly popular locales for vacationing. When the wind blows and
the rain freezes and the winter seems endless, the thoughts of northerners
from Finland to Vancouver turn to charter flights and the search for sun
and sand and uninhibited fun. Certain criteria appear to be obligatory;
for instance, the New Year's Eve after-dinner show at the Tangerine Beach

Hotel included a limbo dancer. What the limbo has to do with Sri Lanka is anybody's guess, but to the assembled Greek, Italian, and other tourists the limbo seemed just about right for a tropical night on a tropical beach.

If the social history of the rise of the tropical beach as a travel destination has not yet been written, it ought to be. A whole range of factors must have played a role, including the crucial invention of air-conditioning, increasingly easier and cheaper transportation, and the introduction of the concept of vacation as compared to the traditional leisured lifestyle of the upper classes. These, combined with significant changes in dress and social and sexual codes, have all led to the commonplace sight of members of industrial societies at play in a de facto nude Garden of Eden for two weeks each year.

There is probably a chicken-and-egg relationship at play here, as exposure to possibilities led to changes in habits and attitudes, which led to greater possibilities—first in thought then in practice. The two great world wars of this century probably played an important role, as large numbers of people, mostly young men, were lifted out of their expected life and transported hither and yon to strange and exotic locales. Some suffered and died, but others had their perspectives permanently changed by real-life experiences. *South Pacific* was not only a successful Broadway play but also an expurgated report on many a young serviceman's out-of-the-ordinary experience. As they sang after the First World War, "How you gonna keep 'em down on the farm after they've seen Paree?" After World War II the answer was that you could most of the time, as long as they got two weeks a year to spend cavorting around a tropical beach, with limbo dancers, some nudity, lots to drink, and peeling noses. In my youth in Detroit just after that war, the more prosperous went to Florida in midwinter and paraded their suntans for the rest of us in January. Now I watch what used to be called the working class swarm off a chartered flight in Sri Lanka—or Ceylon, as it was called in days of yore (and fewer tourists).

Yet who am I to make snide remarks? At the end of one year my wife and I went to Bangkok on a tourist trip, stayed at tourist hotels, did tourist things, and thoroughly enjoyed ourselves. And we soon went off to do more touristing, this time to India. We took pictures in front of the Gateway to India in Bombay, shopped and wandered around New Delhi, and then spent seven days on the so-called Palace on Wheels, a tourist train of old Indian Princely States' railway cars that made one-week tours of some cities of Rajasthan. While the advertised comfort and accommodations fell somewhat short of palatial, they were reasonably comfortable, and the experience of touring by train was good fun. We took lots of pictures, rode on camels, complained when the promised elephant ride was canceled, and came home quite satisfied. As one of our party said, with an air of weary triumph, "Well, been there; done that," the motto for the modern tourist.

However, the political atmosphere in Sri Lanka when we first arrived had not been a good one for tourism. The country was almost perfectly designed for contemporary tourism, what with sun and beaches and superb countryside, including mountains and jungles, tropical fruits, ancient cities, exotic customs, and even elephants. Unfortunately, it had also been plagued for several years with growing political instability arising from ethnic strife. The Jayewardene government had assiduously cultivated tourism since its election in 1977. A modern tourist infrastructure was rapidly built up in the late 1970s and early 1980s, and the number of tourists grew rapidly. Sadly enough, in 1983, just as the improved infrastructure in Colombo and along the beaches came into being, the violence between Sinhalese and Tamils exploded into widely publicized violence, and tourism began to falter. By 1987 the annual tourist arrival figure was under half of the 1982 high point. The hotels and tourist companies hung on, often by renegotiating their loans with their bankers (easy enough in some cases, as often both were government agencies). Following some improvement, the security situation then deteriorated as the presidential election approached, causing the tourist situation to take a nosedive.

In early December 1986 the Ceylon Tourist Board (like the tea industry, they long ago decided to keep the Ceylon brand name) apparently panicked and hustled most of the tourists out of the country. The proximate cause was a strike action, inspired by the insurgent JVP party, by employees of a couple of hotels along the south coast. Although no "terrorists" directly approached, much less threatened, any tourists, the image of thousands of tourists stranded at unstaffed hotels was too much for the authorities to bear. So they announced that tourists should leave the island, hastily mobilized buses, gathered up several thousand tourists from seaside hotels, and brought the tourists to Colombo. For several days, until they left for home, they filled up Colombo's five-star hotels.

The potential visitor's concern about traveling to Sri Lanka is quite understandable. Since 1983 violence had been growing; the previous two years in particular had been badly marked by widespread and persistent murder and assault. Thousands of people had been killed and wounded, imprisoned, and made to disappear by the activities of insurgent groups, political party irregulars, government security forces, and the riffraff and criminal elements who always seem to surface during periods of public unrest.

However, the curious fact was that this persistent and growing internal turmoil and violence appeared to be conducted by all participants in a manner consciously designed to avoid damage to foreigners—both resident and visiting. The number of incidents involving foreigners in the previous six years could literally be counted on one hand: the American economic assistance couple kidnapped in Jaffna but quickly released unharmed following backroom discussions, those killed in the sabotage of a Sri Lankan civil airliner at Katunayake Airport, the German radio technician hit by chance during a small firefight between insurgents and soldiers near Batticaloa, and three Indian citizens murdered on a sugar plantation in late 1988. Even moderately unpleasant and only potentially dangerous incidents of a chance nature had been rare. A couple of American officials traveling north towards Mannar were stopped by some armed youth and restrained for an hour or so for conversation with the group's leader, given Orange Fanta to drink, and then sent on their way. A few other foreigners had had similar brief encounters with insurgents, but they were chance encounters with no serious results. The same was true with respect to government security forces: a foreigner was occasionally stopped and questioned at roadblocks or by chance, but little if any harassment resulted and no foreigner was seriously threatened, much less hurt.

Old hotels had become quite the fashion around the world. Restored to previous standards of elegance and without the stigma of contemporary plastic and chrome, they were able to charge premium rates. Sri Lanka had a respectable number of such establishments; witness the six-page section on Ceylon in the glossy book entitled *Hotels and Palaces of the Orient*. Apart from the Galle Face and the Mount Lavinia hotels, however, they were more provincial colonial establishments than grand places. The Galle Face Hotel had been somewhat restored, but not well enough to attract the upscale world traveler.

Some of the other older hotels in the country were even more interesting. The Taprobane in Colombo (the old Grand Oriental) had a marvelous location overlooking the port in the center of the early twentieth century downtown. But it had been renovated some years earlier and is possibly the worst example of such work around. The Hill Club in Nuwara Eliya probably did not need restoration. It stood in a pristine state as the epitome of the old colonial club. It also functioned as a sort of foreign tourist hotel, as well as a club for its now completely indigenous membership. Next door to the Hill Club was the Grand Hotel, a fine example of a basically attractive Edwardian hotel, but it needed work, particularly in the rooms. The Hotel Suisse in the city of Kandy was another fine example of an early twentieth-century British colonial hotel, not in terribly bad shape but in need of some loving care. The Bandarawela Hotel was an especially fine example of British upcountry colonial or out-station hotel, reminding me very much of the Norfolk in Nairobi. The entrance, dining room, bar, and general layout were evocative and comfortable. I would only polish up the bathrooms a bit (I am an American, after all). My one visit there was on a cool, misty, rainy day, a nice change from Colombo's perpetual tropical clime and reminiscent of the Kenyan highlands.

Two truly magnificent relics remained that cried out for sensitive restoration—the Queen's Hotel in Kandy and the New Oriental in Galle. Both dated from well back in the nineteenth century, and both had seriously deteriorated. Staying in either was a triumph of romanticism. Their settings were perfect; the Queen's in the center of Kandy, looking out to the lake and the Temple of the Tooth, while the New Oriental overlooked the parapet and the old harbor. One hopes they will survive and be restored, while at the same time one fears that the needed restoration could easily ruin them. I am sure there are romantics who would like to see both remain as they were, crumbling but authentic. However, such establishments eventually die and disappear. If they are to survive, they need to be restored to economic health, which means attracting customers. We should not forget that these places were built as commercial institutions, not as museums of a bygone era. Restoring them to life as functioning and profitable hotels would be an honest act.

We saw out our first year at the Oriental Hotel in Bangkok, along with colleagues from Colombo and friends from England. Not knowing Bangkok very well, we had taken potluck on hotel reservations and ended up with a Cook's tour of Bangkok hotels, staying in three during our seven-day stay. They were all very nice, but best was the Oriental. The Regency and the Hilton had nice rooms and good service, but the combination of a more dramatic ambiance and the superb location on the river made the Oriental something special, despite its somewhat vulgar self-praise as the best hotel in the world. In any case, there we were on New Year's Eve, enjoying a marvelous dinner in a truly fabulous setting.

The country continued to suffer from expanding violence during the year, as various political and ethnic conflicts went without solution. Yet 1988 ended on a note of optimism, however qualified. The central short-term question of the year concerned the future of representative government. The country's political system had been for years under severe strain from internal pressures and actual armed attacks from antidemocratic forces. Having two armed insurgent groups was a bit excessive for a country of this size, even in this violent era. The constitutional deadlines for presidential and parliamentary elections were approaching, and it was an openly discussed question among the country's citizens as well as outside observers as to whether the situation would permit the holding of reasonably honest and legitimate elections. The question was often phrased in terms of the awesome choice of bullets or ballots.

The issue remained in the forefront of public interest throughout the year. As violence escalated, the capability of the government to hold the elections became a burning question in the minds of many. The mood in the country, particularly in Colombo, in the weeks preceding the presidential election became increasingly somber. Many Sri Lankans predicted catastrophe, including uncontrolled violence and government collapse. Some left the country, and the mood affected the expatriate and diplomatic communities. A number of them, or at least their dependents, quietly went on vacation out of the island. In the classic phrase, the atmosphere was tense, and fear was palpable.

In addition, government opponents repeatedly charged that the will to hold elections was also lacking. "Will he or won't he?" was the question people asked about President Jayewardene's responsibility to the constitution. In the event, he did. Despite tragically large numbers of deaths and murders, the presidential election was held in December. Although it was flawed by less than perfect procedures and marred by violence, the center did hold, and a new president of acceptable legitimacy was elected.

The successful presidential election almost immediately cleared the air. The new president, Ranasinghe Premadasa, was of the country's more conservative national party, and his success reassured the more affluent. Moreover, the mere success of the process itself appeared to have had a salutary effect on public morale, even though the violence in the country continued. For several weeks the violence rate appeared to have dropped, although it turned out later that only the newspaper and television reporting had been curtailed. The general mood was thus one of relief following a fever through the last weeks of December. The holiday mood during Christmas, a very popular holiday in this largely Buddhist city, and New Year's Eve was almost normal.

For all the carping that can be and has been voiced, the election was a victory for democracy and representative government. That the victory was less than clear-cut and involved compromises and shortcomings was, after all, in the best tradition of working democracies. It did not by any means signal the end of the country's many problems—far from it—but it did mean that the democratic political process had survived, and hope remained that those problems might yet be addressed in less than apocalyptic terms.

Politics aside, a most striking aspect of Sri Lanka was the degree to which it resembled other comparatively small, old, and cohesive nations. I perceived that same combination of ancient heritage, sense of community, and cautious resentment of bigger neighbors that I had felt in Belgium and Portugal. In all three there is the enormous pride of a separate, individual national personality combined with a touchiness about its lack of outside recognition. The Portuguese deeply resented any intimation that they were provincial Spaniards, just as the Sinhalese bristle at those who confuse them with the Indians.

The sense of national personality is strong and based on a long communal memory. That the Sinhalese nevertheless understand their difficult situation is obvious. At the end of a long luncheon discussion with some Sri Lankan colleagues from the Ministry of Foreign Affairs, I remarked that their geographical situation reminded me of the comment by a Mexican president: "Poor Mexico, so far from God and so close to the United States." They broke out in enthusiastic if rueful laughter. Old countries, albeit small, with old civilizations do have their charm.

12

The Diplomatic Village

Diplomats, like every other professional group, have a "village" instinct. They tend to gather together whenever possible and share common experiences and perceptions. Lawyers and doctors do it, and so do diplomats. Like all my colleagues, Americans and those from other countries, I have often participated in this professional camaraderie at every post. Colombo presented an especially clear-cut example of this phenomenon. Its diplomatic community was large enough to have it fully blossom, while being small enough to avoid being submerged in a larger community like Washington or Paris.

The diplomatic system has been around for most of modern history and long ago worked out a set of operating rules and procedures, usually covered under the rubric of protocol. This system is accepted by almost everyone, except occasional revolutionary regimes in the first flush of victory. One of the primary objectives of the diplomatic protocol system is to deal with the vexing problem of precedence among representatives of formally equal and sovereign nations. In truth, nations are not equal, and it has always been difficult for the ambassador of Luxembourg, for instance (or his contemporary African counterpart), to obtain status equivalent to that afforded the representative of a great power. The problem is dealt with by adopting the principle of precedence at post, that is, based on the dates that new envoys presents their credentials. Ambassadors take their place in line or at the table in accordance with their arrival at the capital of assignment—not with the wealth or size of their country—and everyone can avoid undignified haggling over real or assumed slights to one's country in the form of slights to oneself. (For those who do not believe such matters are important, I suggest a quick review of modern history, including the question of the shape of the table in the Vietnam War negotiations.)

This system is eminently workable, resolutely noncontroversial, and occasionally productive of amusing situations, such as the deliberate policy of Nicaragua to keep the same ambassador in Washington for twenty-seven years so that he remained the unchallenged dean of the diplomatic corps. However, while formal organization of the corps is by precedence, there also exists in every capital city an often strikingly different pecking order among diplomats that reflects a combination of judgments about the real importance of the sending country and the quality of bilateral ties. The representatives of great powers are always figures of standing within a resident diplomatic community; there is no place in the world where the American or Russian ambassador is a figure not worth noting. On the other hand, middle-grade powers can be placed at different levels in different places: the French ambassador is generally the most important diplomat in any francophone West African country, but he or she is a marginal figure in, say, Sri Lanka. History and current interests determine this role.

The situation in Colombo provided a nice illustration of this phenomenon. The American and Russian ambassadors were obviously important representatives, expecting and receiving all courtesies and quite good access from the local government, a steady stream of invitations from the best levels of the local society, the attention of journalists, and a general deference appropriate to their status and the prestige of their countries. The British high commissioner (Sri Lanka is a member of the Commonwealth, which exchanges high commissioners rather than ambassadors) enjoyed a good deal of prestige arising from the historical ties between the two countries, the persistent Anglophile nature of its population, and the willingness of England to provide significant financial assistance and a sympathetic ear. The ties between former colonies and former metropoles are often quite enduring.

The Japanese also flew very high, if only because they were prepared to pay for the privilege by assuming the role of the largest—by far—aid donor to Sri Lanka. Others fell in more or less behind: the Scandinavians provided quite a bit of aid and in consequence enjoyed a much higher status than one might expect; the Cuban ambassador occupied a special, prestigious position for a combination of complex political and personal reasons; and the rest more or less grouped themselves into not very well-defined circles, with people like the Romanian and Polish chargés and the PLO rep somewhere on the outermost fringes.

But the top of the heap, the cock of the walk, the undisputed Top Dip in Colombo was the high commissioner of India. His status was dramatic proof of the old adage (by General de Gaulle?) that politics is geography. Sri Lanka, in addition, is a small country located near—very near—a very large country, and one with pretensions to a role as a great power. Sri Lanka is, after all, a South Asian country, and South Asia means, in political as well as cultural and historical terms, India. This situation was obvious and natural, enhanced by current events as India became heavily involved in Sri Lanka's internal problem of ethnic conflict.

The reality of this role could be seen any night at any large cocktail reception or other public function. Upon the Indian high commissioner's arrival, swarms of other diplomats—regardless of nationality, political views, or alliances—bustled to his side to bathe in his presence and, even more important, his information. He was always surrounded by a gaggle of diplomats (unless a collection of local personalities got to him first) posing questions and mentally drafting telegrams to be sent next day to their head offices. Information to report to one's own government is the stuff of life to the professional diplomat. However, for most embassies limited staff and limited contact with the local government severely restrict their direct access to the movers and shakers, and therefore to firsthand information (and to firsthand compared to secondhand rumors). A professional diplomat's day is made by the transmission of the telegram or dispatch that begins, "Last night at dinner, the president said . . ." Alas, most members of any diplomatic corps have few opportunities to write such messages. (Hence the importance of annual dinners for the diplomatic corps given by many heads of state: the next morning even the most modest representative of the most modest country can begin a telegram with those magic words.)

Now, Top Dips fulfill for their less well-placed colleagues a somewhat similar role. How many telegrams must have gone out of Saigon to obscure foreign ministries with the words, "Last night the American ambassador told me . . ."? And this was the role played by the Indian high commissioner in Colombo. As he was a talented professional with excellent personal and professional manners, he accepted this responsibility with grace and charm and always had a few choice tidbits for his colleagues. Almost every large reception, therefore, was graced by the sight of this rather short, rotund diplomat, puffing on his ever-present pipe, surrounded by a circle of invariably taller fellow ambassadors hanging on his words as he generously fed them the latest on local developments and Indian perspectives. All the participants were aware that in other countries and other times these roles have been and would be reversed as professional camaraderie plays its role in human affairs.

Nowadays, Asians give the biggest diplomatic cocktail receptions, most specifically the Japanese and the South Koreans. At least that was the practice in Colombo in those years. For instance, the Japanese embassy gave a national day party that was exceeded that year only by Hilton when it formally inaugurated its new hotel. Among the nicest touches at Japanese receptions in those days were the booths that served fresh tempura shrimp. It was in the waiting line for tempura shrimp that the Soviet ambassador commented to the American ambassador that if General MacArthur had not been so stubborn about Soviet participation in the Japanese occupation back in 1945, neither of them would be waiting patiently in line for their shrimp.

The South Korean ambassadorial couple were extremely smart, expensively well dressed and coiffured, and expansive. He was never seen without a dark suit, white shirt, and somber tie. At one particular South Korean Embassy dinner the guests were largely, if my memory serves, diplomats. Almost everyone had been on post in Colombo for some time, and the air was relaxed and easy among good acquaintances, if not friends. The Dutch ambassador was an ebullient type and his wife a charming, gracious, and popular lady. They had been in Colombo for an extensive tour and were now going home to retirement. The nationalities present ranged across the continents and ideologies. Such dinners were common (I went through the round myself, in October of 1989, as my departure approached) and, by and large, quite pleasant.

In a sense, they were community rituals, much like weddings and confirmations in most communities. Diplomats are a professional class, but we also create a mobile community. We share common experiences and a common attitude and live similar lives. If we do not know each other before this post, we probably know someone in common; someone one played tennis with in Dakar or bridge with in Moscow or something like that. Departures are part of our life and we note them with some care and attention.

This particular evening at the South Koreans' went especially well. The mood was warm and collegial from the very beginning over drinks. Then at the dinner table it passed beyond the usual congeniality into true warmth and sense of community. Maybe it was the Dutch ambassador's unusually boisterous (even for him) air, matched by the Yugoslav ambassador's equally high sense of laughter and pleasure. Even my stories got better than the usual response. In any case, the atmosphere was warm and cozy as well as cheerful and gay. A sense of friendship filled the room, in addition to the usual mood of mutual understanding and easy acceptance. It was an exceptionally nice evening; one to treasure among those best memories of a diplomatic life. Rewards sometimes come in small packages and transient modes, like a special sunset or a bunch of flowers, a cold beer at the right time, a good stroke at tennis—or an especially pleasant evening among congenial fellow souls.

Embassies are about people as well as policies and politics. In the more mundane aspects of diplomatic life, one is involved with individuals or small groups. Being boss in an embassy—management as contemporary jargon would have it—thus means dealing with people in three senses: outside the embassy, in the conventional concept of diplomats meeting, greeting, interviewing, and avoiding; inside the embassy, as a professional colleague; and, finally, as supervisor of both American and local national employees.

The first activity is, as noted, rather traditional for diplomats and has been written about often. I rather like the comment that "diplomats are the only people paid to loiter in antechambers." True; even if the function of antechambers and the word itself are out of fashion, it has been replaced by newer but similar phenomena: tree plantings, honorary degree ceremonies, political gatherings of many types, conferences, building openings, cocktail parties, and the "business lunch."

Many countries operate fairly small diplomatic missions, the sort of diplomatic post that consists of a chief of mission (ambassador), one or at most two other senior officers (ministers, counselors, and such), a second or third secretary or two, a couple of clerical and technical support personnel (code clerks and such), and a handful of locally engaged staff. Nice little operations run either in a collegial (e.g., Canadian) or authoritarian (e.g., German) manner.

American diplomatic posts have long ceased being anything like that. The Russians are even worse, but most countries—even quite important ones like Great Britain, France, and Japan—operate smallish embassies in most places. The American embassy in Sri Lanka, for instance, is probably bigger than the overwhelming majority of other people's embassies in Washington, which everyone considers the world's premier diplomatic location. When I was in Colombo, we numbered approximately seventy directly employed American staff, from ambassador to communications officers (called code clerks in the olden days), including Marine security guards. The number of locally employed employees was approaching four hundred, counting our local security guard detachment. Add to the American employees their dependents, and one soon realizes that the ambassador is mayor of a small community, with his deputy chief of mission as town manager.

Max Weber pointed it out a long time ago: over time, large bureaucratic organizations spend more and more time on internal concerns than on the business for which they were created. An American embassy is clearly such a community. An increasing amount of an American diplomat's time, especially as he or she goes up in rank, is therefore taken up by internal housekeeping chores, from questions of housing assignments to celebration of American holidays and complaints about the nurse. For example, it is true, but still difficult to accept, that we are now required to apply purely Washington-based standards and practices to the renting of houses across the spectrum of the world's countries as if Colombo, for example, were Washington.

Another aspect of diplomatic life is the symbiotic relationship with the local community. Diplomats are not tourists or expatriates, but professional foreigners. We have a special status fully recognized by the local government and community as "official foreigners," in law and practice. We are not visitors, but a special kind of resident—temporary, yes, but also permanent in that the specific individuals change but the "seat" is always filled. So collectively we become part of the local community. Generally, we live in the community, in local neighborhoods, as in Brussels, where we lived in an apartment in an in-town neighborhood. Mostly we lived in houses (size and fashionableness of neighborhood depending on rank). Later, however, as an ambassadorial family in Guinea-Bissau, we lived in a two-bedroom apartment on the fifth floor above the embassy offices on the first floor. As this office building, the tallest in town, had no elevator, healthy physical exercise was built into our daily life.

In Colombo we experienced a living style closer to the image (mostly imaginary!) people have of diplomats. The American ambassador's residence, Jefferson House, and my own house, the deputy chief of mission's residence, were located in a neighborhood called Cinnamon Gardens.

It is called Cinnamon Gardens, a charming name dating back to the nineteenth century, because, reportedly, cinnamon trees were cultivated there. It is also called Colombo 7. Both are local terms for what the French call *"le tout Paris"* or *le tout* of whatever city one is talking about. Whether called Colombo 7 or Cinnamon Gardens, it is a pleasant and attractive neighborhood with a varied collection of houses, ranging from gracious turn-of-the-century villas to newer and smaller villas pitched onto the corners of the larger lots of the older homes. When Cinnamon Gardens was first opened up as an upscale residential neighborhood, the rich Ceylonese (as they were then called) built their large homes with stables and servants' quarters and sweeping driveways on large almost exurban plots. However, rising taxes and the value of land soon made these large plots of residential property too valuable to remain untouched. By the 1950s Colombo 7 was dividing up these plots and giving away sections to children, nephews, and nieces, who built the modern villas referred to above. Cinnamon Gardens is now somewhat congested but still quite upmarket.

Around the corner from the DCM residence lived a Sri Lankan friend from a distinguished family. As he sat in his modern ranch-style bungalow, he loved to recount the history of Cinnamon Gardens and point out through the trees the old family manse, now surrounded by houses like his. His family once lived—as did most of their class—in a central city neighborhood called the Pettah. At some time in the late nineteenth century, the British colonial authorities decided to reorganize the central city and urged a number of the Pettah residents to move away to a new posh residential district in the Cinnamon Gardens area, offering advantageous terms. My friend's family took up the offer, obtained a fifteen-acre plot, built themselves a large and gracious house, and later made a fortune selling off sections when Cinnamon Gardens became the place to live. My friend noted with gratitude that that colonial government decision may well have been what kept his family comfortably well off during much of the ensuing century. The American residences are part of that history—property bought at advantageous prices after World War II in the late 1940s.

Another element of the role of an embassy, in this case the American embassy, is involvement with the local private business community, beginning with one's own nationals. Sri Lanka had only a small American business community, so we did not have a formal business group such as an American Chamber of Commerce. However, there was the American Business Circle—the ABC—which consisted of somewhere between twenty and thirty businessmen of various nationalities (mostly Sri Lankan) who headed or represented American firms, plus a handful of official Americans. Membership requirements were rather elastic, with no fees attached, and the ABC's primary activity was a monthly lunch hosted in turn by individual members. The luncheon was a jolly affair, usually held in one of Colombo's five-star hotels, and consisted of drinks, lunch, and then the most minimal of business meetings over dessert. Attendance was quite good as the members viewed the affair as a pleasant and useful occasion for the exchange of gossip and maintenance of contacts.

Two events, or rather developments, marked ABC activities in 1987. The first consisted of a discreet competition among some of the members that started early in the year when a luncheon at the Interconti-nental Hotel was noticeably tasty, especially a towering construction of ice cream, fresh fruit, and whipped cream that ended the meal. It was noticed that despite the cries of protest from this largely middle-aged group of gentlemen (two lady members notwithstanding), the dessert disappeared rapidly. The next month's host took up the challenge, sched-uled his lunch also at the Intercon, and instructed the hotel's general manager (a member of the ABC, by the way) to surpass the previous month's luncheon. The manager made a valiant and successful effort, and by the next month the competition was on. The members commented and enjoyed the development for a few months, but then—by general consensus—the race was called off. Consciences, if not waistlines, were becoming outraged.

Not to say that the ABC returned to any sort of recognizable auster-ity. The luncheons remained well watered and well within the genre of business lunch. But the dangers of escalation were avoided by mutual agreement. Disarmament negotiators take note.

The year 1987 was also notable for the American Business Circle for the "Great Formalization Debate." Early in the year, the question was posed as to whether or not the ABC should transform itself into a regular American Chamber of Commerce or some similar and more formal organization. The possibility was raised by a representative of the Sri Lankan Greater Economic Organization of Colombo and supported by a visiting representative from the International Chamber of Commerce. Sides were chosen. (Three sides actually: pro, con, and bemusedly neutral.) A study committee was appointed, reports were submitted, and the ABC pursued its stately schedule of monthly luncheons with "Formalization" as the major subject of the business period. As the months went by, the discussion became increasingly complicated and intricate. The arguments for and against became quite refined—and the middle uncommitted group became increasingly uncommitted. All of this was pursued with great good humor, it must be said, and the members of the ABC became rather fond of the ongoing and potentially endless discussion.

As the year came to its end, the group decided—almost regretfully—that a decision must be taken. A reasonable compromise was reached, which essentially said that the ABC would not become more formalized but would attempt to project a more formal presence in the local community—largely, it would seem, by ordering some stationery with an ABC logo. Everyone was actually quite pleased with this decision, and the result was cheered and toasted. And so the American Business Circle of Colombo ended 1987 with the satisfaction of having spent the year in much bonhomie and just enough seriousness.

Another persistent component of diplomatic life is the American Citizen Abroad. Sri Lanka is far away, and we did not have large numbers or tourists or expatriates. One day in December, however, we received our by-now-annual invitation to preside over a graduation ceremony for a class of American acupuncturists. A group of six had just completed a three-month course at a local clinic-school run by a world-famous Sri Lankan acupuncturist. The ambassador had gone the previous year but decided that attendance once was sufficient evidence of devotion to duty and offered the opportunity to others. I took it up and on the appointed day went off to serve as Chief Guest.

The ceremony involved a small central core of borrowed Western academic formality set in the midst of an essentially casual Asian hospital scene. The acupuncture clinic was held largely in the open air, with local patients but both local and foreign students. While the patients and most students pursued their usual activities, a semicircle of seven chairs, six Americans wearing academic robes and me, created a small tableau. When the doctor of acupuncture-cum-professor showed up, we went quickly into a brisk ceremony where I handed out diplomas, pictures were taken, and a few words spoken by Professor-Doctor Jayasuriya. I congratulated everyone, exchanged a few words with each (where are you from, where are you going to practice, how did you find the experience). They were a mixed bag of Americans, mostly from the West. Obviously sincere and gratified by their new status, they glowed at being addressed as doctor. (It is not my role in life to enforce AMA standards, and I have spent much of my adult life employing whatever titles people expect.) From beginning to end, the whole event did not take more than thirty minutes.

As I said, the six Americans, mixed in sex and race but possibly not too differentiated by class, were all pleased with themselves and, armed with their new dignity, looking forward to taking up practice—some as pure acupuncturists and others mixing their new skill into a broader holistic type of medical practice. Three of them however, all female, intended to stay on in Sri Lanka for a while and pursue some advanced work. I wished them the best of luck and continued success, passed out my calling card, and said farewell.

Within two weeks I heard from two of the new graduates, in my status as their Contact in High Places. One ran into trouble when her bank in California failed to transfer necessary living funds and she found herself in difficulty meeting her bills. She came to call, my calling card in hand. I guided her down to the consular officer (who, after all, is paid to do this sort of work), but became accustomed to her dropping in. Another wanted to return to California with a Sri Lankan friend with whom she had a significant relationship. Unfortunately, her simple but perfectly natural view of the visa procedure ran afoul of the United States Immigration and Naturalization Act. She, too, came to call, to consult, and to ask for assistance. I tried to explain, sent her down to the consular officer, and found out the next day she had decided to cut through our visa regulation jungle and married the young man.

Actually, I found these newly minted acupuncturists rather attractive people. They had a sturdy enthusiasm and a healthy optimism, and their pretensions as medical practitioners were probably no more ill-founded than those of many others.

The Extra Holiday. Traditional Buddhist custom or practice, at least among Sri Lankan Sinhalese, identifies the monthly full moon as a religious holiday. Each full moon—called a full-moon *poya* day—is identified with a religious event and treated as a public holiday. At the same time, of course, weekends are regular holidays in the Western manner, and diplomats celebrate their own national holidays. Therefore, we who lived in Sri Lanka benefited from a particularly generous pattern of nonworking days.

To a Westerner, the weekend pattern is, if no longer sacred, at least a regular pattern that requires no thought or conscious planning. The weekends come steadily without surprise, and one builds expectation of them into one's daily life. *Poya* days, however, are exotic and come irregularly, at least to Westerners. Every once in a while, once a month, a *poya* day pops up, sometimes in the middle of the week, sometimes on weekends, providing us expatriates with the bonus of a surprise holiday. This pleasant attribute of living in a foreign country is probably one of the causes for the old canard about diplomats leading an excessively leisured existence. In any case, the *poya* days seem irregular to us and provide a cheerful little "surprise" every month. After a while, I suppose one becomes used to *poya* days and includes them in one's life and personal planning.

Poodle Faking and Cookie Pushing. Leave for Rest and Recuperation (aka recreation or relaxation)—R&R—was quite an innovation when first introduced back in the 1960s. The extra air ticket and the chance to break up the assignment with a bit of exotic world travel was a much-appreciated benefit of service in some of the more isolated diplomatic posts. The availability of R&R fed both the ego (here I am serving on the frontier; not in one of those soft, overstaffed European posts) and the body (next month we are off for four weeks in Greece!). But time passes, and the most exotic posts (leaving out one or two) are now all equipped with commissaries and swimming pools and tourists. R&R has become a standard benefit, available to every Foreign Service post, except possibly Paris, and the R&R ticket, what with the changes in international air service and ticketing procedures, now permits the traveler to get back to the continental United States.

Assignment to Sri Lanka came after six years in Washington. We decided to take R&R in early August and almost inevitably worked out a holiday plan that involved return to the United States, as parental obligations became pressing. However, we also wanted to do some traveling in Europe and tried to combine both, as well as a short stop in Washington. (Somehow, if one is going to the States it seems only natural to drop in on the department in Washington and check in on one's friends, the general mood, and assignment possibilities.) So, there it was: three weeks running around Europe from Brussels to Lisbon, a week in Washington, then separate visits to parents located on opposite sides of the continent, and finally separate return voyages back to post. Even as a prospect it seemed a bit hurried, and the outbreak of a dramatic bit of arms and politics in Sri Lanka shortened the trip by ten days, thereby requiring some curtailment and even faster movement.

It all ended up in a private version of "If it's Tuesday this must be Belgium." We saw a lot of friends, did a bit of sightseeing and shopping—but all briefly and with a sense of rush. Washington was hectic (what else?) and the family visits (never my cup of tea at the best of times) dutiful. I returned back to Colombo with a sigh of relief. My wife wandered in about a month later, having spent that extra time visiting her family. We brooded over this trip in the following months. We had, after all, used up a good amount of leave and spent an even larger amount of money, and were left with a letdown feeling. It had not been a good vacation; we had done a bit of everything but not enough of anything to be really fun and relaxing. We had fallen into the R&R trap. Since one could make it back to the States, one should, and that turns R&R into a form of home leave. The only trouble was that we had only been out of the States for one year and really did not want home leave. We wanted to tour rural Portugal with some friends, wander around Paris like tourists, and spend time with other friends in Brussels and London. We wanted a European vacation of the sort that Foreign Service people used to have. Instead we performed like suburbanites with a couple of weeks to spend on that long-planned European vacation.

This revelation depressed us. We swore an oath that next year would be different. We would not rush back to the U.S. (may avoid the place, in fact) but would go off for "four weeks in Greece" and pretend that the Diplomatic Life is as it used to be.

Admin work. Among the many tasks of an embassy staff is the career's less glamorous: in a word, administration. It is an old and honored tradition among bureaucrats to bemoan the deterioration of standards. In addition, true-blue diplomats have always been somewhat disdainful of administrative tasks; and the growing intrusiveness of administration (or management, as it is now called in an attempt to give it a classier air) has not diluted that attitude. It seems that we spend more and more of our time on internal household tasks, and even some of the external activities are of an administrative character, such as negotiating "right to work" agreements for spouses and dependents. We spend an awful lot of time taking care of ourselves. Some of this activity reflects changes in the world and in the working conditions of contemporary diplomacy. Certainly pay and allowances are better, and a number of benefits, ranging from increased medical care to educational concerns, do require new rules, regulations and, staff.

And yet, and yet . . . Do we really need all that we are getting, and is that package of "all" making us happier and/or better diplomats? Our collective performance on the administrative side is not impressive. The dramatic security program mandated by Congress in a panicked response to the rise of political terrorism has been an administrative nightmare. Now security programs are being abandoned in midstream as money runs out, although no one appears quite sure where it ran out to. For instance, we spent a certain amount of time (too much) at the end of one year of agonizing over the question of security guards at the houses of full-time direct-hire mission employees—essentially our American staff. That it was the experts in Washington, with little reference to our field judgment, who had originally insisted upon the installation of twenty-four-hour guard service was irrelevant. What was important now was that Washington was running out of money and informed us that our guard program budget had been cut.

After studying the problem, we came to the conclusion that the money would not stretch to continue the full twenty-four-hour coverage then in practice and that cutbacks would be necessary. Unfortunately, two developments had occurred that made implementation of that decision somewhat delicate. First, like all good Americans, most of our staff appeared to believe that a privilege or benefit once granted becomes a constitutional right. Withdrawal causes anguish and irritation. Secondly, the security situation in Sri Lanka had changed in the previous year or so, producing a heightened feeling of tension, especially in light of the upcoming presidential elections. It was, quite objectively, no time to cut back on residential security coverage.

We wrestled with this little problem through the last months of the year, avoiding a final decision in light of the growing tension and violence in the country. At regular intervals we held meetings on the subject that produced no results other than airing of divergent views alive in the community, eating up a good deal of time. Because of the security situation in the country we were not able, in fact, to make any change in our system and so continued merrily to chew up the funds at an unsustainable rate. Like Micawber, we kept waiting for something to turn up. Finally, when the end of the year brought no resolution, we would carry the problem into 1989.

The apparent aimlessness of this activity in the name of the American Republic and the people was, and is, disheartening. And yet it was only marginally incompetent compared to the great Chancery Roof and 44 Galle Road projects. The embassy chancery (a word now replaced by the all-inclusive "embassy," a further evidence of the decline of standards) was quite new, having been occupied only in 1984. But the roof had been leaking since 1986, and all efforts to stop the leakage had failed. Experts and study teams came and went; proposals of varying degrees of complexity were proposed, and the leaking continued. In the closing months of 1988, the responsible experts proposed an elaborate fifty-three-week construction program to build a new roof. The project was supposed to begin sometime in early 1989 and be completed sometime in 1990. That schedule was never fulfilled, and by the time I left Colombo four years later, the United States government still had not been able to fix a leaking roof.

Our performance on the Great Roof Problem was fully matched by an admittedly more complicated situation involving office housing for three U.S. government agencies operating in Sri Lanka and housed outside the new chancery. Without going into details, suffice it to say that the two buildings then occupied, especially the old chancery at 44 Galle Road, were threatening to damage the health of their occupants (via asbestos poisoning) and to actually fall down. Several ways of preventing these catastrophes became immersed in a sea of bureaucratic complexity, and we appeared unable to resolve the complicating claims and budget problems. A comprehensive solution had been reached in 1987 but came apart in 1988. Though in mid-1988 a new comprehensive solution was painfully worked out, accepted, and approved by all concerned, little movement in implementation had been seen by the end of December. This project was expected to take upwards of two years to complete, which would again mean years to resolve a relatively straightforward problem. It had not been resolved by the time I left Colombo.

It is all so depressing. Attempts to describe the process immediately call up images of wading through swamps or Kafkaesque nightmares, of endless meetings, redrafted memoranda, telegrams, and little noticeable progress. And all of this diligent effort was essentially peripheral, not touching the substantive work for which we were paid. It was a triumph of form over substance.

It is difficult to avoid the conclusion that technical progress in communications and word processing and the rise of management as a separate and distinct discipline can be self-defeating phenomena. It no longer appears possible to leave field posts to handle their local affairs. Both stricter standards of management accountability and vastly enlarged headquarters facilities to field communications have resulted in a dramatic increase in micromanagement, a phrase and a concept that did not even exist a few years ago. There must be some corollary of Parkinson's Law in all of this.

13

Ethnic Strife in the "Blessed Isle"

Gradually overriding all other considerations was the continuing and intensifying ethnic conflict between the majority Sinhalese and the minority Tamils. It is an ancient tension in the country, going back thousands of years (according to the two communities). Interestingly, both communities express the same sense of grievance; that they are minority communities threatened with oppression and even extinction. The Tamil claim to this status is based on their minority population position in the country, exacerbated by claims of oppressive Sinhalese majority government measures taken after independence. The Sinhalese claim is based on a longer historical memory and refers to centuries if not millennia of invasion and attacks from the vastly larger Tamil community of South India. As these two communities differ in religion, language, customs, and (so they claim) race, the tie of living together on the same island is under constant strain.

It is the central issue of the day and has earned the country a place—admittedly not of the top priority—in the international media. Up to the late 1980s it was fought out within relatively clear limits. As of late 1986 it had not yet become a full-fledged war between two national or racial communities, which it later did. There was still a controlled air about it, with each side feeling its way along. The government clearly directed its efforts to dealing with a limited number of insurgents (or terrorists, if you will) while distinguishing them (at least in theory) from the general mass of Sri Lankan Tamils. Visitors were constantly reminded how many Tamils live outside of the north and the east, in fact, in Colombo itself. But the Tamil rebels had essentially assumed control of the Jaffna peninsula and created a de facto government.

There was an air of walking along the edge of a precipice, a fear of falling over into a situation of open warfare between the two communities. The militant leadership claimed that this had already happened, and it became even more true later after we had left Sri Lanka. Looking around the world, one is inclined to be pessimistic about the possibility of two communities with differences and attitudes such as these coming to a reasonable working relationship. They have done so at various times in the past, and the genuine working democracy that exists offers a framework for conciliation. This would require on the part of the Sinhalese a bit more self-confidence and willingness to be generous to the Tamil minority. On the part of the Tamils, it would require getting down off the high horse derived from the "Rice Christian" position they occupied during the British colonial period. They must accept that they are and always will be a minority. An opportunity to achieve this understanding surfaced years after we had left Sri Lanka and the Sinhalese government won a bloody victory after full-scale warfare.

By early 1987 the "Tamil Tigers," or LTTE, pretty much dominated the situation in the north, having eliminated, that is killed or cowed, most of their Tamil competitors. In January they attempted to alter the de facto cease-fire in Jaffna by openly usurping certain civil functions, for instance, by creating their own traffic police. They appeared shocked when the GOSL responded by cutting off fuel shipments to the Jaffna peninsula. It was interesting for observers to note that the Tigers and many of their supporters and sympathizers appeared to hold the curious view that it was somehow permissible for them to practice rebellion but reprehensible for the government to retaliate. Curious indeed.

Beginning in November of the previous year, the Sri Lankan security forces demonstrated increasing aggressiveness, culminating in May of 1987 in a well-planned attack that resulted in the recovery of a significant portion of the Northern Peninsula. The Tigers cried foul play and reacted with a propaganda campaign charging the SL army with deliberate and extensive brutality and genocide. Charges and countercharges flew back and forth, with both sides obviously mixing truth with misinformation. When the dust settled after this offensive, it was clear that the initiative as well as a certain amount of territory had shifted from the Tigers to the government.

The next question on everyone's mind was whether or not the government intended to move towards a military solution of the conflict and assault Jaffna City, as it had assaulted Vadamarachi. For several years the argument over the virtues of a military as opposed to a political solution of the Tamil insurgency had been somewhat moot, as few thought the army could obtain a military victory. The apparent military successes of late 1986 and early 1987 caused many to reconsider this option, and both private and public discourse focused on the rumors of an impending assault on Jaffna. This possibility obviously worried the Indian government, which floated rumors and news leaks designed to preempt a Sri Lankan offensive.

The period from late April to late July 1987 were confused and full of emotion and anticipation. Then in late July the Indian prime minister and the Sri Lankan president signed the Indo–Sri Lanka Peace Accord, and a peacekeeping force of Indian soldiers arrived in Sri Lanka. Almost immediately all hell broke loose in the streets of Colombo, as masses of Sri Lankans expressed their outrage at the real and implied insults contained in the accord and the presence of Indian troops on Sri Lankan soil. The storm in the streets soon abated. While acceptance of the accord within Sri Lankan society was at best limited, outside interests, including the United States, Great Britain, China, Japan, most of the European Community, private groups, and individuals, rushed to applaud the accord and the presumed end to the vexing problem of ethnic conflict in Sri Lanka. Few governments other than the Sri Lankan and Indian, and few peoples other than the Sri Lankans and the Tamils of India, had ever really considered the problem a major one. Everyone else wished that the conflict would be resolved in some fashion—any fashion—and go away.

September arrived and everyone waited to see how events would turn out. It was clear that the peace accord was a gamble—a "Sahib's Pact" between Gandhi and Jayewardene. The Tamil militants had had their arms twisted by the Indian government, and President Jayewardene obviously counted on his prestige, actual power, and lack of an alternative to get away with the deal. In August and September, the Indian peacekeeping force tried to put the deal across and failed. By the end of September, it was increasingly clear that the Tamil Tigers would not accept the accord. They stepped up pressure on the Indians, at first, ironically, by use of nonviolent confrontational tactics dating from India's own heroic independence struggle. The pressures grew, the inevitable incidents occurred, and blood was spilled—first that of anti-LTTE Tamil militants, then of Tamil Tiger prisoners of the government, followed by Sinhalese soldiers held prisoner by the Tigers, then almost everyone.

In October the Indian army was ordered into battle against the Tamil Tigers. The Indians had misjudged or mishandled the Tigers and had now moved all the way from sympathetic support and clandestine arming of the Tigers through mediation to armed opposition. Once again history and events have proven the truth of the old saw about the best-laid plans of mice and men. Irritated and exasperated, the Indian army moved forward to implement its will, only to discover that the task was much more difficult than expected. By the end of the year they had indeed "pacified" the Jaffna Peninsula, but the Tigers remained alive and well in other parts of the island. Indian casualties had been high, and the reports of civilian casualties became the foundation of charges of human rights abuses by the Indian army. The Indian peacekeeping force—now numbering almost fifty thousand men—was the butt of criticism and sarcastic humor. In an interesting outbreak of *schadenfreude*, even fervently nationalist Sinhalese were expressing satisfaction at the discomfiture of the Indian army at the hands of a ragged group of young Tamils.

Meanwhile, the dramatic events surrounding the conflict with the Tamil insurgents and the involvement of India in Sri Lankan affairs appeared to open up opportunities for the country's other antigovernment opposition, the Sinhalese Janatha Vimukthi Peramuna (JVP), or People's Liberation Front. They had been slowly coming back into consciousness in the previous couple of years; now they moved right back onto the front pages with a steadily mounting series of attacks and assassinations of government and ruling party cadres in the island's southern regions. Fervently Sinhalese and antigovernment, they now presented themselves as another challenge to Jayewardene and the United National Party government. Two armed insurgencies in a country of fifteen million, occupying an island roughly the size of West Virginia, is really too much. One did not know whether to laugh or cry.

But somehow, despite all the criticisms and complaints, the rather interesting figure of J. R. Jayewardene continued to dominate the scene. He had made his move in making a deal with Indian prime minister Rajiv Gandhi. It was an unpopular move and, in one sense, threw him onto the mercy of New Delhi. On the other hand, New Delhi was discovering that, as in jujitsu, the unexpected can happen, and by the end of the year at least some people were beginning to wonder who had conned whom. The Indians had an army on the ground, they had "conquered" Jaffna, and they had justification for doing so in the form of a bilateral agreement between the two relevant heads of government. But the Tigers still roamed the countryside, no political agreement was in sight, and the Indians were discovering the truth of the old statement that you can do many things with a bayonet except sit on it. Meanwhile, Jayewardene remained calm and even passive, waiting for the Indians to fulfill their part of the deal.

Then, in November, the Indian defense minister visited Colombo and joined J.R. in a televised press conference, one of the occasional events intended to prove that both governments knew what they were doing and that all was going according to plan. J.R. sat at the center of the table, exuding that almost bored air he affected, with his eyes hooded and that marvelous nose dominating the table. In reply to one question he used the phrase "The quality of mercy is not strained." A journalist piped up with, "What was that you said?" and J.R. played out a lovely scene of the weary schoolteacher instructing a particularly dim student. First, he repeated the line, then paused, then quoted the whole speech from which it comes; then paused again and said, "Shakespeare"; then paused once again and said, "*Merchant of Venice*"; and finally gave the scene reference. All without a flicker of expression.

So, the year ended with a drastically changed security situation. Warfare had flared up, India and Sri Lanka had faced each other down, a new international agreement was in place, and an Indian army was in the country in fulfillment of new—and serious—obligations assumed by the government of India. Despite a continuing sharp little war in Jaffna between Indians and Tamil rebels, a hint of change had begun, with increasing emphasis on electoral politics and dealmaking. But young men with guns had dominated the year 1987.

Since about mid-1985, the northern city of Jaffna—the traditional center of Tamil Sri Lanka—had been the "forbidden land" for most foreigners, and for foreign diplomats in particular. The deteriorating security situation made it difficult to visit the area, both because of the actual physical danger (admittedly relatively low, as foreigners were not actually targets) and the potential political implications of too much obvious attention to the area and the insurgents, who were in de facto control. The media formed the one excepted category. From December 1984 through July 1985, big-name journalists came flying in from New Delhi, Singapore, and other points in a classic demonstration of parachute journalism. (There are few regularly assigned foreign correspondents in Sri Lanka.) Each outbreak of violence would bring in a new wave for a quick survey and a couple of articles. The prime objective of these folk— after they had made the rounds of the regular contacts in Colombo—was a quick trip to Jaffna, including, they hoped, a meeting with some Tamil Tigers. In the relatively quiet period of January and February, this exercise took on the character of a guided tour. The journalist would express his desire to visit Jaffna to the Sri Lankan military authorities, who would "book" a seat on one of the daily military flights north. In Jaffna, the army liaison officer in the fort would telephone the Tiger headquarters and explain who was visiting that day.

Arrangements would be made, and an army liaison officer would accompany the journalist(s) to the turnover gate where, several yards away, an LTTE liaison officer would be waiting. After completion of the Tiger-conducted tour, the visitor would be returned to the fort in time to catch his Sri Lankan air force flight back to Colombo. It was a cozy arrangement, and soon had become almost as automatic as the Eastern Shuttle between Washington and New York.

This neat arrangement lasted for several months until increasing Sri Lankan military activity, the signing of the Indo–Sri Lankan Peace Accord at the end of July, and the subsequent arrival of the Indian peacekeeping force had closed it down. In August only Indian journalists were permitted into the Jaffna Peninsula—under careful supervision of the IPKF. However, the opportunity to visit soon became open to resident diplomats, and the scramble was on. Now diplomats could hold their own, with eyewitness reports from Jaffna; and the first sentences began to form in various minds' eyes ("Yesterday I flew to Jaffna, the first American/British/Soviet/Swedish diplomat to do so in three years. We arrived as dusk fell and soon I was in earnest conversation with . . ."). These first visits took place in an atmosphere of euphoria. The Indian army was in place, and its beneficent influence was calming tensions and permitting a return to normalcy. The Indians—with agreement from the Sri Lankans, more or less—wished the world to observe this development and quickly arranged for "delegations" of foreign diplomats and military attachés to make flying visits to Jaffna. That the Indians were obviously serving their own purposes did not detract from the interest of these outside observers to see for themselves what was happening. Everyone assumed that the rule was "caveat emptor."

In the American embassy there was a discreet scramble to see who could get there first. While displaying casualness towards the possibility, all the substantive officers were itching to be the first American official into Jaffna in several years. One of the political officers made it first. Her eagerness to go was touching and amusing, as was her almost palpable worry that one of her seniors (whom she generally viewed as doddering antiques) would pull rank and go instead.

I then went off on a five-week leave, and by the time I returned in early September several others had made brief visits to Jaffna and other points in the north. To my delight, a similar opportunity opened up for me soon after my return. One morning, quite early, I found myself at Colombo's old airport in the company of diplomatic colleagues from Japan, the UK, Australia, and Sweden, who had agreed to share the costs of a small airplane. Armed with government permission, off we went for a two-day visit to Jaffna. It was an interesting enough trip and equipped me with sufficient on-the-ground expertise to hold up my head in professional discussions in the ensuing weeks. The most interesting event was our group meeting with a senior official of the LTTE Tigers. He was quite smooth and effective, and only went beyond his obvious brief to charm us when asked about the LTTE's political intentions in the event that it were to constitute a government.

All in all, the entire trip was certainly worthwhile, but again demonstrated the essentially anecdotal character of much diplomatic observation. We build theories and interpretations on what we see and whom we talk to. That down the street or at another party something else is happening is a truism that diplomats should never forget.

This relatively happy (for the foreigner) situation persisted in a country awash with domestic violence. Two separate and distinct insurgent groups waged terrorist and guerrilla war against the government, one of them successfully enough to bring about the introduction of a fifty thousand–strong foreign army. Political activists engaged in campaign violence, including murder. Action and reaction followed in quick succession, yet the foreigner wandered about the major cities and much of the countryside in blissful safety. It was almost as if all of the practitioners of violence had reached an agreement that their conflict was strictly intramural and outsiders need not to be involved. Ambushes and murders occurred, and the next day a bus meandered down the road to deposit a group of tourists at a beach hotel. Diplomatic observers spread out through the countryside and returned to Colombo disappointed, with nary a terrorist having been spotted. It was almost as if everybody imposed a form of the peace of God when a foreigner hove into view.

This is quite a rare situation in today's world. Internal conflict and violence are certainly widespread, with a number of the world's countries suffering from some level of politically connected violence—from the Middle East to Sikh terrorists to separatist guerrilla armies in the Sudan to the classic Latin American "revolt in the backland" and urban guerrillas. Usually foreigners are at some risk, and specific foreigners especially so. Americans in particular are often viewed as legitimate targets because of a generalized anti-Americanism or the perception of a specific American political or economic role in the country in question.

That was not the case in Sri Lanka at that time except for Indian citizens, because of the highly unpopular presence of an Indian army on Sri Lankan soil. I have no explanation for this curious state of affairs. The various insurgent groups indulged in a certain amount of modish anti-imperialist political sloganeering, but it seemed almost pro forma and did not lead to action. It may be that the issues at stake were truly local, and the antagonists saw no reason to reach out to make a point or punish a perceived enemy. In a sense it was reminiscent of the nineteenth century, when diplomats and other foreigners could travel through exotic climes by and large exempted from local squabbles.

In any case, this situation posed two problems for embassies in Colombo: how to reassure their own nationals that the appropriate attitude towards the security situation was one of concern but not alarm, and how to phrase advice to potential visitors that threaded its way between providing adequate caution and avoiding alarmist statements. This required careful drafting of travelers' advice sent back to headquarters for general distribution—drafting as delicate as that required for important diplomatic notes and congressional testimony.

Still, the local violence did come close from time to time. One day in mid-February I was sitting at home leafing through a magazine waiting for a luncheon guest to arrive when my steward came into the sitting room and said that the 12:45 news in Sinhala had announced that my guest had just been shot dead in front of his house. He was an interesting, relatively new young political leader who was also the country's most popular film star. I had run into him at the Australian National Day reception a few weeks before and followed up a long chat with an invitation to continue our discussion over lunch one day. All of that was quite a normal incident in the life of a working diplomat; the disruption of our plans by violent death was not. Certainly, this death was not the first in Sri Lanka, only the first that had come close to me. It was also not the last, as more political killings followed over the course of the year. In any case, my involvement was professional and purely fortuitous, as I did not know the man well.

In the following days, I adopted the appropriate public face but found it increasingly difficult to do so, like most people, and especially Sri Lankans, who were much more cynical if not callous. For months after the event friends, colleagues, and acquaintances expressed mock horror at the possibility that I might invite them to lunch.

Another interesting sidelight to this incident was the manner in which my involvement—that is, the American diplomat to whose house the dead man was heading when assaulted—did not become a significant subject of comment or reaction. This was particularly noteworthy, as the murdered man was a political figure of the left and his now revealed and seemingly intimate relationship with an American diplomat could well have become some sort of scandal in Sri Lanka's rather complicated political life. But it did not. There were some rumors and some gossip, even some newspaper references, but by and large the American connection did not in itself become an issue. This was another example of the curious manner in which Sri Lanka's various political (and increasingly violent) conflicts were pursued with comparatively little reference to foreigners other than Indians.

The year 1989 began—in a political sense—on an upbeat note. The sense of relief that followed the more-or-less successful presidential elections continued into the New Year. Parliamentary elections were scheduled and held in February, resulting in a victory for the ruling United National Party—to the surprise of few. While the victory was marred, in the minds of many, by charges of fraud and manipulation, at least most observers (such as the American embassy) felt that the elections had been reasonably representative.

The general mood was upheld by a sense that the violence in the country had subsided significantly. The official and newspaper reporting indicated an encouragingly lower level of violence, and Colombo at least was eager to accept this view. However, hints, then rumor, and then general opinion began to say that the impression was false, and that the violence level was not down, merely the reporting. Government management of the press had been quite effective for a time.

By the end of February the newly elected president, Ranasinghe Premadasa, was joined in Parliament by a majority of his own party and turned to organizing his government. In fairly rapid fashion he did a number of interesting things that demonstrated—for good or ill—that a new government had indeed taken office. He deliberately appointed some of the major political figures of the previous UNP government to backwater assignments. His own major appointments were notable for their lack of reputation or political weight, and he appointed a relative newcomer to the joint portfolios of foreign affairs and defense. Combined with a drastic realignment and reshuffling of the senior civil service, it was clear that Premadasa was setting up his own administration. The Old Establishment was not amused.

An unusual aspect of the new administration was the role played by Premadasa's wife. From the beginning, she was present in a public and prominent way that raised eyebrows—a sort of co-ruler more than a president's spouse. Her prominence on television and in the newspapers was striking, and tongues began to wag. The most striking (to a Westerner) story was that her horoscope was exceptionally powerful and necessary to Premadasa's success. For several months the president's active program of public appearances with his wife in a prominent role was the single most interesting subject of gossip—replacing even the activities of the Indians and the JVP.

Then, suddenly, she disappeared from TV, the newspapers, and all public appearances. Explanations were not long in appearing, some of them rather scandalous, whether true or not. The fact is that in March she disappeared and as of the end of the year remained out of the public eye. Whatever happened, the rest of the world will have to be content with a mystery and lots of gossip.

The political situation deteriorated steadily throughout the year, for reasons too numerous to recount—some old, some new, some internal, some external. Violence for the first part of the year escalated steadily as the northern part of the country appeared to take on a life of its own. Insurgents and government forces acted and reacted. Throughout it all, attention focused on President Premadasa's efforts to govern. In 1988 the central question had been whether the country's democratic and pluralistic political system could surmount its many problems, including attacks upon it, and hold elections. It did, although the elections were closely contested.

In 1989 the question of the future of democratic government was in the air. Sri Lanka provided more than adequate evidence, as if anyone needed it, that man individually and collectively is not a particularly reasonable creature. After all, as the most repeated comment in Colombo put it, how could so much misery and tragedy take place in such a beautiful country? No answer was forthcoming at the time, except an occasional wry reference to the line in the early-nineteenth-century poem, "Where every prospect pleases, and only man is vile." The poem was written about the new English colony of Ceylon at the time.

Although the security situation deteriorated, life in Colombo remained largely unaffected, especially for the urban elite and the expatriate community. The People's Liberation Front (JVP) called numerous general strikes (*hartals*), to which the government responded with curfews. The *hartals* were quite effective, and Colombo resembled a ghost town on some days. All this peaked at the end of July, when President Premadasa organized a diplomatic confrontation with India. Afterwards the government imposed a nightly curfew, although the original time for the curfew to begin was later extended to nine, ten, and then finally midnight. Once it had been moved from six to ten o'clock, the curfew had little effect on Colombo social life, except that everyone was home and tucked in at a more respectable hour. This was much commented on, and people speculated whether they really wanted to return to later hours.

Even the casinos and the discos in the big hotels had little problem, as their clientele were largely people from Singapore and points east who flew in for the purpose of gambling and were already staying at the hotels. The discos also attracted the city's gilded youth. With the excuse of the curfew, which then lasted until four in the morning, they went out before eleven and stayed until the curfew lifted.

For most of the city's inhabitants, the round of *hartals* and curfews had been less amusing. The JVP threatened punishment, namely death, for those who violated their strike calls. The first public service hit by such calls was public transportation, which was vital in this society where people traveled hours from the countryside and small towns to work in the capital. The *hartals* forced the closing of shops, imposing another hardship on the poorer families, who had to earn their pay and do their shopping each day. While Colombo 7, the shorthand reference to the upper class, danced and kept on with its dinner parties, the country suffered. Individuals agonized over the choice of trying to make it to work or going without income and possibly food for the family.

Certainly the JVP had developed an effective program of using force to immobilize the country and challenge the government. When bus drivers were called out on strike, and they refused, the JVP discovered they only had to kill a handful the next day *"pour encourager les autres."* They applied this technique to various elements of the society, including the civil servants, and only came to grief when they threatened and killed families of soldiers and policemen. With an almost audible cry of anger, the security forces turned into vengeful enforcers and demanded retaliation "ten for one." This initiated an active period of effective campaigning against the JVP that cost them the initiative, partially broke the climate of fear in the country, and strengthened the government's hand. Unfortunately, it also resulted in large numbers of bodies scattered around the highways and back roads. The weekly death tolls doubled and tripled. By early October Sri Lanka had become the *Economist*'s standard for a country in serious internal trouble, almost replacing Lebanon. By the end of the year the JVP had been defeated with much bloodshed on both sides—defeated, but not eliminated, persisting as an essentially clandestine radical opposition.

And still life went on in Colombo, and tourists continued to arrive, and the bookings were promising for the winter season. Friends and relatives wrote and called with concern for our safety after each TV report or newspaper article, and we calmed them down with soothing remarks about the peculiar local situation and the privileged situation of foreigners. One gets used to things if they happen gradually. That year's murder rate would have appalled us two years before, but now we almost accepted it, together with the strikes and curfews. I would imagine it was like that in many trouble spots in the world. Was it like that in Europe before World War II? Or in the Chicago of the 1930s?

14

Winding Up

For over a year I had been discussing climbing Sri Pada (Adam's Peak) with several friends. This is the highest point on the island and a religious shrine, especially for Buddhists but for others as well (there is a footprint of the Buddha on top, one of the three places he set foot in Sri Lanka). Climbing it is an act of earning grace, especially during the lunar month of March–April. Its summit is over 7,000 feet, but the climb (rather the walk) up begins at about 3,500 feet.

Traditionally one tries to climb after midnight so as to be at the top for sunrise, which on clear days creates a pyramid-shaped shadow that reaches down to the ocean some thirty miles away.

Two of us left Colombo one Friday afternoon in mid-January to make the climb. We had arranged to have dinner at a tea plantation manager's bungalow near Adam's Peak and then leave for the jump-off point after midnight. However, the manager advised us to leave somewhat earlier as the crowds were already rather large and the climb took at least four or five hours. We reached the parking lot at about midnight and began our climb up. As promised it began easily, and the steps never really did become too steep; certainly it was not rock or mountain climbing in any sense. However, the effort did become increasingly fatiguing as the steps became steeper. My friend set a stiff pace, and by 1:30 a.m. we appeared to be about two-thirds or more of the way up. As I was slowing down, my friend decided to go on, leaving me with the two escorts from the tea plantation.

On I struggled, stopping more and more frequently for breath. About forty minutes later my friend appeared on his way back. He had reached the top but decided it was too cold to wait for me or for sunrise. We had tea in a tea *kiosque*, and he continued down to the car while I continued up. Another hour or so found me at the top, breathing and sweating heavily despite the many pauses. I looked around, regarded the many devotees curled up in blankets and jackets, decided that the wind was indeed too strong and the cold too biting to wait another three hours or so for sunrise, and turned to go down.

Then began a real Calvary. I had been told, and did not believe, that the trip down was worse than the trip up, and so it proved. At first it was lively stepping down instead of lifting one's body up another step. But then the steady pounding of the body and the foot hitting the stone steps began to take its toll. After a while I was convinced that the mountain had grown in the past hour. By the time I reached the parked car (where my friend was sleeping in the back seat) I was exhausted, with extremely sore feet, legs, and thighs. I woke my friend and our driver, said goodbye to our guides, and headed off for Colombo in the dark.

The drive back was pleasant; we dozed in the back seat and then woke to have breakfast at a guesthouse overlooking the location where the movie *The Bridge on the River Kwai* was shot many years ago. We were sorry to have missed the sunrise, but it really would have been a mistake to have waited, shivering, on the mountaintop. Still, we were glad to have gone and to have made that pilgrimage. The mistake we made was in listening to the tea plantation manager's estimate of the time it would take to make it to the top. He did not realize that my friend was a Gurkha from Nepal.

I had not quite realized the significance of that either. With someone else we would have taken four hours up and three hours down, like the little old ladies we kept passing. But no, I had to go with a mountain-bred walker who does this sort of thing for relaxation on his holidays at home in Nepal. I was sore for days.

Fonseka and the Parked Car. One evening we pulled out of the gate, en route to some dinner or other, my driver Fonseka at the wheel as usual. We came up to the main street, Albert Crescent, and turned right to go down a bit and then turn around the center island to head back towards Horton Place. As we came around and passed by the wall of our house, I noticed a car parked on the other side of the street with its lights off but with someone sitting behind the wheel. Suddenly conscious of the security warnings about surveillance, I asked Fonseka to go around once more, right at Independence, down Albert Crescent, right around the island and back past the parked car. Fonseka said little—he rarely did—and drove as asked. This time I clearly noted the parked car, with no lights and the figure behind the wheel, parked along the wall along the back of my garden. I asked Fonseka to go around once more so that I could get the license number, with the idea in mind that I would call our security officer to alert our guards and ask the police to check. As we came around again, the car's lights came on and it pulled away, but not before I got the license plate number. Fonseka appeared reluctant to go around a third time, and I was getting increasingly vocal in demanding to know what was up. With the car gone, I let the matter drop for the moment, although I had every intention of alerting the security officer and the guards in case that particular car should appear again.

The next morning, however, all was explained. As we left for the office, Fonseka diffidently (he is a quiet, well-mannered, and reserved young man) raised the subject of last night's sighting of the parked car. I encouraged him to go on, and he explained that perhaps I had not noticed that just down the street was a covered bus stop. I said I had but asked so what. Fonseka then alluded to the fact that young men and boys tended to frequent that bus stop, and older men in cars sometimes came by or waited nearby. At that point, the penny dropped, and I suddenly realized that a homosexual pickup point existed around the corner from my house. I started to laugh, realizing why Fonseka had appeared a bit hesitant to circle the block the third time, why he made no comment when I speculated about surveillance, and why he had not explained the situation at the time. Madame was in the car, and Fonseka is both too well-brought-up and too reserved to mention such subjects in the presence of a lady. Who says that manners and delicacy are no more?

Personal Projects. I started two personal projects in Sri Lanka, one official and one private. One involved a mongoose and one, Jaguars.

The worldwide traffic in narcotics has become a matter of some concern for the United States government, and among the embassy's various tasks is that of liaison and coordination with the local authorities on the subject. It was not yet a major problem in Sri Lanka, nor was the country an exporter or a major transit point. Nevertheless, these were relative terms, and the Sri Lankan government was worried that narcotics activity in the country was growing, and both governments were concerned about the increasing evidence that at least one of the Tamil separatist groups was funding its activities by drug smuggling from South Asia to Europe.

Soon after my arrival in Colombo, a young colleague who held the narcotics portfolio (among his other duties) arranged a luncheon with four of his most important contacts in the narcotics area, including police and customs. We discussed various aspects of the problem and our bilateral cooperation in the field. At one point we discussed inspection and control mechanisms and airports and ports, and especially the virtues of specially trained sniffer dogs. The subject interested me, as I had some knowledge of the subject from my days in counterterrorism. We all realized that useful as these creatures are, they had disadvantages, notably scarcity, cost of procurement and maintenance, difficulty of adaptation to a tropical climate, and the cultural reaction of Muslims to dogs. I cannot remember exactly who first broached the thought (although I would like to take credit), but suddenly we were discussing the possibility of replacing sniffer dogs in Sri Lanka and elsewhere in the Asia with an indigenous animal, the mongoose.

The more we talked, the more the idea seemed worth pursuing, as the senior policeman present claimed experience with local mongooses as pets and insisted that they were clever, trainable, and notable for their ability to smell.

The next day I raised the subject with my young colleague and asked him to draft a telegram to the Bureau of Narcotics Matters in the department, proposing an experimental project to train mongooses in sniffing narcotics. He appeared surprised, as he had thought our previous day's conversation was simply a lark. He was also obviously a bit embarrassed at the thought of drafting a telegram to the Department of State on what appeared a rather frivolous subject. I assured him that there really was something to explore here, that nothing was frivolous if properly phrased, and that the department's Bureau of Narcotics was flush with money and short of projects.

So he went out to do some research. First, we had to determine if the plural of mongoose was mongeese or mongooses. The answer is mongooses. Then he contacted the local zoo and found the director interested in the idea and prepared to offer staff and space. Through the zoo director he found a young Sri Lankan PhD in zoology at Peradeniya University who was delighted at the thought of directing the project. The police offered cooperation and the necessary small amounts of narcotics for the training. So, there we were, all the details in place. My colleague, now more or less officially appointed as Mongoose Project Coordinator, made some quick calculations and estimated that we could start the project and run it for one year for about $2,000. I felt that was too small a sum to appear serious, so I upped it to $10,000 in the telegram. With some trepidation on his part, and glee mixed with satisfaction on mine, we sent the message off.

The first result was a spate of articles in various newspapers and magazines, to include the *Washington Post* and *Time*. Obviously someone in Washington had leaked our proposal almost within minutes of reading it. The articles were humorous in tone, but not unfavorable. The best one was headlined "Rikki-Tikki-Tavi replaces Rin Tin Tin." I thought that was rather a good line. The next result was approval of the project and authorization of our requested $10,000. I was gratified and the rest of the embassy amused.

The project itself was carried through for about one year, with mixed results. We confirmed that mongooses could indeed learn to identify hidden drugs and point them out to the handlers. However, we were never able to get hold of more than half a dozen young mongooses to train, and our sample was not large enough to determine the reliability of the little animals. (We also had some losses in the training program. One of the most promising of the trainee mongooses got loose from his cage one night, wandered around the corner, and found himself face to face with a huge Bengal tiger, who roared him out of his entire training and into a nervous breakdown.) Washington sent out a specialist in dog training, who inspected our project, confirmed that the results were incomplete but promising, and recommended a further authorization of funds and an expansion of the program. At this point, however, the department lost its nerve (or interest; the U.S. government is not very good at small projects). But the local Sri Lankan authorities remained interested and promised to continue at a reduced level.

It's a pity that the project did not take off. I still think the idea has real possibilities. Still, the PhD promised to write a paper on what he learned about mongooses, and maybe we advanced human knowledge a tiny bit. In any case, newspaper articles on the project continued to appear from time to time, and my young colleague may have learned something about the nature of bureaucracies.

My Jaguar. Sri Lanka was an old car museum, mostly of British models. First, one noticed the ever-present little Morris 1000. It had been years since that that car was seen anywhere, except in the darkest corners of the British Isles. Yet here they were, all over the streets of Colombo, mostly painted black and mostly serving as taxicabs. But the Morrises were only the beginning. Old Jaguar and Mercedes sedans could be seen, usually from the 1960s, but sometimes a delicious old remnant of the forties or fifties or even the prewar era. Some of the older Mercedes sedans immediately reminded the viewer of World War II movies, and you expected to see someone in black boots descend. Every once in a while even rarer cars were seen, for instance, toylike Austin 7s from the thirties and MG two-seaters from the late forties. The reason these older cars remained in service and operating was twofold: the economic conditions of the sixties and seventies made it particularly advantageous to keep older cars running. In addition, there was nostalgia for the old days and an active interest in the older cars themselves. The owner of the Galle Face Hotel was very proud of a prewar Austin owned by Prince Philip (bought for fifteen pounds when the prince was a young naval officer on duty in Colombo just before the war).

Some cars were family heirlooms. A neighbor and friend went out to his garage every now and then to crank up and go for a spin in a 1914 Pipe—a Belgian car whose very name is lost to history. His grandfather bought it on his honeymoon trip to Europe, and an uncle drove it around town until the mid-1950s. The car was a member of the family as much as a vehicle. He kept it in working condition and often invited me to cruise around town on quiet Sunday mornings.

A young officer in the embassy responded to the opportunities offered by this situation to search out and purchase an MG-TD for restoration. Inspired by his initiative, and an old unfulfilled passion to own a Jaguar, I followed his example and began to search for the model I wanted. This search led to some interesting contacts, as I discovered the existence of a whole subculture of old car buffs in Colombo. One kept discovering that Sri Lanka was not your standard Less Developed Country.

I had always lusted after the Mark II model of the Jaguar. When I discovered that some were available in Sri Lanka and that restoration capabilities were also available—at a very low cost—I decided to make the purchase and restoration of an old Jaguar sedan my personal project for the Sri Lankan tour. After about nine months of searching and checking out some old cars (almost being diverted by a couple of Mercedes 170s from the late 1940s) I finally settled on a Jaguar Mark I sedan, which I purchased in August 1987.

Why I ended up with a Mark I rather than a Mark II was probably due to the fault of my impatience. The cars are similar, although the Mark II is, I think, better looking. Nevertheless, I bought the Mark I on the advice of my technical assistant in this project, the owner-manager of the company that would be doing the work. He was a young (thirty-fiveish) Sri Lankan graduate of Cambridge who loved old cars. Anyway, I took his advice and will always be a little sorry. I do that sort of thing often. Among other things, it turned out that he underestimated the differences between the Mark I and the Mark II. In fact, Jaguar made many changes between the two models; and as the Mark I was never produced in large numbers, the changes all increased the cost and difficulty in obtaining new and/or used spare parts. It certainly increased the complexity and the time necessary to complete it. On the other hand, the Mark I is somewhat rarer, so what the hell.

The restoration project began in August 1987, and by mid-October 1989, as I approached departure for my next post, the car was not quite finished. The two events—my departure and the completion of the restoration—shared a close finish.

All in all, however, the project was a lot of fun. I spent a fair amount of time peering into the innards of my car and others. I also spent a certain amount of time calling on Jaguar spare parts dealers in England and the United States, writing and telephoning others in the world of Jaguar lovers. I cannot claim to have learned anything about the mechanical side, but I have learned the old rule—vital for those who are having things done for them. You do not have to know anything about the subject itself, but you have to know what you want and what questions to ask. I estimate that a couple of questions I did not ask added many months and untold costs to the project. Oh, well.

About a year before the end of my tour I actually thought that the project was close to its finish. I foolishly began to talk again about the car and its expected completion. (I had talked quite a bit about it at various dinner tables the first year of work and then tailed off.) Now it was again a subject of conversation. I discovered that when I did not raise the subject, others did. Apparently, it had become a bit of a legend around town. Certainly, my ambassador took every public opportunity to pronounce that the whole thing was a fraud, and that no Jaguar actually existed.

Anyway, completion was near, and apparently the car would make it to New York. Therein lay a problem I had not expected. I had not envisioned being assigned to New York, where I would not like to have any sort of car—much less a cream white, leather interior, completely restored 1956 Jaguar Mark I saloon. What in God's name was I going to do with it there? Friends who know New York said it would not last thirty minutes on the street before being stolen or trashed. But it was a lovely project, and I had met some very nice people doing it, and I enjoyed myself. (My experience back in New York and Washington with this car was neither enjoyable nor successful, but that is a story for another day.)

People. Whatever we do is largely about people, in various ways. Shortly after arrival in Colombo, I began the thrice-weekly Sinhala-language lessons that seemed to be expected of me. The ambassador and others were taking the course as well, and it did seem to be the thing to do. I continued doggedly throughout my three years, although my progress in the language was minimal. I have never been an especially successful learner of languages for their own sake, and the atmosphere in Sri Lanka was not supportive. Peace Corps volunteers in the villages do well, but senior diplomats in Colombo do not. Our interlocutors, by and large, speak excellent English and (often) meager Sinhala themselves. Our servants and subordinates speak at minimum useful English and react with embarrassed smiles when we attempt our first halting words of Sinhala. Most Sinhalese—and I have had this confirmed by many Sri Lankan friends—cannot conceive of a foreigner speaking their language and therefore do not hear it even when it is being uttered. How different from, say, the Spanish-speaking peoples, whose first reaction to hearing a Gringo say *"Buenos días"* is to proclaim him a new Lope de Vega.

I made little progress in learning any useful Sinhala and turned the sessions into an informal seminar on Sri Lankan society. My teacher for the first year was a well-known local character actor, if a poor teacher, and taught me about Sinhalese family names and certain attitudes and customs. My second teacher never made much of a mark at all, but in any case, did not last long. My third teacher was a charming, educated Sinhalese schoolteacher and mother. She was also an excellent teacher, and I even began to learn some spoken Sinhalese (if I had started with her, I might have made real progress). However, our discussions of the day's events, of Sinhalese words and phrases, of local moods and attitudes, and of local jokes and rumors were all informative and amusing. If I never made any real progress in spoken Sinhala, I had many a pleasant hour early in the morning just talking over events with someone not quite a friend, not quite an employee, not quite a teacher. It was, I assure any readers who are taxpayers, well worthwhile.

Another aspect of people management involved the dismissal of a local employee, a Foreign Service National, as we call them. He had been boss of our warehouse for many years, but it was increasingly clear he had been promoted above his level of competence. Having performed well as boss of the furniture-moving crew, he had been promoted and never managed to handle the broader administrative and recordkeeping tasks. But he was both nice and willing. Generations (in the Foreign Service, that usually means two years) of relatively junior administrative officers had put up with him, either covering the administrative work themselves, or letting it slide, or a combination of the two.

Finally, an aggressive young officer decided to bite the bullet and place our hapless FSN on a one-year program to learn the skills of his job or be fired. The year passed, and it was obvious that he could not make the grade. A dismissal notice was issued, regretfully but firmly. The situation now became complicated, as our now former employee—obviously with the advice and encouragement of another more experienced FSN—appealed his dismissal to the Embassy Employment Review Panel. Most of us were unaware of the pertinent regulations and even the existence of the board, even those of us who sat on it. But the appeal was duly made and the process had to be pursued.

We members of the board were all somewhat uneasy once we had reviewed the file. First, the appellant's attractive character and long, faithful service was painfully evident. Second, in his eagerness our young administrative officer had clearly cut a few corners and transgressed due process. Nevertheless, it was also equally clear that the appellant (a) could not do the job, (b) had never really done the job, and (c) his inability to do so was becoming increasingly burdensome to the post. We compromised at first by allowing the appeal process to run out lengthily and painfully. Over several weeks, we spent hours in interviews and review of documents and detailed discussion over the appropriateness of the relevant job description, the opportunities given the appellant to pull up his socks, and the handling of his final testing and dismissal. Finally, with no alternative available, we had to confirm the dismissal notice, making some administrative (and financial) arrangements to compensate at least partially for any improper procedures. (That is, he got another month's pay out of us.)

We admitted that our painstaking effort in this case was partially to salve our consciences about the firing of this nice man (firing a crook is easy). American Foreign Service types are not hard-nosed business executives, nor should they be. Nevertheless, we also agreed the procedure we had followed had been educational. We had learned quite a bit about our own regulations, a good deal about one of our administrative operations, something about our locally employed colleagues, and a little bit more about ourselves.

Dealing with one's American colleagues is a relatively more complicated and never-ending task. This is always true for everyone in every walk of life, but the environment is especially intense for diplomats because of the relatively isolated and yet public atmosphere of a diplomatic post. On post, the diplomatic staff (in our case, American) are operating in someone else's world, but as an extension of their own—a little bit of bureaucratic America detached from the main, so to speak.

The relationships are complicated by the fact that within the larger body of the mission (or consulate) there are subdivisions of section and function (administrative, political, and consular affairs) and home agency or department (State Department, Agency for International Development, military attachés, and so forth). This is surprising to most people who believe that embassies are filled only with diplomats. In fact, on a worldwide basis, only approximately 20 to 25 percent of the American staff are State Department Foreign Service. The rest come from the mob of other agencies that deal with foreign affairs because the nation has a need for their services, or because that is where the drama is in today's government. Therefore, the inevitable range of personal relationships, from full understanding and cooperation to nasty backbiting, is intermingled with an equivalent range of institutional squabbling. The two are often intertwined, as two officers find their personal chemistry bad and their organizational objectives competitive.

It is interesting, edifying, and even amusing, therefore, to watch the shift of relationships as officers come and go. For instance, I had a very easy and comfortable relationship with one colleague, the head of another agency. He left and his replacement and I found that our relationship soon became somewhat uneasy and always on the edge of conflict. Why? I have my own opinions, of course, which placed the blame on him, and I may even be right. Still, only a slight shift in personal characteristics can bring about a new situation without anyone wishing it so.

All human beings share roughly the same set of characteristics, but the mixture is different, much like the physical characteristics of the human face. All have the same components—nose, eyes, mouth—yet even among those of a homogeneous group, the occurrence of two similar faces is rare (twins aside, of course; but they only prove the point). So apparently it is with personalities. Slight but numerous differences in personality and emotional traits produce different characters and thus a different set of relationships within a community. A Foreign Service post is a small community, and the tone and atmosphere in it therefore changes and flows as people come and go. Awareness of this fluidity and some success in channeling it have become recognized parts of modern leadership and management. I found it an absorbing and continually difficult task and can only claim reasonable success.

One reason for my modest claim came to my attention as my final days in Colombo drew near. My ambassador, Jim Spain, was a widower of somewhat crusty habits and Old Service attitudes like the importance of duty. My wife and I did not have children and shared what I like to think are Old Service manners. The political tensions of the past few years had caused some strains, between the ambassador and me on the one side and some of the younger members of the community on the other over differing ideas toward career responsibilities and (probably most important) children at post. My replacement had arrived at post, and, apart from his other virtues, he came equipped with two (charming) teenaged daughters. The obvious reaction of some staff was that the arrival of one of their own signaled a more sympathetic Front Office in the offing. (Possibly, but they may have been fooling themselves.)

Much of the mood at a post depends upon the quantity and quality of humor that individuals bring to it. For instance, if one agency head with whom I had an uneasy relationship had ever shown any ability to laugh at himself, his agency, the embassy, the world, or me, we might have gotten along much better. An excess of unmitigated seriousness may be career enhancing, but it does create a personality "of an enormous boringness," as a Portuguese colleague used to say.

My final year included other minor official and personal adventures. I had hoped to do more traveling, but the combination of the political situation and official responsibilities precluded my having much success. I did finally get to Trincomalee Harbor; it was impressive, but not in the sense most people in this part of the world believe. To many Sri Lankans and many Indians, the name alone calls up dramatic pages of history, of the Empire, of the Raj, of the sweep of fleets and armies in pursuit of empire. They still believe it to be of potential strategic importance and that the great powers are lusting for its possession. Actually, in the modern world it is of little or no military use to anyone, and certainly not worth much of a price. But history and feelings of self-importance dissipate slowly, and many find ulterior motives in unrelated American actions and statements, or the lack of them, at any given moment—either is open to interpretation.

But Trinco Harbor was superb. And what struck me was its potential as a tourist center—a potential Acapulco of the East. All the potential for a water sports center is present and nothing serious in the way of development would need to be cleared away. Wellington's troops and the Bombay Marine are gone; battalions of German tourists await.

Ambassador Spain retired in June, and I assumed responsibility as chargé d'affaires, pending a new ambassador. Though his arrival was delayed, I departed Colombo a few weeks beforehand. Too bad—I was rather looking forward to handing over, as too few opportunities exist to complete assignments formally. Normally we just move on to the next post. But I would have enjoyed driving out to the airport in the Cadillac with the American flag and the chargé's flag flying, meeting the newly assigned ambassador at the steps of his airplane, and then driving back into town with the ambassadorial flag replacing the chargé's. We have little enough ceremony in life.

The departure of Ambassador Spain opened up an interesting period for me. His seniority and reputation had provided somewhat of a screen against home-headquarters meddling. With his departure the full force hit me, and what a depressing phenomenon it was. The department and presumably most, if not all, of the U.S. government had become obsessed with a sort of self-protective CYA mindset. One had the impression that most people in Washington were spending their time identifying possible problems on which to zero in with a pompous new regulation, warning, or guidance message. Having done so, they could sit back and say, "See what a good boy am I!" Meanwhile the system was drowning in paper and rules. Max Weber again.

Occasionally, this situation offers a moment of pure joy. An inspection team had been scheduled for some months, with a tentative date of November. In late September they decided to come in mid-October, leaving me somewhat less than enthusiastic, as their visit would coincide with my last two weeks at post. Instead of concentrating on wrapping up my affairs and saying goodbye, my last days in Sri Lanka would be complicated by the care and feeding of an inspection team. I was not amused.

Still, sometimes a merciful universe intervenes. The day prior to the team's arrival, we discovered that the department had failed to provide us with the inspectors' security clearance information, although a recent onerous and meddlesome telegram had informed us that no official visitor was to be given unescorted access to official facilities without such a security notice as part of their authorizing telegrams. We dutifully notified the department of this shortcoming, waited patiently, and found ourselves facing the inspectors on their first day without a reply. In other words, the inspectors lacked authority to inspect by virtue of this new department regulation. Oh joy! After a few minutes of preliminary exchange of gossip (two of the four inspectors were old friends) I turned serious and mentioned that we had a problem: to wit, the new regulation and their lack of clearance. They were not amused, but our side enjoyed ourselves thoroughly.

Meanwhile, the packers for my move had come and gone, and the accumulated goods of this assignment were on their way to the next. At this point the house was a bit empty and certainly depersonalized, rather like a hotel room waiting for the next guest. We had lived there happily for three years and three months, and it was time to move on. We had done this a number of times in the past, but it gets more difficult each time, especially as we had found it an especially satisfying assignment. We were sorry to leave, and sad. We had not merely been *en poste* in Sri Lanka; we had *lived* there. We were leaving friends and familiar sights that we would miss.

As we were packing, political developments continued apace, including political developments of some promise. In less than two weeks, though, I would have to check in the *New York Times* to see what was happening in Sri Lanka. As that news was sporadic and would appear only if dramatic in character (bang-bang journalism, generally), I slowly found I had drifted away from those events. Sri Lanka would join other memories of places and situations and, like them, become somewhat frozen in time. My Sri Lanka would join my Kenya, my Zambia, my Belgium, my Zaire, Angola, Mexico, Cape Verde, and Guinea-Bissau.

That is my world.

15

Turtle Bay

In the run-up to leaving Colombo, I had contacted people about a follow-up job. It was soon clear I would not be offered a chief-of-mission position, but two interesting possibilities surfaced. One was an office directorship in the Bureau of Intelligence Research, and the other was as head of the Social and Economic Section of the U.S. Mission to the United Nations in New York, both interesting and tempting for various reasons. In the end I took the guarded advice of an old friend, in fact the person who offered me the INR job. He was a classic New Yorker and could not resist reminding me of the attractions of New York as a place to live. I realized my career was approaching its end in any case. Time was running out, and Aida was as attracted by the idea of living in New York as I was, so we decided to head to Manhattan. We never regretted that decision.

The first thing I discovered about New York was that I immediately felt at home. We had arrived in November 1989, the day before Macy's Thanksgiving Day parade, having stopped by Washington to pick up some winter clothes from Security Storage. New York, indeed all of the East Coast, was experiencing a record-breaking snowstorm. We left our hotel the next morning and went out to see the parade, despite banks of snow all over town. The parade—the first time we had ever seen it—was fun, and I noticed that I felt right at home in New York. I had visited the city in the past, but always as a tourist. Now, possibly because I knew we had arrived to stay for some time, I viewed the city differently and felt excited and comfortable at the prospect of living there. It was a feeling that never left me during our four years in New York. On visits ever since I feel like I am returning to, not visiting, Manhattan.

In previous long-distance telephone conversations with the administrative office of the U.S. Mission to the United Nations (USUN, as it is generally referred to), we had agreed on a mission-leased apartment on the Upper East Side—my introduction to the complicated social and economic geography of Manhattan. I had no idea of the implications of that sort of address, but more knowledgeable friends and relatives provided guidance. When our household effects arrived from Security Storage, we soon settled into the life of Manhattan apartment dwellers. This was not difficult to do, as our permanent home in Washington was an apartment and we had fond memories of apartment living in Brussels.

We soon discovered that the New York version of apartment living had its quirks and differences, almost all good. Manhattan is essentially an apartment city and is so organized. Regardless of New York's reputation as a hard place, it is easy to live in. Out the door, down the elevator, and one finds all of life's necessities—cleaners, drug stores, grocers, hardware, specialty shops, locksmiths, other services, and lots of pubs and restaurants—within a two-block radius. In fact, there are usually two or three of each within spitting distance, so one quickly gets into the New York habit of selecting the ones that are yours. This is a variation on the well-known New York passion for searching out the best new little restaurant that your friends haven't heard of yet. New Yorkers are in a perpetual search for the "best" address or supplier. This is not only a game of oneupmanship; it also reflects the fact that in almost all activities high standards of performance really do exist in New York—from opera to dry-cleaning.

The professional side of life was a little more difficult. At least at first, multilateral diplomacy differs quite a bit from the bilateral experience I had acquired in thirty-some years in the Foreign Service. As deputy U.S. representative to the Economic and Social Council (ECOSOC) and minister-counselor for Economic and Social Affairs (multilateral diplomacy goes in for long titles) my new responsibilities focused on the UN's intergovernmental bodies dealing with economic and social matters in ECOSOC itself, in the Second and Third Committees of the General Assembly, and with a plethora of what are called Specialized Agencies, Funds, and Programs. The specialized agencies, funds, and programs are a collection of UN organizations dealing with economic and social matters, many of which, such as UNICEF and UNHCR, are better known than the UN itself. My predecessor was still at post when I arrived and generously shared his experience as he attempted to fit me into my new world. It was a daunting task, as my initial reaction to that new world was one of disorientation and confusion, combined with incredulity. So much for thirty years of diplomatic experience!

To understand this "new world" of mine the reader may require some background explanation on the United Nations environment and my place in it. Even though I was a professional diplomat of long experience, I knew little about the United Nations. I needn't feel abashed by this lack of knowledge, as it is common among almost everyone, including usually well-informed people such as journalists and politicians. The essential characteristic of the UN is that it exists on two levels—the intergovernmental and the bureaucratic. The intergovernmental level constitutes the political organization, where governments (the member states) meet. It has the authority to dispose of money and other resources. This is the UN of the Security Council, the General Assembly, and the other intergovernmental bodies. It is a permanent convention, or conference, of nation-states.

The other UN consists of a bewildering array of organizations with complicated names (UN Development Program, UN High Commission for Refugees, the International Labor Organization, and so on), all doing good work and nominally headed by the secretary general of the United Nations, a political figure of some prestige and little power. In fact, the whole UN system is remarkably devoid of power, authority, or resources. The UN organization cannot levy taxes or pass regulations, much less give orders. Its programs in public health, development, and related fields depend upon grudging annual contributions by member states. In the political and moral areas, it has no army or police but depends completely on moral suasion, political and economic influence, or military pressure exercised on its behalf by member states. In the end, it is they who decide and they who enforce.

That anyone can fear this UN and its imaginary fleet of black helicopters is beyond belief.

The UN world is global, with personnel and employees all over the world: distributing food and medicine, running peacekeeping operations, testing soil samples, fighting terrorism and drug traffickers, protecting human rights, and always pursing complicated bureaucratic procedures. UN employees, after all, are international civil servants.

New York is one of the UN's three headquarters, the other two being Geneva and Vienna. New York is by the far the "most equal" of the three, although Geneva grumbles at that ranking. But the Security Council, the General Assembly, and the secretary general and central organization are located in New York, and it is difficult for the other two sites to compete in prestige and importance.

It was to this central United Nations that I was now posted and in which I would live and work for several years. The UN headquarters is located in the Turtle Bay area of midtown Manhattan along the East River on a site donated by Nelson Rockefeller. Its major building, the Secretariat, is an architectural icon well known around the world and one of New York's major tourist sites, a fact ignored by those who grumble about various aspects of the UN presence in New York, such as traffic jams and diplomats who appear to park wherever they wish. New Yorkers dislike seeing foreigners with a license to do this, as they prefer to reserve that privilege for themselves. Grouped around the well-known UN headquarters building are a number of other edifices the UN owns or rents, plus a number of permanent missions (or embassies), mostly spread out in the adjoining streets. Some of these missions consist of office suites of varying degrees of luxury, while the United States and others have built freestanding buildings. The Uganda mission was right next to the U.S. mission and was one floor higher, reputedly by direct order of Uganda's one-time president, Idi Amin.

Many diplomats and UN staff also live in the neighborhood, although most live further afield, with not a few residing in New York's commuter suburbs. The key characteristic of this UN neighborhood of a few square blocks of Manhattan is the presence of thousands of diplomats, UN officials, and assorted onlookers—not to mention tourists—through much of the working day and well into the evening hours. They spend their days in their offices and conference rooms, in the innumerable meeting rooms and halls of the UN itself, and in the equally numerous Manhattan restaurants and bars. As important as the concentration of officials is their composition. A large percentage are diplomats, and most of the rest are international civil servants. It is the diplomats, however, who tend to set the tone, as they are by and large a more prestigious crowd than mere civil servants. Furthermore, many of the UN senior officials are diplomats by training and background (and often intend to return to that profession). Finally, as the UN is in essence a permanent conference of nation-states, the diplomats are in a real sense the true core of the UN system. As noted, all authority and power in the UN flows from its member states, and the diplomats posted to their missions in New York are the visible representation of that authority.

One way to look at the UN in New York is to see it as a diplomatic community, such as one can find in any major capital, albeit bigger, and one that exists without being accredited to a national government. In a sense, therefore, the UN in New York is classic diplomacy in its purest form, without the distraction of a local government and real-time political and economic developments and pressures. For those who have experience of such things, I suggest they remember the monthly luncheon meeting of the Corps Diplomatique common in many capital cities and multiply it by several factors. Professional diplomats love it.

As a senior officer of the U.S. mission, I was a fully paid-up member of this community. The American mission is naturally an important element of this community. Despite the existence of what could be called an anti-American majority in the UN community (the Soviet bloc plus many Third World countries) and an anti-UN attitude shared by many in the American body politic, the United States as one of the two major world powers and a permanent member of the Security Council with veto power, not to mention being the host country, remains a major player in UN events. This role is illustrated by the thirteen-story USUN mission located on the corner of First Avenue and Forty-Fourth Street, directly across the street from the delegates' entrance to the United Nations. No other country's UN mission is nestled so closely.

Though a senior officer of USUN with the rank of minister-counselor and head of a section (Economic-Commercial), I was only fifth in the mission's pecking order. Above me were the four officers with ambassadorial title: the permanent representative himself, Thomas Pickering, his deputy, Alex Watson, and two others—one of whom, Jonathan Moore, the United States representative to the Economic and Social Council, was my immediate boss. USUN was (and is) a large mission, with several hundred staff members, including seven others at my rank of minister-counselor. Few other missions were as large, except of course for those of the Soviet Union and China. We Americans filled up seven pages in the UN Diplomatic List, the Soviets six, and the Chinese five. This ratio could be found around the world in most capital cities and reflected in some way the world-power pecking order.

I arrived in the middle of the annual General Assembly, which runs from September through December, usually ending just before the Christmas holiday. According to local legend, this schedule was set in the earliest days of the UN and was based upon the transatlantic sailing schedules and the desire of most senior and special delegates to return home for the holidays. The tradition continues, and the UNGA is a high-pressure diplomatic conference. While not the Congress of Vienna, the concentration of chiefs of state and government at the beginning of the GA is impressive; even American presidents show up to open the session. After they leave, the permanent missions, augmented by special delegates and additional staff, throw themselves into an orgy of meetings, which produce hundreds of resolutions. Underneath the formal conference rooms shown on TV and to tourists, there are several floors of small rooms where the delegates meet in what seem to be an unending series of "official-informal" and "informal-informal" meetings, where the exquisitely nuanced language of UN resolutions is negotiated. The work of the GA is formally confirmed in the major committees (Political, Special Political, Economic, Social, Financial, Legal, Trusteeship), but it is mostly done in this swirling world of working committees.

Working hours at the UN are actually quite long throughout the year, but during the GA they are staggering. During a General Assembly twelve-hour days are normal, and working around the clock is not unknown. My longest negotiation was a two-week negotiation on UN reform, with increasingly longer days culminating in a five-day weekend during which I got home twice (for a total of about six hours).

It was, and I presume still is, a hothouse atmosphere. Delegates (diplomats) ran from meeting to meeting from early morning to late evening, carrying sheaves of papers. Some delegates from missions located relatively far from First Avenue would arrive in the morning with large briefcases full of papers and remain at the UN all day, going from meeting to meeting, interspersed with coffee, lunch, and cocktail breaks. For others, meetings were intermingled with quick trips back to the mission to check up on instructions from home and consultations with colleagues and home offices. The long days included luncheons, cocktail parties, and dinners little different from meetings, except that food and drink were being served. The delegates' lounge (and bar), coffeehouse, and dining room were mere extensions of the meeting rooms. The work done in the committees expanded outside to the wide world of Manhattan's bars and restaurants. Spouses were generally absent from these affairs (by choice I believe) during the GA as the conversation was little more than extended negotiation and information-sharing about negotiations—one hundred percent shop talk. After most evening drinks parties, most of us went back to the office or to the meeting rooms for continued negotiations.

When I arrived in the midst of this diplomatic madness, my predecessor was still on the job and stayed for several weeks to break me in. Even with his solicitous guidance, it was a daunting experience. It was not so much the hothouse atmosphere, the sheer number of players, or the pace of activity as the apparent subject matter. Each document I looked at and every meeting I attended seemed both arcane and incoherent. The subjects were mostly new to me—deep-sea fishing, Palestinian rights, UNDP development strategy, NGO accreditation to the UN, elections to obscure UN bodies, and so on. As a long-serving diplomat I was used to jumping into new environments and dealing with new subjects; the problem here was the manner in which these subjects were being dealt with in the intergovernmental world of the UN.

As my initiation occurred well into the life of this particular General Assembly, the activity under way was the basic work of such organizations—the drafting of resolutions, hundreds of resolutions—each one submitted by one or more delegations with the objective of getting on the record one or several viewpoints. In addition to the nominal subject of the resolution, there might often be an additional political subtext. A draft resolution on UNDP strategic planning, for example, might include language validating the role of the Palestine Liberation Organization in UN development projects or implying the right of Pakistan to some sort of formal status in Indian-controlled Kashmir. Israeli diplomats would be on the lookout for the former and Indian representatives for the latter.

For these reasons the drafting of UN resolutions was and is a tedious business involving beady-eyed diplomats carefully vetting every word in every sentence. Long hours are spent negotiating language, before resolutions are formally presented for vote in the appropriate committee of the General Assembly. The convention since the late 1980s has been to seek consensus, meaning that resolutions would be passed with no negative votes, if not unanimously. Though obviously not always possible, this is achieved in a remarkably large number of cases. Such resolutions are thus written in a special, careful language of compromise. Nuances are everything in UN drafting, and often fairly dramatic decisions are couched in language requiring expert knowledge to decipher.

Or at least this is the claim of protagonists. One of the most famous of these resolutions is Security Council Resolution 242, which was passed following the 1967 war in the Middle East. It calls for Israel to pull back from "occupied territories." The debate as to what that phrase means continues to this day in almost every meeting of the GA into which the Arab bloc can introduce it—all the occupied territory or some of the occupied territories? Naturally, each side claims its interpretation is the valid one.

During my first year at USUN, we spent a lot of time on a proposal to create a new UN department to deal with humanitarian intervention. The idea was to provide greater UN capability to deal with both natural and manmade disasters that threatened large numbers of people with death or privation—famines, floods, civil wars, the collapse of governments, and the like. The proposal was to create a new department designed to pull together and manage this type of UN crisis management and to authorize the UN to intervene in natural and manmade catastrophes. While there was a general agreement about the desirability of this proposal, there was at the same time great concern among members of the Group of 77 (the countries of the Third World, of whom more will be said later), who feared that the new authority and capability to intervene in humanitarian disasters was really a cover for the renewed effort of the First World (the West, the rich, and the former colonialists) to intervene in the internal affairs of the newly independent.

The resolution creating the new Department of Humanitarian Affairs took over one year to negotiate, and the final language was carefully designed to ensure—in the minds of the Group of 77—that it did not authorize meddling in internal affairs of member states. This careful qualification is occasionally thrown out the window when member states, including those belonging to the Group of 77, want to interfere in the affairs of their neighbors, such as Arab states with respect to Israel, some African states in the case of the Great Lakes genocide, and lots of people in the case of Indonesia and East Timor.

The vast majority of resolutions can be seen objectively as tempests in a teapot. Important resolutions are few and far between, though with a few exceptions such as "Uniting for Peace" back in the Korean War days and several resolutions on global warming, which raised that issue to a position of priority in international affairs.

But viewed in its totality, as an ongoing conversation among nation-states and increasingly now among the general public through pressure groups, every country can strut its brief hour upon the stage—can, at the UN, have its moment at the rostrum to express its views and its concerns. No subject is missed: child health, ethnic aspirations, economic development and the relief of poverty, government corruption, preservation of native cultures, disarmament, the role of women, colonialism and neocolonialism, deep-sea fishing, the preservation of cultural artifacts, and on and on. It is true that concrete decisions and actions do not often emerge from these discussions, but they often do result from other meetings and venues. But intergovernmental treatment in the GA, ECOSOC, and other UN bodies constitute the global town hall meeting in which concerns get raised.

The anti-UN crowd in the United States ignores this aspect of the UN. "A talking shop" is a common dismissive title for the UN, as if talking and open discussion were not a traditional and important characteristic of civilized, not to mention democratic, countries. Interestingly, the importance a country places on the UN and this multinational conversation is almost inversely related to that country's weight or power in the world. The smaller, poorer, and/or weaker a country, the more value it places on the UN and its participation. This is not surprising, as Thucydides long ago pointed out the limited role available to small countries in the international arena. The UN (apart from the important distinction of the Security Council) is organized on a one-state/one-vote principle embodying the theoretical and legal equality of sovereign states. Therefore, even the smallest of governments and countries have their seats at the table. This is not a small achievement in a world struggling to implement ideas of democracy and human rights.

The converse of the importance given to the UN by small states is the comparative disinterest with which larger countries view the organization. Still, most countries, even quite important ones, grant the UN a reasonable role in their worldview. The United States, however, comes close to disdain in its attitude.

This is true despite the central role the U.S. played in creating the UN, the importance we gave it through the 1950s, and the Clinton administration's attempt (largely verbal and not especially effective) to multilateralize American foreign policy following the implosion of the Soviet Union. The reasons for the loss of U.S. passion for the UN are complex, but two are particularly important. First, the end of colonialism in the 1950s and 1960s produced a vast influx of new countries into the UN, countries with leaders motivated by emotional anti-Westernism. The U.S. lost its ability to produce dependable majorities in UN bodies, and many Americans decided therefore to take their marbles and go home. That attitude was supported by many Americans' realization that the UN was full of foreigners, and that they did not always agree with American interests—another reason, in the minds of many, to take our marbles and leave.

Despite this history, service at USUN at the end of the Cold War was an exciting experience. As the Soviet Union disintegrated, so did the Soviet bloc at the UN. The Soviet Permanent Mission became the Permanent Mission of the Russian Republic. The hitherto obedient permanent missions of the Ukraine and Belarus started to show signs of independence. The other Soviet bloc missions turned independent overnight, it seemed. From slavish diplomatic foot soldiers of the Soviets, they quickly became almost obstreperous spokespersons for their newly "democratic and capitalistic" governments, for democracy and capitalism were now the only ideological games in town.

The turnaround in the behavior of the now Russian mission was most striking. Seemingly bereft of instructions from Moscow, Russian diplomats in New York turned to the U.S. mission for guidance. They always seemed to be hanging around us, chatting in a friendly fashion and being almost embarrassingly cooperative on a wide range of issues. This new behavior appeared to be especially sincere on the part of the younger officers. They gave the impression of being relieved at dropping their old attitudes and language. I soon made a number of new friends among the Russian mission staff working in the Second and Third Committees, friendships that remained well into my retirement. Some Russian observers, experts, and analysts had been saying for years that Communist ideology was dead in the USSR and that the bureaucratic elite and working class alike had pretty much abandoned ideology and adopted a more or less cynical attitude towards the government and official positions. Our new extensive professional and personal interaction with Russian diplomats in the early 1990s confirmed that analysis.

The varying reactions among what we used to call the satellite countries of Eastern Europe were amusing to track. For a while, some of these East European embassies appeared to be engaged in intramural combat between the old staff and the newer arrivals representing the post–Cold War government taking control in their capitals. Most East European embassies were quickly "democratized," but it was amusing to watch, for instance, the tugging that went on between the two competing cliques in the Polish Embassy. The rest of us watched how Polish positions on certain subjects varied depending on which Polish diplomat showed up for a meeting.

Even more striking was the two-year transition of the relationship between the Russians, the Belarusians, and the Ukrainians. The horrible 1986 nuclear accident at Chernobyl in the Ukraine was the subject of a Russian-Belarusian-Ukrainian-sponsored resolution in ECOSOC to obtain general world recognition of the gravity of the accident and, not incidentally, financial assistance from the world community through UN agencies. The resolution was originally drafted so as to call for assistance in language that implied that member states would have at least the moral obligation to provide additional financial contributions to the relevant UN agencies (especially the World Health Organization and the International Atomic Energy Agency) for the benefit of Belarus and Ukraine—the country that had suffered the most damage from Chernobyl. The Belarusian and Ukrainian interests were obvious, as was the Russian. The new Russian Federation was embarrassed by the accident, impoverished with the collapse of the USSR, and being held responsible by the other two as the heir to the USSR. The ECOSOC resolution ploy was an attempt by Moscow to demonstrate its concern and sympathy and obtain some financial relief from the Belarusian and Ukrainian claims.

The ploy was obvious, and the rest of the (rich) world was willing to provide bilateral assistance and to authorize UN assistance within existing budgets. That was the rub: within existing budgets. The U.S. government took a strong stand on this issue; and, as the chief of the ECOSOC section, I ended up in a two-year negotiation with the three delegations. It was a typical UN negotiation, with many meetings and seemingly endless verbal maneuvering, which finally produced a resolution that expressed strong sympathy for the victims of Chernobyl, authorized UN agencies to provide as much assistance as possible within existing budgets, and urged countries to provide bilateral assistance to Belarus and the Ukraine. The phrase "within existing budgets" was the key phrase, as it meant that no one (and most especially the U.S.) was obligated to provide additional money.

The locally interesting aspect of this development was the shift in relations among the diplomats from the three countries. At the beginning, the Russian diplomat did all the talking, while the representatives from Belarus and the Ukraine sat silent and nodded. This was the traditional role of diplomats from those two nominally independent countries. After some months, as the venue of our essentially bilateral discussions continued, mostly in UN coffee bars in New York or Geneva, the Belarusian delegate began to become agitated and forceful, expressing opinions independent of his Russian colleague. Some months later the character of the talks went through another change as the Ukrainian permanent representative took a direct hand. From then on he led the negotiation, with the support of the Belarusian delegate, while the Russian delegate kept silent and participated only with his presence and occasional technical comments. In the two years from 1990 to 1992, these talks reflected the fundamental change in relationships between Moscow, Kiev, and Minsk. The Soviet empire had well and truly dissolved.

The closed world of UN diplomats was marked by two characteristics: the substance was global, while the focus was on local processes. The subject might be the role of women in development, but the activity under way was the phrasing of the prospective resolution and vote solicitation. In the rarified world of the UN diplomatic community, success is represented by an adopted resolution.

Comfortably ensconced in New York, the delegates varied in their degree of cynicism—from none to complete. Delegates from countries with competent, well-organized ministries of foreign affairs usually worked under instructions from their capital, while others freewheeled to an astonishing degree. U.S. delegates were the most instructed. Our capital was just a couple of hundred miles down the road—one hour by shuttle airplane—without even the need to use an area code when telephoning. Russian and Chinese delegates appeared to operate under a tight leash, but the rest of the crowd seemed to have more local running room. Delegates of smaller countries with limited diplomatic traditions (mostly small and poor countries) actually seemed to operate as diplomatic entrepreneurs, voting by personal preference on a few issues and trading their votes with their peers on most others. This was especially true of the members of the Group of 77—the nonaligned or Third World countries. Meeting in their own caucus, on any given subject they would generally adopt the position of the country or countries most interested, in the expectation that they would each receive similar consideration on issues they cared about. The Group of 77 adopted Latin American issues favored by Latin American countries, African issues favored by Africans, and so forth.

Naturally, this did not work all the time. The Group of 77 had to be essentially neutral on Cyprus and Kashmir, but they could quite consistently come down hard on the Palestinian side of Middle East issues. Generally speaking, the U.S. emerged as the target of most of these positions, or at least did so until the end of the Cold War.

Another complicating factor was that of personal ambitions and relations. Delegates did favors for each other, in the way that diplomats often do, in the expectation of having them returned sometime in the future. In New York the returned favor might be voting support on another issue, or it could take the form of preferment or support for a UN job. Many diplomats prefer or find it advantageous at a given time to leave their country's service and move into the international job sphere. UN jobs are reasonably well paid and most diplomats find that they like living in New York (or Geneva or Rome). In some cases diplomats find that returning home can be dangerous if they have fallen out of favor with an irascible tyrant. UN jobs are distributed to some degree by geography, so senior diplomats from smaller countries can often find a haven in the UN bureaucracy—if they haven't blotted their copybook so as to make themselves unwelcome.

All of these motivational crosscurrents created a lively and intimate atmosphere. We were all constantly interacting in our UN "neighborhoods"—the political people in the First and Special Political Committees, the economic and social people in the Second and Third and ECOSOC committees, the lawyers off on their own somewhere. Each of these subcultures had its audience and bureaucratic interlocutors in relevant sections of the UN Secretariat. It was all very jolly and collegial, as well as intense.

As noted, I arrived in the midst of a General Assembly and remained in a state of shock through the end of it in December. There were so many subjects, so many esoteric and arcane discussions, and so many as yet unknown players to deal with. Fortunately, the most senior management of the mission was experienced, sensible, and quite professional. My immediate boss, Jonathan Moore, was one of our five ambassadors and the one with the title of U.S. representative to ECOSOC. He was not a professional Foreign Service officer but had a great deal of government experience, a good sense of humor, and zest for policy and negotiation. He and I got along famously, sharing a similar view of the world and finding that we both actually enjoyed what we were doing.

Thomas Pickering, our permanent representative and head of the mission, was one of the most senior officers in the Foreign Service and a legend in his own time. A local legend told around the mission was that after his first staff meeting, one senior officer had turned to another and asked how he was going to like working for a boss who knew everyone's job better than its occupant. Withal, he was a delightful and warm human being. When a few years later a well-founded rumor had him being considered by President Clinton for the position of secretary of state, a rare prospect for a career diplomat, knowledgeable commentators in the academic, think tank, and media worlds and in Washington government circles were openly in favor. That he was not selected was not in the end surprising, American politics being what it is. But he nevertheless ended up as the under secretary for political affairs—the number three position in the State Department, usually considered the highest position open to any career diplomat. Still, many believe an opportunity was missed.

My peers at the minister-counselor level varied in quality and helpfulness but by and large earned their pay. My own staff possessed varying degrees of experience but were willing, hardworking, and more than competent. Certainly the mission as a whole compared favorably with my previous experience in the State Department. It was at least equal to other government agencies and clearly superior to the private-sector bureaucracies of large companies. The enduring legend of the superior qualities of private-sector employees is just that—a carefully fostered fiction. Aside from questions of competence is the matter of conscientiousness and devotion to duty. These qualities still exist among the majority of Foreign Service people.

My time at the UN soon assumed a more or less regular pattern. September meant the opening of a General Assembly, when the mission went into high gear, accelerating until the final burst of activity just before Christmas. Some went away over the holidays, but we stayed in

New York, which is magical over the holidays. I had looked up a college classmate soon after I arrived, and we discovered that our wives liked each other even better than we did. Herb and Debbie Schneider were quintessential New Yorkers, so we tagged along together, roaming Manhattan. We began a tradition of spending New Year's Eve together, dinner and dancing, sometimes in New York and sometimes elsewhere: Philadelphia, Washington, Annapolis, and later Honolulu. This continued for years until my wife became ill.

The UN year, beginning right after Labor Day, picked up speed quickly. From the opening of the General Assembly in mid-September until it closed just before Christmas, we operated flat out. Even the city of New York itself felt the pace, as additional staff, delegations, and visitors augmented UN missions. Tourists flooded the UN halls and meeting rooms—and taxis—and hotel and restaurant reservations became harder to get. Despite the complaints of some about "all those diplomats parking wherever they wish," the city's businesses and taxi drivers notice when they are gone. January is a comparatively quiet month in New York, and not just because of the weather. New York mayors have calculated the net economic benefit of UN headquarters, and it is substantial. However, complaining about the UN enables the mayor to argue for more federal support, such as for police. It also allows other politicians to appear to agree with some of their more nationalistic supporters without having to worry that the UN cash cow will actually leave New York.

According to local tradition, the UN had been a relatively quiet place between General Assemblies until the late 1980s. The end of the Cold War changed things, making delegations and UN staff busy all year round. January or February would bring the annual meeting of the Commission on Human Rights, which met in Geneva. Many delegates and staff from New York would attend. Spring would bring annual meetings of the boards of directors of various specialized agencies, funds, and programs such as UNHCR, UNICEF, and UNDP. Soon summer would arrive and with it the annual meeting of ECOSOC. This meeting would alternate between New York and Geneva, with Geneva referred to as ECOSOC summer camp.

By the time ECOSOC was over, it was time for August vacations (sacred to Europeans and popular with everyone else). August in New York at the UN was quiet, but soon September approached, loins were girded for the next General Assembly, and the round began again.

ECOSOC is one of the UN's main bodies, a Charter-established intergovernmental body. It was conceived of as the economic counterpart to the Security Council, but it did not have permanent members and was not equipped with the authority of that body. Fairly soon its original fifteen-state membership was expanded to fifty-four. The resulting voting control exercised de facto by the members of the Non-Aligned Movement doomed the body to irrelevance in the eyes of the U.S. and other rich developed countries. The West declined to have either their national or global economic policies subject to control by votes in ECOSOC. By the late 1960s the members of the Non-Aligned Movement, supported by the Socialist bloc, had adopted a policy that called for perpetually increasing economic concessions and contributions by the rich countries. Thus, ECOSOC remained throughout the Cold War the very model of the UN "talking shop" so disliked by many American observers.

The end of the Cold War appeared to offer the chance of a rebirth of ECOSOC. The free-market model was triumphant and, for the moment, the Third World demand for First World largess was muffled. Jumping at the opportunity, in 1989 the five Nordic nations (Sweden, Norway, Denmark, Finland, and Iceland) introduced a program of reform and revitalization of ECOSOC. In proposing to trim and rationalize the complex jungle of ECOSOC committees and subcommittees, and by concentrating and expanding ECOSOC's authority over its putative bureaucratic charges, they hoped that ECOSOC and therefore the UN could play a more active and constructive role in the brave new post–Cold War world. In the end, the Nordic effort resulted in a reform resolution that fell short of the original ambitious hopes. Still, it did produce some improvements in ECOSOC's organization and processes, enabling it to play a more active role in international economic and development affairs. Specifically, for those interested in the internal operations of the UN world, ECOSOC was empowered as the body responsible for four major UN organizations: UNDP, UNICEF, UN Women's Program, and the World Food Program. This shift of authority up from the governing bodies of these organizations to ECOSOC was the first significant reversal of the fifty-year trend, which had seen authority flow away from ECOSOC. The reformers hoped that this (actually quite modest) change would enable member states to agree on and implement more coherent relations between these development and humanitarian assistance organizations—organizations well known to prefer separate lives, as if they did not belong to the same world family.

The ambitions of the reformers did not come to pass. Most of the Third World still wanted the First World to write blank checks, and the First World still preferred to direct the world economy through institutions such as the World Bank, where voting is based on more than one-country/one-vote principles. As a result, the UN member states, including the U.S., have not used the adopted reforms aggressively or imaginatively

While not a subject deemed worthy of much attention by the *New York Times* or, for that matter, by many in Washington, the Nordic ECOSOC revitalization effort was important and exciting for me as head of USUN's economic section and as the deputy U.S. representative to ECOSOC. The game may not have loomed important on the world scene, but played for itself it was a fast-paced exercise in professional multilateral diplomacy. Within the enclosed world of the UN, it was actually a major subject. Permanent Representative Pickering, a thorough professional with wide-ranging interests, thought the reform proposals intriguing and full of potential. He gave us a license to support the Nordics, despite a less than enthusiastic Washington. (This was after all, a Republican administration with political appointees viscerally opposed to anything UN, including John Bolton, the assistant secretary responsible for UN affairs. Why he took that job was always a mystery to many of us, but perhaps he saw it as his responsibility to protect America from the UN.)

ECOSOC reform and revitalization occupied much of my time over the next year or so. Meetings and negotiations went on almost continuously, in the General Assembly, in ECOSOC itself, and informally in the time in between the formal intergovernmental meetings. The lineup was interesting, as it did not reflect the traditional Cold War patterns. The United States staunchly lined up in support of the Nordics, as did some of the Latin Americans and a scattering of countries without reference to ideological commitments, although they were by and large reasonably successful economies. The members of the European Community were reasonably supportive, although some of the bigger ones, such as France and the United Kingdom, were somewhat lukewarm. The British attitude was, I believe, largely the reflection of my counterpart, a rather snooty Englishman who still resented the loss of Empire and the rise of the United States. The French were motivated, I think, by a kind of "not invented here" syndrome, combined with a resentment that the U.S. was in cahoots with several countries who had traditionally joined the French in looking down at the uncouth Americans. Interestingly, the Russians and several East Europeans were quite supportive, for numerous reasons, I suppose, but also for the sheer pleasure of partnership with the U.S.

There were no opponents per se to reform, but a large number of Third World countries were suspicious, as usual. They had committed themselves for decades in fruitless support of the dream of a New World Economic Order in which the exploitations of the colonial and neocolonialist periods would finally be replaced by a representative West that would shower resources and technology on the countries of the Third World. The Soviet bloc had for years voted, with tongue in cheek, in favor of an endless stream of General Assembly and ECOSOC resolutions on this subject. Now the Russian Federation and the other successor states of the Socialist bloc abandoned this crusade, leaving the Group of 77 desolate and clueless in the post–Cold War world. A number of newly successful countries—the Asian Tigers, some of the Latin Americans, and a few others like Morocco—were quite prepared to leave behind old attitudes and join in efforts at revitalizing the United Nations.

While this ECOSOC reform effort took up a majority of our time for a year or so, we carried the debate from one ECOSOC session to another for a couple more years. None of this activity reached the media. Near the end, as we approached some sort of success, I tried to interest a serious journalist from a serious paper, but nothing was ever printed. I was not surprised—who would want to read this "inside baseball" story?

Some of our other UN scuffles were more colorful, although none of them achieved publication either. Though Israel's founding had been legitimized by the United Nations, it has had an increasingly difficult relationship with the UN ever since. The formation of the Group of 77 in the UN, composed of the countries of the Third World including all Arab states, has resulted in Israel's being marginalized in the UN's intergovernmental bodies. As noted, countries are nominated for membership in various intergovernmental bodies, such as the Commission on Human Rights and ECOSOC itself, by the regional groupings. Israel, not surprisingly, has not been accepted into its regional group and has never been nominated or elected to anything. It may attend meetings of the numerous UN bodies, but cannot participate as a voting member, except in the General Assembly. This exclusion, combined with the flood of Arab-sponsored resolutions in recent years, has produced a strong Israeli distrust of the UN and contributed to its sense of isolation.

A major turning point in Israel's role in the UN was the passage in 1975 of the GA resolution equating Zionism with racism. Although resisted by the U.S. and other Western countries, it was passed by the Group of 77 majority. Successive American administrations worked to revoke this resolution but were never able to obtain the needed votes until the early 1990s. But we did test the waters in ECOSOC in 1990. After consulting with our Israeli colleagues, we decided that the voting alignments had shifted sufficiently to enable us to get Israel elected to a minor ECOSOC subcommittee. For reasons I do not remember, this subcommittee did not select its members via nominations by regional groups, and Israel was able to put its name in for nomination. The Arab bloc obviously opposed the nomination and quickly tried to mobilize the Group of 77; but times had changed, and they were unsuccessful. We lobbied intensively, with the U.S. delegation taking the lead; following a dramatic debate in the full ECOSOC plenary in

Geneva, Israel was elected. Interestingly, the Arab delegates who spoke in opposition did so with a resigned air, as if they knew the old game was up. The next year, 1991, the U.S. delegation mounted a full-court press in the General Assembly, which successfully reversed the offending Zionism-is-racism resolution. All this occurred in the early 1990s at a time of real optimism about prospects for peace in the Middle East.

Our little success in ECOSOC served me well. But the next year I foolishly allowed myself to get into an open discussion with a representative of the PLO. This was not permissible for American delegates, as we did not then recognize the PLO, and I stood in serious danger of reprimand or worse. However, my Israeli colleagues told me not to worry, they would protect me back in Jerusalem and if necessary in Washington. Nothing ever came of my *faux pas*, but it was worrisome for a short while.

Knowledgeable readers will have noted by now that I have not mentioned some of the really dramatic events that occurred at the UN during my time there, such as the U.S. response to the Iraqi invasion of Kuwait, and that I only marginally discussed the successful USG effort to revoke the infamous Zionism-terrorism resolution of 1976. It was not because as a member of the U.S. mission I was not involved in those issues, but because the main action took place in the political section and the ambassador's suite. These were essentially "political" issues being dealt with in the Security Council and the UN political committees, not in the economic and social committees where my colleagues and I hung out. We supported our positions in our own areas, but the main action was political. The old hierarchy of political-versus-economic in diplomacy held firm. We consoled ourselves by accepting our roles as spear carriers, backing up the principal singers.

Nonetheless, some of our comparatively minor riffs were not without interest. The UN Charter grants international nongovernmental organizations an associate status, which entitled them to attend meetings and even sometimes address the assembled delegates. One of the first such associated NGOs, back in the late 1940s, was Lions International. By 1990 the number of such associates totaled somewhat over a thousand and doubled to over two thousand with the NGO explosion of the 1990s. With the green and human rights movements, the number had reached over five thousand by 2018. A subcommittee of ECOSOC rules on their applications according to set criteria, such as documentation of their multinational status, and the process is generally a fairly dull chore.

At the 1991 ECOSOC session, consternation hit the subcommittee when the International Gay and Lesbian League applied for associate status. It turned out that they met the written criteria. The Nordic and other progressive delegates stoutly affirmed that they would vote yes. Other delegates squirmed in their seats. As the American delegate, I sat with a Cheshire grin. I had thrown the question back to Washington, and the Clinton administration in its early and idealistic days, instructed us to vote in favor (but not to make any public comments, favorable or otherwise). One group of delegates was truly in agony, though. The Arab delegates were appalled. Apart from any cultural, religious, or political objections, there was apparently a serious linguistic problem. According to an Arabic-speaking colleague, the words *gay* and *lesbian* could only be translated into Arabic by words so vulgar that they could not be pronounced in public, certainly not by dignified Arab diplomats in UN meeting rooms. Or so I was told. Arab opposition, therefore, had to be couched in elaborate euphemisms and the ensuing debate was obviously one of enormous embarrassment.

In the end, the International Gay and Lesbian League was granted associate status, if only because no one could figure out a reason to deny them and face the inevitable outrage of liberal circles. But a year or so later, a bomb exploded, figuratively speaking. It seems that one of the league's constituent organizations was composed of pedophilic pederasts, the Man-Boy Love Association. This was too much. Now it was everyone's turn to be embarrassed. Several American congressmen huffed and puffed, and few were willing to stand by the original decision. Accordingly, the International Gay and Lesbian League was disassociated.

As I indicated, ECOSOC is a sideshow, but there are those of us who loved it.

16

Washington *Entr'actes*

Although most of what I am recounting in this disjointed memoir is about my life in the Foreign Service on official duty outside the United States, it also covers various periods spent in the States, mostly in Washington. These stateside assignments were the connective tissue, so to speak, between the foreign elements of a Foreign Service career. I spent three years in the Africa Bureau between Zambia and Brussels. Another such period, a relatively short one of eighteen months, followed my early transfer from Lubumbashi back to the Bureau of African Affairs as deputy director of the Office of Central African Affairs. The cutting short of my Lubumbashi tour was for various bureaucratic reasons of no great historic import, and as it was at the request of my superiors, not a bad mark. To the contrary, as events proved.

For diplomats, headquarters assignments are just as interesting and important in their own way as overseas postings, but they lack the exotica of foreign assignments. The Department of State, while a comparatively small U.S. government (USG) department, consists nevertheless of thousands of people engaged in what seems a bewildering number of bureaucratic tasks and activities. After all, the "mission" of the Department of State is essentially the whole world and what goes on in it. Especially for a global power like the United States, not a bird can fall anywhere without somehow being of interest and, sometimes, of importance. The breadth of this responsibility, shared only by the White House and to a degree the CIA, distinguishes State from the other departments and explains its comparative weakness in bureaucratic and political terms. All the other departments, including Defense, have narrower and more readily comprehensible missions, combined with a domestic constituency of people and interests connected with that mission. The military-industrial complex comes most readily to mind.

When assigned to Washington in 1966 to the Office of East African Affairs, I did not go there directly but went instead on a six-month detour to the Foreign Service Institute for its new six-month course in economics. Based on my Nairobi tour, I was now slotted as an economic-commercial specialist. This was before the current system of formal career specialties, or "cones," was created and when such specializations existed but were somewhat informal. Nevertheless, there was a well-established pecking order: political, economic, consular, administrative. I was now safely ensconced in the substantive or "real diplomat" part of the community (political, economic), though not branded with the most prestigious tribal label (political officer).

The economics course was the first and perhaps only serious substantive course then at FSI, whose catalogue mostly consists of language programs and a potpourri of short "tradecraft" courses covering, inter alia, how to issue visas and perform administrative tasks. Several courses covered foreign cultures and political developments, but these were often for days or weeks rather than months and somewhat superficial. The economics course was quite different: six months of full-time study intended to provide the equivalent of an undergraduate major of thirty-plus academic hours. The faculty were professional academics, not FSOs or civil servants on temporary duty. The class hours were long and the study requirements heavy. The course was initiated in the mid-1960s to meet a felt need for FSOs with basic economic literacy, a quality in short supply among the mostly humanities-trained recruits to the Foreign Service. Since the department believed in the importance of economic matters in contemporary diplomacy and could not manage to recruit enough new officers with the requisite background, it decided to provide the background by means of an in-service training program. I cannot speak to what improvement this program has made in the design and implementation of U.S. foreign and economic policy over the past thirty-some years—there are too many variables and too many cooks—but FSI's economics course continues today; and it has earned a reputation as solid, serious, and very professional.

For various reasons, I was no more than an average student. Still, I remember the experience with gratitude as it provided the necessary foundational background for work I did throughout my career. For many years I was an economic-commercial officer, a role unlike that of an economist. Even when I was not nominally functioning in the economic or commercial field, the background and intellectual orientation of the FSI course enriched my perspective of contemporary developments wherever I was by ensuring that I always included an economic perspective. This was true for many of my fellow students. In performing these functions, both significantly increasing general economic literacy in the professional diplomatic service and providing the first steps in the development of professional Foreign Service economists, the course has been and continues to be an enormous success.

That tour in the department was a standard one for a youngish FSO. I was not wafted up to the high visibility jobs on the seventh floor in the Executive Secretariat or the staff of a senior principal (the path of those already identified as "water walkers"); but the position of Kenya desk officer in the Africa Bureau was quite respectable. "Desk officer" is not an official title; that is country officer. But desk officer is the traditional term, and one much respected in foreign offices and other organizations that deal in international affairs. While relatively junior (except for the senior officer on a very big country desk—say the USSR in the old days), the desk officers occupy a central position in all that is happening between the U.S. and "their" country. Desk officers are in the middle of whatever is going on, and the professional satisfactions are generally enormous. It is a conventional attitude among FSOs that Washington duty is onerous and distasteful, as real diplomacy is practiced and lived in the field, and so Washington assignments are required but never sought—

though Washington assignments are often sought for professional and personal reasons.

That first Washington assignment of mine also produced an amusing and educational experience involving my wife and the State Department's Bureau of Security. Aida had taken a job as a personal assistant to the ambassador of Guinea-Conakry, and I had dutifully informed the department. (In those days there were many special requirements for spouses, clearly gender related.) In due course I received a letter from the Bureau of Security that my wife's job would appear to be somewhat chancy for security reasons, that is, working for a foreign government and especially one with a suspicious political alignment. (Guinea-Conakry under the leadership of Sekou Touré was a notably vocal member of the Non-Aligned Movement.) The letter suggested that for this reason she should leave the job. As I dithered about my reply, a more knowledgeable colleague noted that, as the letter merely suggested that Aida quit her job, I should call their bluff. So I replied in writing that I appreciated their concern but felt that in fact Aida's employment was not a security risk. Therefore, I would leave it completely up to her to decide on her situation. On the advice of my friend, I then added that if the Bureau of Security judged the risk to be real and instructed us both, we would of course comply. No further word was ever forthcoming from the Bureau of Security.

Kenya desk officer was a good job, and I thoroughly enjoyed it. Nothing spectacular or historic happened on my watch, as Kenya gingerly continued to adapt itself to independence. Some countries under more radical leadership, like that of Kwame Nkrumah in Ghana, quickly took on a new national persona and attempted to adopt a distinctive role in the international community. Kenya, however, was under the leadership of Jomo Kenyatta, who became an essentially conservative politician once independence had been achieved. Close to seventy when Kenya obtained independence, he had lived through the period from the arrival of the first European hunters and settlers all the way to independence. Referred to as "Mzee" (respected elder), he wore double-breasted English-cut suits, with a rose in his lapel.

Whether Kenyatta's style was influenced by the settler attitude mentioned earlier or was the result of his earlier life in London, he certainly reinforced it. The transition from the colonial Kenya to the now independent Kenya therefore moved slowly. This presented the U.S. government with few problems, so the life of the Kenya desk officer was fairly peaceful. All these years later, only three incidents come to mind. The assassination of the prominent political figure Tom Mboya, though dramatic, did not significantly affect U.S.-Kenyan relations nor require any meaningful action on our part, other than drafting appropriate condolence messages. The slow dissolution of the East African Community was important but, again, not something requiring USG action of any significance.

The one action I do remember most vividly was more amusing than important. It involved Kenyatta's first anniversary in office, which the government of Kenya decided to make a major event. Our ambassador, William Attwood, quite properly felt that this was the occasion to make a mark with a notable present. But what? I was tasked with divining this special gift. My first thought was to find an automobile accessory for Kenyatta's well-known and much-loved personal car—a 1945 or '46 model Hudson, the one with the distinctive body shape. But we could not find anything for this now rare vehicle, the company itself having disappeared. Next, I turned to another of Kenyatta's well-known personal passions—roses. He always had one in his lapel, taken mostly from his own personally cultivated rosebushes. Here we were more successful, as the largest rose-cultivating company in the U.S. responded magnificently by naming a newly developed variety "the Jomo Kenyatta Rose" and providing us with three bushes of the new variety. They were duly sent to Nairobi for presentation by our ambassador and were received with much appreciation. I wonder if they are still being cultivated in Kenya.

As mentioned earlier, I somehow always seemed to arrive after historic events and then leave before the next round. So shortly after I arrived back at the department from Zaire in 1976, again to the Africa Bureau, the legendary Katanga Gendarmes, who had been in exile in Angola since the days of the Katanga secession, decided to return to Zaire. They crossed the border and started down the Zairian Copperbelt, heading towards Lubumbashi. Several weeks of crisis ensued as the inept Zairian government and army tried to deal with the invasion, with less than fully enthusiastic support from the U.S., Belgian, and French governments. Eventually the invasion petered out. I had missed another "historic" event and only got to watch and participate as one of the Washington mob.

This Washington tour turned out to be dramatically cut short with my nomination as ambassador to the republics of Guinea-Bissau and Cape Verde. Not only was this offer welcome, it was also quite a surprise, as officers of my grade (at that time, equivalent to an army colonel) were normally not appointed as ambassadors. Apparently, the Powers That Be in the upper levers of the department had decided that it would be good policy, or at least an interesting experiment, to appoint relatively junior officers as ambassadors, albeit to small, mostly African countries. I was, I believe, the second of the "baby ambassadors."

It was a matter of chance of course. Guinea-Bissau and Cape Verde had become independent the previous year and the first American ambassador, Melissa Wells, was only six months into her appointment. However, she had been precipitously called back to Washington to take on a senior position at our mission to the UN, and the job was thus suddenly vacant. And there I was ready to hand in the department, and a Portuguese speaker to boot. A quick nomination, a short and uneventful Senate confirmation hearing, and I was off to Bissau via a stop in Lisbon to check in with the American ambassador to Portugal and have some interviews with the Portuguese Ministry of Foreign Affairs.

These rotations were, and still are, common in the Foreign Service and in most diplomatic services. Although often cut short or extended for the "needs of the Service," it's usually two to three years in a place, then off to another or back to Washington. Occasionally special assignments crop up to graduate university training or a private industry organization, or the U.S. Congress for some. And then come occasional visits to the Foreign Service Institute for short courses of one sort or another in addition to language training.

People often ask about this constant movement, wondering why and questioning its value. At the same time, many ask about the tradeoff between having enough time in country to learn about it while avoiding the presumed danger of "localitis" (somehow no longer thinking like a "real American," a surprisingly common suspicion held by many of our fellow Americans). But the danger of localitis is real—not only going "native" but also going stale and probably, more important, becoming too narrow. One of the functions of a professional career service is to cultivate a cadre, a bench, so to speak, of experienced senior officials both to lead and to manage the system and to serve as professional advisors to the political leadership. Such a bench cannot be created and nourished unless the personnel in the system are given varied experience and professional education over the years. Fifteen years in Paris or in Guinea-Bissau may create a truly in-depth expert on France or Guinea-Bissau but will not provide the broad-scale strategic expert that is needed at the senior levels. (The Guinea-Bissaus of the world just don't provide embassies of sufficient size to provide the requisite range of experience for career development or opportunities for promotion.)

Accordingly, we have the normal practice of rotation and the Foreign Service requirement of "worldwide availability" (which, together with rank-in-person like the military, is a defining characteristic of the Foreign Service). All this makes personnel management in the Department of State a nightmare. Some people worry about that more than others.

So off I went to Bissau and Cape Verde for three years. The two countries had just become independent and had no serious outstanding problems with or for the United States. I spent most of my time and energy on "housekeeping" matters, getting the two embassies physically established and operating in an impoverished environment. But the opportunity to write discursive "Letters from . . ." was obvious, and they are the source for the earlier chapters on those countries.

My three years in Guinea-Bissau, followed by assignment to the National War College at Fort McNair in Washington, illustrate the Foreign Service practice of regularly sending FSOs to the military senior colleges, although not usually after serving as chiefs of mission. But as I had been one of the "baby ambassadors," the rules were somewhat different, I suppose. My year at Fort McNair was fascinating in many ways and a serious introduction to the professional U.S. military. So, naturally, I wrote a "Letter from Fort McNair," which was published in the Internet journal *American Diplomacy* and forms the basis of that chapter.

I returned to the department from Fort McNair in 1980 and, after a few months in desultory activity in a nondescript office supposedly concerned with state government relations, ended up in the relatively new office of the Coordinator for Combating Terrorism (S/CT) as one of the two deputy coordinators. This was during an early period of the terrorism threat, when we were concerned with what was called the "boutique terrorists" of Europe and Latin America: the Red Brigades and their ilk. This was an important task, probably the most important one of my career, although its career impact was disappointing in the long run.

Although most of my State Department assignments were unexceptional in department terms, that was not true of the counterterrorism assignment. S/CT was a small office at that time, only about a dozen personnel, and I was brought on to design and implement a new initiative—a USG assistance program for combating terrorism. The idea was to create a program whereby the United States would work with like-minded governments in fighting terrorist organizations.

Complicated problems of legal authority stemmed from legislation dating back to the Vietnam War that prohibited certain kinds of USG support to foreign police and required congressional action for the necessary authority, as well as budget support. I was responsible for drafting the necessary legislation and defining and designing the new program, which we named the Anti-Terrorism Assistance program, or ATA. The work involved relations with members of Congress and their staffs and a wide range of officials in other agencies—Defense, Treasury, and various federal security organizations. Most unusually and enjoyably, it involved extensive interaction with police officials in Washington, New York, and other places because the program focused on the role of the police in combating terrorism. After Congress passed the appropriate legislation and we had designed the program, we reached out to our counterparts in other countries. Our first contact was with the Italians, who had just succeeded in rescuing an American general who had been kidnapped by the Italian Red Brigades.

The ATA program took off nicely, with an initial annual budget of $2 million, which has grown over the years to about $200 million. Unfortunately, the original concept and objective of the program was later changed. ATA had begun as a USG assistance program designed to facilitate expanded intergovernmental cooperation on combating terrorism. The money and resources for technical assistance were intended as walking-around money to sweeten bilateral policy coordination. Some years after I left, the program was handed over to the department's security branch, which turned it into a security officer assistance program. The policy coordination aspect was dropped. As the years passed and the terrorist program expanded, especially after 9/11, the loss of this foreign policy tool left the door open for the increasingly dominant role of the military. That probably would have happened anyway, but surely the unnecessary abandonment of a civilian instrument of policy and programs was a self-inflicted wound.

Nevertheless, it was a most satisfactory job while it lasted.

With the ATA program launched and three years having passed, reassignment time came up again in 1985. With my counterterrorism experience I was now a "terrorism expert," at least in government terms, and I was offered a Distinguished Senior Fellow position at a prominent think tank, the Center for Strategic and International Studies (CSIS). The department was willing, so off I went down to the legendary K Street corridor to join the think tank world, a common enough activity, as FSOs often spend an "excursion" year at a think tank, in Congress, at a university, or under a special program at a private company. I certainly enjoyed it, and spent my time attending conferences, doing research, writing articles and monographs, and contributing to CSIS publications.

The year passed quickly, and I soon became engaged in the search for a new assignment. Nothing very exciting came up and, most pointedly, no offers of another ambassadorial appointment. Soon it became clear that none would be forthcoming: my day in the sun was over. Then I received a call from Jim Spain, a colleague and friend who was the recently appointed ambassador to Sri Lanka, offering me the position as his deputy chief of mission. I liked the idea of working with him, and Sri Lanka was an attractive country, so I accepted. (Aida's father had visited Ceylon many years before as an official of Iran Air, and his story about his visit had stuck in her mind.) Sri Lanka did turn out to be one of our most interesting and enjoyable posts.

When my allotted time in Sri Lanka approached an end, the usual scouting around for a new job began. When the choice finally came down to an office directorship in the Bureau of Intelligence and Research or a job at the U.S. mission to the UN, we happily fastened on the opportunity to live in New York. Our time there was as exciting and fascinating an experience as any. USUN and Manhattan turned out to be career high points in terms of personal satisfaction.

Both New York and the UN were new and different experiences in many ways, as I attempted to explain why in the previous chapter. My UN experience led to some of my postretirement work on several UN projects, including missions to Rome, Azerbaijan, Armenia, and Georgia. I also became a fan of the UN and took every opportunity I could to explain and defend it to skeptical fellow Americans. I especially enjoyed the opportunity to engage people on the subject, often a contentious experience, when lecturing on cruise ships.

But the USUN assignment ended in due course, and my allotted time in the Foreign Service was approaching its conclusion. For the remaining couple of years (I was approaching the mandatory retirement age, but saw no reason to retire before I had to) I was assigned to the Institute for National Security Studies, a government think tank at Fort McNair, for which my time at CSIS had served as a prelude of sorts. And so, with the pompous title of Visiting Senior Fellow (think tanks love these academic-sounding titles), I spent my time attending conferences, doing research, and writing. One could say I ended my diplomatic career not with a bang but an academic whimper.

17

Three Years before the Mast

I spent the first years of my retirement in a manner common to many of my colleagues. We stayed in Washington because we both thought of it as our home, and we had had no other place calling to us. Aida went to work as a volunteer at the White House and began a career as a real estate broker.

I did some contract work with the United Nations and the U.S. military. The most interesting parts of the UN work involved missions to Azerbaijan, Georgia, and Armenia with the UN Development Program (UNDP) to assist these newly independent countries (former members of the Union of Soviet Socialist Republics) in setting up their own government bureaucracies. My role was to advise on setting up their ministries of foreign affairs. I don't know if my efforts were productive in the long run, but these visits to the fabled mountain countries of the Caucasus were satisfying experiences, especially for Aida, an Armenian of the Armenian diaspora.

With the military I served as a technical expert, role player, and lecturer in their exercises and professional schools, which the military take very seriously. There is a cottage industry for retired diplomats as subject matter experts in the "war games" and classes at their schools.

Then came 9/11 and an offer I could not, and did not want to, refuse. An idea I had floated in a military exercise at Joint Forces Command in the summer of 2000 had flourished in the military world and was now to be put into practice. The idea was to facilitate civilian-military cooperation and coordination by creating a new element or office composed largely of civilian officials seconded to the military combatant commands from their home agencies—State most obviously, but also Treasury and CIA, and perhaps some others. The idea was to provide the military commander with in-house expertise from other relevant agencies as well as expanded coordination links through these detailed personnel. The planning people at Joint Forces had massaged the idea, and, with the consequent focus on terrorism after 9/11, created the Joint Interagency Coordination Group on Counter-Terrorism, or JIACG-CT. The several combatant commands were enjoined by their masters in the Department of Defense to turn their attention to the terrorist challenge and create JIACGs to help with the job.

State was somewhat leery of this innovation and, pleading the traditional shortage of officers, turned to the retired ranks. As a result I was called into the Combatting Terrorism office in State and offered a six-month job as State's representative to the newly formed JIACG at the U.S. Pacific Command in Honolulu. It should not come as a surprise that I jumped at the opportunity, my wife enthusiastically concurring.

The invitation to go to Hawaii for six months on a State Department temporary assignment to the U.S. Pacific Command (USPACOM) was what is called a WAE (When Actually Employed) contract. It was supposed to be for only six months, but as the months passed and more permanent arrangements failed to jell, PACOM kept asking State to extend me until an active-duty Foreign Service officer finally arrived in September 2005. I do not know if I set a record for a temporary duty assignment, but thirty-nine months should at least put me in the running.

This offer was more appropriate than State realized. As a senior mentor at the 2000 annual command exercise of the Joint Forces Command, I had formulated the concept of an interagency staff directorate, tentatively labeled JX, to improve interagency coordination. Joint Forces took up the concept and in March 2001 issued a White Paper on it, renaming the proposed entity the Joint Interagency Coordination Group.

Following September 11, the major military commands were instructed to create these new units and to ask other departments to assign civilian personnel. The initial response was unenthusiastic; State, as noted, pleaded lack of available personnel and money but eventually worked out contract arrangements to employ retired officers.

So off I went to Hawaii as the State Department representative in the JIACG-CT. I arrived in Honolulu just before July 4 and was warmly received, with an amusing combination of respect combined with reserve and caution. FSOs are not completely unknown at regional combatant commands. Political advisors (POLADS), now called foreign policy advisors (FPAS), have been around for generations. POLADS, however, reside in the upper reaches of the command, mingling with the most senior officers, while I was embedded (to use the current terminology) among the working staff.

USPACOM is one of the regional combatant commands (COCOMS), organizational creatures unlike anything existing in State. They are the war fighters, the actual forces positioned to perform operations, including war itself. Distinct from the departments (Army, Navy, Air Force, and so on) and the services, the combatant commands report directly to the president through the secretary of defense and do not handle the recruiting, training, equipping, or any of the mundane but necessary "household" tasks of the military. Readers may know them by their old appellation of CINCDOMS, headed by CINCS, or commanders-in-chief. However, Secretary of Defense Donald Rumsfeld decided, quite logically, that there was only one commander-in-chief in the American government, and that was the president. So CINCS became COCOM commanders, as in Commander, U.S. Pacific Command, and Commander, U.S. Central Command.

The COCOMS are joint commands (purple, as compared, for example, to green for the army and blue for the air force), staffed by officers from all the military services. Due to its heavy focus on naval warfare (the Asia-Pacific Area of Operation is very watery) the Pacific Command (PACOM) always had a heavily naval character. The office of the commander, for instance, is generally referred to as the "bridge," and the many naval personnel working in the headquarters building refer to "heads" and "decks" instead of "johns" and "floors."

PACOM personnel are largely military, so the pecking order is clear, with rank constituting the signposts of their life and behavior. It was interesting to see them automatically insert a "sir" the very day a peer moved up in rank. This was not an act of currying favor, rather merely showing the respect that one gives, as one also expects it. (There was also a lower caste of contractors numbering in dozens if not hundreds. They are mostly retired military now double-dipping and jocularly referred to as contractor slime.)

Distinctions are made not only between ranks but also between seniority within ranks. This is especially true of colonels or navy captains, where the significant difference is whether the officer holds a major command, such as an army brigade. Officers are often referred to by number, as in 0–4 (major) or 0–6 (colonel). Generals or admirals are usually referred to as GOs (general officers) or Flags (flag officers).

The staff falls into three distinct classes: "action officers," 0–6s, and GOs or Flags. Action officers are majors or lieutenant colonels, or their naval equivalents, with full colonels or navy captains generally serving as section or unit bosses. Senior 0–6s also belong to something called the Council of Colonels, a senior vetting group with no official standing but of great weight. The GOs and Flags are treated almost as a different species and are usually referred to by their job designation; for example, the director of operations is "3," as the Directorate of Operations is the J3. There are some enlisted personnel, mostly senior sergeants, but junior officers are rarely seen in the corridors.

The military world is full of subcommunities, beginning with the services themselves—army, navy, air force, Marines. However, these identities are further refined by more specific differentiations—warriors and "horse holders," or combat arms and support services. These categories are refined still further—not merely between pilots and intelligence types, but different types of pilots, as in the air force, for example, B-2 pilots, fighter pilots, or transport pilots. In the navy, pilots are differentiated from service sailors and submariners, while A-7 pilots form a different community from F-18 pilots. Armored cavalry is different from light infantry or artillery and from heavy field artillery. And then there are the support services: military police, logisticians, planners, engineers, and so on. These communities constitute the primary environment in which they are trained and promoted. Differences are muted as individuals move up the ranks and become subject to broader responsibilities and education, but they remain important. Promotion takes place within these communities, even to general and admiral.

These communities have generally accepted characteristics. When I commented to a young major on the differing leadership styles of our co-bosses, an army colonel and a navy captain, I was assuming the difference was one of individual personality. He pointed out, however, that the difference arose from their professional backgrounds, specifically that the decision cycle of a fighter pilot (the navy captain) was measured in seconds, while that of an infantry officer (the colonel) in hours and days.

Sometimes called "Bubba" communities, reflecting the heavy Southern influence in the American military world as well as a sort of self-deprecating humor, these communities are somewhat comparable to political officers or Arabists in the Foreign Service. It is just that the military world is so large that the phenomenon is that much more robust.

As a forty-year veteran of the Department of State, I thought I was comfortable with large bureaucracies. However, USPACOM alone consists of over three hundred thousand military personnel, not to mention civilians and contractors, and disposes of amounts of money and materiel unimaginable to FSOs. For instance, when after 9/11 PACOM set up its JIACG out of existing resources, the commander "scraped up" forty bodies and $2 million. In my occasional "State Department 101" presentations to PACOM personnel, I would emphasize this vast difference in resources as a major factor explaining the difference in organizational cultures. They always appeared somewhat bemused when I told them that FSOS view the military as unbelievably rich and therefore a good touch, if you could only figure out how to do it. They naturally consider themselves short of resources to accomplish all they need and/or want to do. Military organizations are extremely expensive.

The COCOMS have a complicated relationship with the Pentagon, beginning with the usual tension between headquarters and the field—not too dissimilar to that obtaining between embassies and the State Department. This inherent tension is exacerbated by the fact that the COCOM commander is a very senior "four star" with a major responsibility who reports directly, by law, to the secretary of defense and the president. He is senior to everyone in the military chain of command, except perhaps the actual members of the Joint Chiefs of Staff. Obviously, the president and the secretary of defense can give direct orders to the COCOM, but everyone else must ask, suggest, or negotiate.

Planning is a word spelled with a capital P in the Defense Department world, a formal process pursued in accordance with publications such as Joint Pub 3–07, "Joint Doctrine for Military Operations Other than War," A separate officer caste exists that does planning as their occupational specialty. As the authors of *Defense Is from Mars, State Is from Venus* put it: "Martians use a formal, linear, sequential problem-solving process, a step-by-step guide that ensures a thorough problem analysis and selection of one best course of action in order to achieve the defined end state. Results are published in thick reports."

The "end state" concept more than anything defines military planning. It is so central to the process that intellectual and linguistic contortions are used when the end state is not obvious, for instance when the end state is not merely to defeat the Iraqi army but something like "create a democratic government which provides for economic development, protects human rights, and lives at peace with its neighbors." While obviously desirable, such an end state is essentially meaningless given the discrete time frame and limited military means at hand.

The planning system constitutes the nervous system of the military. Nothing of any importance or weight—and much with neither quality—is done without it having been "planned" by this process. Influencing the American military, then, means influencing the planning process. Waiting until this process is done, and then attempting the difficult task of approving, disapproving, or influencing the final product—essentially asking them to go back to the drawing board—requires serious authority.

The JIACGs were created to moderate this process by introducing the perspectives of other agencies into the military planning process at an early stage. Pursuing greater interagency coordination was not only a military problem, however. Because PACOM was a military command, our attempts to reach out to embassies in an interagency fashion were at first resisted both by the embassies' military attachés and by civilian officers. The attachés tried to keep all interaction with PACOM in their channels, and the civilians cooperated by stating, essentially, that anything coming from PACOM was obviously for the attachés to handle. Regional security officers, Agency for International Development officers, legal attachés, and intelligence types were particularly resistant.

Also important in the military world is the "Schoolhouse," a complex of military training and educational institutions. The professional military spend a significant portion of their career in the Schoolhouse, sometimes as much as 25 percent. The process begins with basic training and progresses to the senior service schools like the National War College and courses for generals and admirals.

The Schoolhouse has both advantages and disadvantages. It is a repository of tradition and doing things by the book—by approved doctrine. It can be viewed as proof of the old charge that generals always fight the last war, especially as the U.S. military are fixated on the need to identify lessons learned from anything they do.

On the other hand, the Schoolhouse is also the venue for serious and often critical contemplation of the military profession. Much innovative thinking has come out of the Schoolhouse. Around the turn of this century, the Schoolhouse was wrestling with the so-called Revolution in Military Affairs, including the need to work more closely with civilian departments along the continuum from classic war fighting to nation building. The traditional American Way of War called for a sharp division between war and peace, but today that approach, if it was ever valid, is no longer acceptable.

The military, those aware of the situation, are puzzled by State's apparent lack of interest in training (along with our disdain of planning) until the resource situation and the mission of State is explained. I usually explained that, first of all, the discrepancy in resources was enormous. They could understand the lack of funds, but the personnel question often puzzled them until I pointed that that while the military were not unlike the fire department, which stands around polishing its equipment until it is called into action, State is like a police force which is on duty at all times. I would make that point vividly when I recounted the reported blank expressions on the faces of State Department officers when newly appointed Secretary of State Colin Powell asked about the department's "training float."

The military staff culture reflects all of these characteristics. The size and complexity of the military staffs and the staff processes involved would astound the Napoleonic-era soldiers who invented the Western military staff system. However, not only is the "directorate" system itself large and complicated, it is supplemented by a Topsy-like growth of ad hoc and/or temporary staff organizations, referred to as B2C2WG or "Boards and Bureaus, Cells and Committees, and Working Groups." Each of these creatures is focused on a specific subject, such as information operations, is composed of representatives from the relevant directorates, and is designated by the commander with varying degrees of authority. In one sense, B2C2WG is a matrix organization superimposed on a hierarchical structure. It is a confusing environment for the outsider, and even for the military themselves.

Another striking characteristic of the American military staff culture is the centrality of the PowerPoint slide presentation. The written memorandum has been largely replaced by the PowerPoint presentation, prepared by action officers and then presented for correction and approval ("rudder steer" in naval parlance) at every level above until it reaches its final destination. All officers must know how to prepare PowerPoint slides, and those with exceptional skills are known as PowerPoint rangers. Jokes are made about medals and ribbons awarded for particularly striking slides, and "Death by PowerPoint" is a common comment on a meeting or a conference.

The dominance of PowerPoint culture in the military is sharply contrasted with its absence in civilian agencies in general and the State Department in particular. State Department officers who show up in military venues to give a briefing usually preface their remarks with a mock apology for not having any PowerPoint slides and being therefore forced to make a purely verbal presentation.

Them and Me. Although most military officers are by and large innocent of personal experience with State Department types, they hold a gratifying general respect for the Department of State. The classic essay *Defense Is from Mars, State Is from Venus* always gets a good reception from military audiences. Their end state—obsessed and formal planning-bound culture, their professional focus on concrete activities, their conservative instincts, and a general lack of contact with FSOs combine to produce ignorance rather than animosity. However, I always found that actual contact produces a more sympathetic attitude.

I have some military experience—two years as a company clerk draftee in ancient peacetime days. This very modest military experience actually gave me some credibility among these present-day professionals. They did not disdain it but instead took it as my having done my duty when called upon. I sometimes thought it was more valued than my attendance at the National War College.

So there I was, a superannuated FSO carrying the rank equivalent in protocol terms to a four-star admiral but working side by side with, and under the direction of, colonels. Admittedly I was retired, but the military show respect to retired officers. As my wife always said, they do have excellent manners.

This general attitude quickly manifested itself in two welcome aspects. The JIACG staff was crammed into an inadequate space in the PACOM headquarters building, a World War II "temporary hospital." Officers worked cheek by jowl in open workspaces just large enough for a computer desk, with the two co-commanders (two very senior o–6s) sharing the only office. Out of consideration for my dignity, they had carefully saved for me a workspace in a corner next to the door to the commanders' office, which by virtue of geography gave me a semblance of privacy.

More important, they had gone to the parking space controller and, on the basis of my title, obtained for me a designated parking space in the most desirable lot on the base—right in front of the headquarters building. Those with experience in bureaucracies will understand the significance of this act. As it happened, I was able to keep that space all through my time in PACOM. When the headquarters moved across the street to the new building in 2004, a nice Navy commander kindly "grandfathered" me (how appropriate!) my parking spot.

All in all, the working atmosphere within PACOM was much more collegial than I had expected. That may be because of B2C2WG, but probably also resulted from the leadership style of Admiral Thomas Fargo, who commanded PACOM during most of my time at Camp Smith. To the very end of my time at PACOM, no one ever gave me a direct order—although I had made it clear that I was a working stiff and more than willing to take on assignments and tasks. I always had to volunteer in some fashion after I realized that I would not have any work to do unless I did. I raised this issue with the commanding colonel, who noted that my value to him would be as a sort of advisor and resident "wise man," not another action officer. I noted that I was quite willing to perform those roles but really needed to have some actual tasks to perform. Eventually tasks appeared, but I always had to seek them out. Giving briefings to foreign visitors, for instance, eventually became my regular duty, but only after I volunteered. Eventually people got around to asking if I "minded" or could find some time to do something or other, always in a diffident tone.

We traveled extensively to consult with embassies and governments on counterterrorism programs. I soon discovered that my role was to act as a door opener to the front office of embassies, a prestige symbol when dealing with foreign officials, and as *bona fides* for the interagency character of our mission. I was, in other words, the Colonel Sanders of the operation, sans white mustache and beard but still in a tropical suit.

Traveling with the military was an experience requiring first of all a threat assessment, which would determine our movement mode while in-country. In most countries some level of threat was identified, and restrictions on our movements were imposed. For instance, sometimes we were restricted to the hotel, traveling to our meetings in a group by bus. Other times we were authorized to move about the city in our spare time only if we doubled up in a "buddy system"—much like summer camp. The first time I ran into this situation, I laughed and thought they were joking. When I realized they weren't, I pleaded with them not to tell any of my former colleagues in the local embassy, as it would ruin what little reputation I had.

In later trips I noted that whether or not any formal restrictions were in place, some of my young military colleagues made a discreet point of keeping a watchful eye on me. I don't think it was about security concerns per se, merely a respectful concern. After one such trip, when one of these young majors and I took a day off to visit Angkor Wat, he later recounted the experience to my wife over drinks and noted that I had "run him ragged through the temples." Not true, of course, but my wife noted with appreciation the message that they were watching over me.

And so . . . As all FSOs know, living in someone else's world is curiously liberating. It was also great fun living up to the military's prejudices and illusions about Foreign Service types. In any case, we learned from each other, and I certainly deepened my understanding and sympathy for our military colleagues. They are essentially serious people, despite the locker-room style they adopt. The difference between diplomats and the military came ever clearer into focus for me. First, there is the fundamental obligation that the military accept, at least in theory, that under certain conditions they will kill and be killed, and this concentrates the mind to some degree. No other profession has this obligation as an essential element of the professional contract, except possibly police.

Another insight, if that is what it is, describes the two professions' mirror image. Military science is simple in theory (you go left, you go right, you kill those guys over there). Implementation, however, is infinitely complicated. (Moving thousands of men and pieces of equipment in order to arrive in certain places at certain times to accomplish specified tasks, while an opponent is trying to frustrate your efforts and do unto you what you hope to do unto him—all being done under immutable physical constraints such as gravity and time and weather.) This insight is not new or original. Clausewitz stated it more succinctly and authoritatively: "Everything in war is simple; everything in war is difficult."

Diplomacy, on the other hand, is extremely complicated in theory (see the shelves of books on history and political science and economics and so on), while the actual process is simple. Some people put some notes in a briefcase and go off to discuss the matter at hand with a couple of other people.

Military activity is essentially short-term, discrete, and finite. Diplomacy is about the relationship between immortal creatures called governments or states—a never-ending process. This difference was reflected in a curious way. I noticed that my military colleagues spent little time discussing events in Afghanistan and Iraq. I was puzzled by this apparent lack of interest about current events I would have thought of intense professional and personal interest. I discreetly inquired about it, contrasting it with the insatiable curiosity of FSOs about everything going on everywhere. Our naval captain boss finally explained that military folk are practical people who focus on the job at hand, and Iraq was not the job at hand for anyone at PACOM. Yes, they were interested and monitored events, but not closely or with any sense that they had to have an opinion. Besides which, most supported the war, so what was there to discuss.

This answer was somewhat disingenuous. Most, but not all, did support the war, but many had become nervous about its path. Still, professional discipline held them to continued support and subdued observation, especially in the presence of an outsider like me.

I didn't experience any war during my time at PACOM, not even secondhand, as all the wars being engaged in by the United States during this period were being conducted elsewhere. But I did have an extended and intensive interaction with America's warriors. It was a rich experience.

All in all, my three years before the mast were memorable—a superb posting. And that would be true even if one discounted that it was in Hawaii.

Epilogue

"He ordered another bottle . . . in honor of a career
so comfortable that it is called The Career and a ministerial
department so superior that it is called The Department."

I repeat this quotation because it sums up my admittedly self-satisfied memory of my career and that of many colleagues of my generation. It was so satisfying in so many ways that many of us found it difficult to let go upon retiring. Positions at think tanks, universities, and private companies beckoned, with opportunities to continue working in the field. Sporadic work back in the government occurred, like my stint with the U.S. military in Hawaii. One favorite activity is playing the American ambassador in U.S. military "war games." (The military have lots of money to do this.) Books, articles, and memoirs have appeared in a steady stream, which obviously I am trying to add to. Some of the most distinguished retired diplomats have become prominent participants in the public arena.

This is what I have done since retiring, albeit at a modest enough level. But the original appeal of and interest in foreign affairs continues almost unabated among us, especially those who have continued to live in the Washington area, tied emotionally to the Beltway.

While I repeat this quotation because it sums up my own memories, I am not sure that opening quotation still applies to the Department of State itself. There is still a certain cachet about diplomacy and recognition that the title of ambassador or assistant secretary of state for European affairs carries more prestige than assistant secretary of education (unless you are a professional educator). The perpetual effort of political partisans to get jobs at State when their party is in power, whether they have any serious credentials or serious interest in the subject of diplomacy, is a constant in Washington. Unfair and not justified, but it does meet the standards of the marketplace. No one is prepared to donate large amounts of money to become the GSA administrator for the western United States.

In addition, there is the crowd of diplomatic and foreign policy "experts" who pursue entrepreneurial careers via the political route rather than in the formal organizations responsible for the country's foreign affairs. Each new administration oversees a lemming-like flow of foreign policy acolytes in and out of the departments. The almost-traditional salting of the country's ambassadorial ranks by political appointees has been matched by the numerous political appointees in the department itself. "To the victors belong the spoils" has revived as an American custom. This growing marketplace for jobs at State was part of the illness that reduced the department's substantive role in foreign policy.

Even calling the career itself comfortable may no longer be possible. The emergence of widespread nonstate violence—terrorism—in the past twenty years has changed the environment. Governments, politicians, and even revolutionaries, for all their machinations, had traditionally left the persons of diplomats alone, as the system served everyone's purposes. Diplomats used to wander around the world pretty much enveloped in a "no-touch" wrapper, along with children and nuns. Except in actual war zones, diplomats could pursue their duties because all desired that they do so. In almost every country, diplomats could mingle with their colleagues and local people quite openly and roam around the cities and countryside with great abandon. Yes, there were irksome limitations in the Soviet bloc and some of the nastier dictatorships; but even in such places, rules were mutually understood and enforced.

This situation was satisfying to diplomats, most of whom had entered the profession out of a combination of desires: public service, a desire to see and participate in history, and a modified form of wanderlust. For those with these ambitions, diplomacy was indeed a "comfortable" career.

And so it seemed to most of my generation, loosely defined as the period from the 1950s to the end of the Cold War. Sitting around even today, we often make comments about that "Golden Age of American Diplomacy." Winning the Cold War as we did contributes to that nostalgic view, given that the Cold War was the central issue we were involved with. Key to that situation was that the U.S. government had adopted a widely accepted "diplomatic" framework for our foreign policy. George Kennan's concept of containment provided a framework for USG behavior that included and undergirded, without being dominated by, the military. Both traditional and new forms of diplomacy (public information, public diplomacy, economic assistance) flourished, and the professional Foreign Service of the United States also flourished in that environment.

The end of the Cold War produced something of an interregnum, when the United States appeared to stand alone on the world stage. By the beginning of the twenty-first century the situation began to change. Political terrorism emanating from the collapsing Arab Middle East and the rise of other powers (returning Russia, China, Brazil, India, and others) complicated the world scene. While the United States is still seen as the world's most important global power as we enter the century's third decade, the political and economic environment is increasingly crowded with other significant players.

As terrorism captured most of the attention, the dramatic and enduring U.S. response in Afghanistan and Iraq turned the government and its policy increasingly toward a military perspective. Twenty years of war, despite President Obama's efforts and President Trump's pronouncements, turned the U.S. into more of a garrison state than we would have imagined. U.S. foreign policy has become increasingly focused on the military instrument, while the Foreign Service and the State Department have correspondingly sunk in stature and role. President Biden launched his administration with a promise to correct this imbalance. We shall see.

Between that shrinking and the effect of widespread terrorist threats, the diplomatic life no longer appears to be so comfortable—or safe. Sadly, the same is true for children and nuns in conflicted areas.

But it remains absorbing for those so inclined. And by those, I mean people motivated by the same enduring interests of service, sense of history, and wanderlust. Obviously, these motivations must be allied with an intellectual interest in foreign affairs, in the continuing activity under way in the international environment, where governments, NGOs, nonstate actors, private sector entities of various kinds, and private citizens interact.

However, taking up this role means taking up obligations. The old phrase about "taking the king's shilling," dating back to the eighteenth century, meant that the bonus for enlisting in the British Army, a shilling coin, meant that private life was over. Your private wishes would now take second place to the desires of the king, meaning the government and officers above you. You were now an agent of the state.

That principle applies today to those who enter government service, a fact that appears to surprise if not discomfit some. Obviously, the limits on personal life and expression are not the same as those of a British soldier of the eighteenth century (although they come closer in the military services), but they are not negligible. The most obvious limitations on one's personal life arise from and are connected to the actual work. Nothing surprising here. Similar conditions apply to anyone working for any large organization: loyalty to the organization, discipline, work ethic, honesty.

Working for the government, especially in diplomacy, requires additional obligations. After all, the fundamental characterization of the diplomat is that of an official representative. The public official aspect is important. The accreditation of the diplomat *en poste* (most obviously for the chief of mission) is as a formal representative, authorized to speak for his or her government. This inevitably puts a heavy burden on the diplomat, which is why diplomats traditionally speak with such circumspection. If your words are official, then you had better be careful. And there is no "off-duty" status in which one may speak as a private individual. Even when one means to speak privately, and the listeners on hand believe it, the mere fact it was spoken makes it of use to those who wish to use it. Diplomats are never assumed to be speaking privately. The most junior third secretary, especially if American, must never be caught repeating publicly even well-known scandals, such as "the well-documented rumors about the sexual habits of the minister of finance."

We all learned this in the day, but the current environment of social media is apparently creating new standards of behavior. Many officials nowadays apparently believe they have a right to private views that can be circulated on the internet. They are wrong. They have taken the king's shilling, and by doing so have accepted limitations on their First Amendment rights. I am told that this is not a popular view among the current generation of younger officers.

As already noted, most of us entered the profession out of a combination of desires: public service, a desire to see and participate in history, and a modest wanderlust. Those ambitions, which I think clearly describe me, probably engendered the sort of lessons or conclusions my experience led me to. I have discussed this at various places in this account, mostly around the role of culture. Recently I ran across the following quotation by Daniel Patrick Moynihan, which pretty much summed up my view: "The central conservative truth is that it is culture, not politics, that determines the success of a society. The central liberal truth is that politics can change a culture and save it from itself."

Culture counts, in other words, probably more than anything else, because culture determines the form of government and public attitudes, and government and public attitudes pretty much determine everything else—in the short run. And politics counts in the longer run because that is one of the major influences on culture. This is an insight that economic development experts in particular refuse to accept.

Nostalgia is not only part of an exercise like this, but also a danger. Recently, while relocating my personal files, I found a thick folder of most if not all of my annual officer evaluation reports, written over these forty-some years. I decided to sit down and read them all. Most people not in government service are without a detailed record of their professional life unless they are obsessive diarists.

This sort of walk down memory lane consisting of official reports creates an occasional surfeit of sweetness. An officer's efficiency reports in a closed, and often small, collegial environment require handling criticism with delicacy, especially as you will have to work with the subject of the report the next day. The legendary caustic observation in a British Army annual officer's evaluation—"If this officer were a horse I would not breed him"—is almost certainly apocryphal.

Reports are often full of overly generous compliments, given the generally high quality of Foreign Service officers. But FSOs are not perfect; imperfections exist and failings occur. Dealing with them in the reports—on which careers depend—is therefore a delicate exercise. There is thus a general tendency to dismiss the efficiency reports as exercises in mutual self-congratulation, useless for realistic evaluation purposes.

This judgment is too easy, too cynical, and unfair. Having served on promotion panels, I have readily discovered comments and observations of value contained within the prose. One sees the truth of this when comparing, as one does, comments by different supervisors over time. Observations, no matter how delicately phrased, reappear, and a picture emerges, though often only after close and careful reading.

I noticed this in browsing through my own collected file. Reports from the first overseas post noted that my drafting (writing) did not meet standards—"needs work." In the Foreign Service world this can be a crushing remark, but it was cushioned by my youth and inexperience. A few years later a completely different supervisor noted that my drafting, while still requiring checking and supervision, was notably improving in the short time I had been at that post. Ten years later I was being lauded for the quality of my drafting, a comment that became standard in my reports over the succeeding years. And my extensive list of published articles confirms that judgment.

Reading these reports, I was surprised to discover how much I had forgotten about my own life. The nature of diplomatic service means that such a record will inevitably tell much of the personal side of one's career, including where one lived and whom one associated with. Reading the file resurrected many, many memories of people and events long past. It also resurrected personal ambitions, disappointments, and regrets, as well as satisfactions and victories, also all long past. But the pain of the disappointments has faded, while the remembered pleasures are gratifying. Additional details only confirm my general satisfaction with a life reasonably well lived.

And much of that general satisfaction comes from the memory of people: professional colleagues, both American and foreign, government officials, neighbors, friends, and the whole range of people one runs across in life as a globe-trotting professional foreigner. Some interactions were intense and long-lasting, some casual and fleeting; but from John Smith of the *London Times* to Arjun Diraniyagala of the 1914 Pipe, they add up to a rich panorama of memories. Which is why I was somewhat dumbfounded during a routine security update after I retired when the young interviewer looked up from her quiz sheet and innocently asked if I knew many foreigners and could provide a list of their names and addresses!

Still I continue to harbor one professional regret. Although I had five African posts in the exciting and dramatic period between 1960 and 1980, I was never present when truly dramatic events took place. I arrived in Kenya after the Mau Mau Rebellion and left before independence. By the time I arrived in Angola in 1965, the initial independence uprising had been effectively quelled and would remain so for several years. I arrived in Zambia, Guinea-Bissau, and Cape Verde not long after independence during the sort of "honeymoon" that often follows such an event. Countries had revolutions or civil conflicts before I arrived or after I left, as in Zaire. Although there were problems and tensions in most of these countries, my tours of assignment turned out to be relatively quiet interregnums. I arrived in Lubumbashi after the late, unlamented Mobutu Sese Seko had turned the economy upside down (and in the process changed his name from Joseph to Mobutu Sese Seko, which we were told meant "the rooster who covers all the chickens in the yard"). And I left several months before the legendary Katanga Gendarmes invaded Shaba Province from their exile in Angola. Despite a long and bloody rebellion, Guinea-Bissau was enjoying the quiet and peaceful first years of independence during my time there. But political strife, a sort of ethnic coup, and the eventual collapse of Bissau as a functioning government began not too long after I left. It is true that the civil war in Sri Lanka in the late 1970s was slowly heating up while I was there, but it was still largely restricted to areas distant from the capital and did not yet seriously threaten the government. The only dramatic historic crisis I participated in professionally was the first Gulf War—but far from the battlefield, in the halls of the United Nations in New York. Not terribly photogenic.

It was all so frustrating for a young man who had joined the Foreign Service to observe history close up and maybe even play a role in it. I finally decided that I was a mirror-image version of the Li'l Abner character, Joe Btfsplk, who created chaos around him wherever he went. Only I had an opposite effect; I wandered through Africa in a tumultuous and historic period seemingly spreading calm and boredom. I even once tried, only semifacetiously, to convince the Africa Bureau to send me to the hottest spots they had, promising that my karma would almost immediately calm the raging mobs, like oil on stormy waters. They never took up my proposal.

Retirement caught up with me in 1995, required by law and my years, and was marked by a smallish ceremony in the office of a deputy director general of the Foreign Service. A few friends were there, drinking champagne I had paid for, and I was presented with the traditional pair of gold-trimmed U.S. flags, the national and the ambassadorial. All quite low key, as the State Department doesn't do retirement ceremonies with the style and splash of the military. Even if the department wished to, who would they get to pass in review?

I left in good humor. I had had my innings, and any regrets were manageable. While it didn't cross my mind that day, I later recalled an incident from my first tour in the Foreign Service when a Foreign Service inspector interviewed me during an office inspection. Given that it was 1959 and this senior FSO was winding up his career as an inspector, his memory went back to the early 1930s, before I was born. The inspection wasn't particularly rigorous, as least not my part of it, and he used part of the time with me to reminisce. As he finished and picked up his notes, he looked at me and said, "Well, if I could do it all over again, start at the beginning, I would."

So would I.

ITHAKA
As you set out for Ithaka
hope the voyage is a long one,
full of adventure, full of discovery.
Laistrygonians and Cyclops,
angry Poseidon—don't be afraid of them:
you'll never find things like that on your way
as long as you keep your thoughts raised high,
as long as a rare excitement
stirs your spirit and your body.
Laistrygonians and Cyclops,
wild Poseidon—you won't encounter them
unless you bring them along inside your soul,
unless your soul sets them up in front of you.

Hope the voyage is a long one.
May there be many a summer morning when,
with what pleasure, what joy,
you come into harbors seen for the first time;
may you stop at Phoenician trading stations
to buy fine things,
mother of pearl and coral, amber and ebony,
sensual perfume of every kind—

as many sensual perfumes as you can;
and may you visit many Egyptian cities
to gather stores of knowledge from their scholars.

Keep Ithaka always in your mind.
Arriving there is what you are destined for.
But do not hurry the journey at all.
Better if it lasts for years,
so you are old by the time you reach the island,
wealthy with all you have gained on the way,
not expecting Ithaka to make you rich.

Ithaka gave you the marvelous journey.
Without her you would not have set out.
She has nothing left to give you now.

And if you find her poor, Ithaka won't have fooled you.
Wise as you will have become, so full of experience,
you will have understood by then what these Ithakas mean.

—C.P. CAVAFY, *Collected Poems*,
    translated by Edmund Keeley and
    Philip Sherrard, edited by George Savidis.

INDEX

Acheson, Dean, 20

acupuncture, 169–70

administrative work, 30–31, 173–74, 200–202

Afghanistan, 252, 256

African independence movement, 40, 48, 50, 52, 54, 56, 60–62. See also *names of specific nations*

African National Congress (ANC), 64

African nationalism, 53, 66, 94

agricultural production, 60, 68, 104–6, 122, 123, 124

airlifts, 37, 65, 67, 84

airline industry, 74

airports, 48, 74, 127, 143

alcohol, 7–8, 42

Les Ambassades (Peyrefitte), 11

American Business Circle (ABC), 168–69

American Diplomacy (online publication), 237

American Foreign Service Association, 23–24

Amin, Idi, 211

Anderson, George, 56

Angola, 30, 34, 47–58, 260, 261. *See also* Luanda, Angola

animism, 97. *See also* religion

Anti-Terrorism Assistance program (ATA), 237–38

apartheid, 62, 65–68, 71

Armenia, 239, 241

Asia Society, 144

Atlanta, Georgia, 74

Attwood, William, 234

Austin 7s (automobiles), 197

Authentic Zairian Revolution, 79

automobiles, 30, 36, 97–98, 100, 105, 196–99, 234. *See also* car accidents

awards for foreign diplomacy, 23–24

Azerbaijan, 239, 241

Bandarawela Hotel, Sri Lanka, 156

Bangkok, Thailand, 153–54, 157

Belarus, 217, 218–19

Belarusian diplomats, 219–20

Belgian colonialism, 50, 51. *See also* Zaire (formerly the Congo)

Belgian Congo. *See* Zaire (formerly the Congo)

Belgium, 73–88. *See also* Brussels, Belgium

Biden, Joe, 256

"Big Men," 60

Fort Lesley J. McNair, 131–32. *See also* National War College

Franklin, Benjamin, 16

Freeman, Charles W., 19

French colonialism, 49, 51, 161

French diplomats, 17, 51, 99

French language, 19, 32, 59, 72. *See also* language

Fukuyama, Francis, 18

Fulbright program, 28

Galle Face Hotel, Sri Lanka, 156–57, 197

Gandhi, Mahatma, 180

gas rationing, 59

Gecamines, 83–84

Geneva, Switzerland, 210, 219, 221, 223, 228

Georgia (country), 239, 241

German language, 76. *See also* language

Ghana, 60, 233

Gilbert, Felix, 21

Glaspie, April, 23

Good, Robert, 59, 72

Grand Hotel, Sri Lanka, 156

Great Leap Forward, 64

Greek communities: in Colombo, 153; in Lusaka, 69; in Zaire, 80, 81, 83

Group of 77, 215, 220, 226, 227

La Guerre des Belges (Du Roy), 75

Guinea-Bissau: agricultural production in, 104–6; class consciousness and consumerism in, 96, 99–102, 106; colonialism in, 56; economy of, 105–6, 112, 114; Marks's position in, 25, 89–91, 116, 235; political community of, 107–8; political

system of, 90–96, 108–13, 260, 261; racial politics in, 95, 97, 109

Gulf War (1990–91), 261

Gurman, Hannah, 20–21

Harrop, Bill, 81

hartals, 188–89

Hawaii, 242–43, 249–51

Heimann, John, 28, 35

Hill Club, Sri Lanka, 156

Hilton Hotel, Colombo, 157, 163

Hinton, Deane, 23

holiday celebrations: in Bissau, 102–3; in Lubumbashi, 82; in New York, 207, 222–23; in Sri Lanka, 158–59, 171–72

Honolulu HI, 242–43

Hotel Suisse, Sri Lanka, 156

Hubert's Highway, 66

humanism, 61, 69

Hussein, Saddam, 23

Immigration and Naturalization Act, 42–43, 171

immigration laws, 42–46, 171

impartiality, 21–22

independence movement in Africa, 40, 48, 50, 52, 54, 56, 60–62. See also *names of specific nations*

India, 154, 162, 214

Indian diplomats, 162, 163, 183, 214

Indo–Sri Lankan Peace Accord, 183

Industrial College, Washington DC, 131, 133

inflation, 124–25

infrastructure projects, 64–67, 71. *See also* railway system

University of Oklahoma, 34, 75

U.S. Agency for International Development (USAID), 36, 59, 124, 247

U.S. Air Force, 42, 132

U.S. Army, 8–9

U.S. border. *See* Texas-Mexico border culture

U.S. Coast Guard, 132, 133

U.S. Department of Defense, 134, 231, 237, 242, 246

U.S. Department of State, 230–31, 254–55. *See also* Foreign Service of the United States

U.S. Information Service (USIS), 36

U.S. Marines, 132, 133–34

U.S. Mission to the United Nations (USUN), 208–29, 239

U.S. Navy, 98, 132, 243–44

U.S. Pacific Command (USPACOM), 26, 242–45, 250

U.S. Treasury Department, 16, 237

Vieira, João Bernardo "Nino," 95, 109

Vienna, Austria, 210, 212

Vietnam War, 23, 25, 161, 237

visa stories, 42–47

Walloons, 75–76. *See also* Belgium

Washington DC, 30–31, 32, 34, 73, 85, 114, 230–40

Watson, Alex, 212

W. Averell Harriman Award, 24

Weber, Max, 166, 204

Wells, Melissa, 89, 235

Wikileaks document release, 21

William R. Rivkin Award, 24

Wilson, Woodrow, 20

World Bank, 225

World Health Organization, 219

Wotton, Henry, 17

Wray, Edrie, 27

writing skills, 12–13, 29. *See also* communication

Zaire (formerly the Congo), 33, 50, 54, 77–88, 235. *See also* Lubumbashi, Zaire

Zambia, 30, 34, 57, 59–72

Zimbabwe, 60